THE Windows NT
Web Server
BOOK

**TOOLS & TECHNIQUES FOR BUILDING
AN INTERNET/INTRANET SITE**

THE Windows NT™
Web Server
BOOK

**TOOLS & TECHNIQUES FOR BUILDING
AN INTERNET/INTRANET SITE**

Larry Budnick

Contributing Authors:
Jonathan Magid
R. Douglas Matthews
Paul Jones
David McConville

VENTANA

The Windows NT Web Server Book:
Tools & Techniques for Building an Internet/Intranet Site
Copyright © 1996 by Larry Budnick & Ventana Communications Group, Inc.

Library of Congress Cataloging-in-Publication Data

The Windows NT Web server book : tools & techniques for building an Internet/intranet site / Larry Budnick ... [et al.].
     p. cm.
   Includes index.
   ISBN 1-56604-342-5
   1. World Wide Web servers. 2. Microsoft Windows NT. I. Budnick, Larry.
TK5105.888.W56 1996
005.75—dc20   96-15266
                                   CIP

First Edition 9 8 7 6 5 4 3 2

Printed in the United States of America

Ventana Communications Group, Inc.
P.O. Box 13964
Research Triangle Park, NC 27709-3964
919/544-9404
FAX 919/544-9472

President / CEO
Josef Woodman

**Vice President of
Content Development**
Karen A. Bluestein

Production Manager
John Cotterman

Technology Operations Manager
Kerry L. B. Foster

Product Marketing Manager
Diane Lennox

Art Director
Marcia Webb

Acquisitions Editor
Sherri Morningstar

Developmental Editor
Eric Edstam

Project Editor
Beth Snowberger

Copy Editor
Eric Edstam

Assistant Editor
JJ Hohn

Technical Director
Dan Brown

Technical Reviewer
Adrian Knotts

Desktop Publisher
Scott Hosa

Proofreader
Sandra Manheimer

Indexer
Mark Kmetzko

Cover Illustration
Tom Draper Design

Dedication

This book is dedicated to my parents, Carl and Clarice Budnick, who gave me the opportunity to succeed and the drive to do so.

About the Authors

Larry Budnick has had more than 15 years of computer systems experience as a systems engineer, developer, and systems integrator. He holds a B.S. in Systems Engineering from Rensselaer Polytechnic Institute, and an M.S. in Computer Engineering from Boston University. He has worked on a variety of computer and communications projects ranging from ISDN telephony to wireless data systems to web site design and implementation. He is currently a manager of an Internet Solutions group in Boston.

Contributing Authors

Jonathan Magid was the system administrator, Webmaster, and programmer for the SunSITE project at the University of North Carolina at Chapel Hill from the project's start in 1992 until September 1995. He now works on Internet search tools for the Center for Network Discovery and Retrieval. He is the author of several articles about the Internet and UNIX, as well as several utilities for administrating information systems.

R. Douglas Matthews worked on the SunSITE project at the University of North Carolina at Chapel Hill from January 1994 to April 1995 as a World Wide Web developer and is currently a Webmaster and CGI programmer for Cisco Systems, Inc. He also cofounded Scratch Disk, Inc., and teaches HTML authoring and Internet classes. Matthews hold a B.A. in Religious Studies from the University of North Carolina at Chapel Hill.

Paul Jones was a lecturer in the School of Journalism and Mass Communication and in the School of Information and Library Science at the University of North Carolina at Chapel Hill. He managed SunSITE.unc.edu from the beginning in 1992 until January 1996. He is now Technical Director at the Institute for Advanced Technology in the Humanities. Jones holds a B.S. in Computer Science from North Carolina State University and an M.F.A. in Poetry from Warren-Wilson College.

David McConville received a B.S. in music from the University of North Carolina at Asheville, with a concentration in audio engineering and music synthesis. He is currently a graduate student in the UNC School of Journalism and Mass Communication and worked as a multimedia developer at the UNC-SunSITE project from June 1994 to August 1995. McConville is the President of the WWW and CD-ROM design and consultation firm Scratch Disk, Inc. (http://www.scratch.com).

Contents

Section III: Adding Interactivity

Section IV: Final Considerations

Section V: Appendices

Introduction

The World Wide Web has emerged as the hottest new information technology. This vast network of hyperlinked multimedia resources spans the globe, bringing information and entertainment to a growing population of users. With this book, you can be a part of it!

You have in your hands everything you need to use the Internet as your very own printing press. The Companion CD-ROM includes all the software you need to create a Web server on your Windows NT workstation. *The Windows NT Web Server Book* will teach you how to use these tools to create a secure and professional-looking presence on the Web, including these secrets of Web-wizardry:

- How Web servers work.

- How to include inline images in your Web pages, and create image maps.

- How to create interactive forms and how to write CGI scripts.

- How to quickly convert and format your "legacy" data for use on the Web.

- How to embed audio and animation in your pages.

As popular as the public Internet and World Wide Web are, many companies are today electing to establish internal web networks, called "intranets." Web technologies can provide a platform-neutral way to distribute information inside a company, whether that company is in a single building or scattered across the world. Most all the information in this book applies to the intranet web sites as well as to the public Internet Web sites.

This Isn't "Just Another Internet Book"

Three years ago, the Internet didn't exist as far as the popular media was concerned. There were no books or articles detailing its wonders, nor were there slick TV spots tempting us with a networked utopia. Research universities and high-tech companies had almost exclusive access to the Internet. If you wanted to create your own Web site, you were forced to learn the complex and arcane language of the UNIX wizard. Even if you knew that you wanted to be wired, it was almost impossible for an individual or small organization to get access.

Today, dozens of Internet books crowd the shelves, and more than 250 Internet Service Providers (ISPs) are in the United States alone. A tremendous amount of material about the Internet is out there, and its quality ranges from carefully edited tour guides to mere conglomerations of network FAQs and text files.

Still, most of these sources have one thing in common: they want to bring you, as a consumer, to this vast amount of information. What they don't do is tell you how to add to it. These guides seem to suggest that only network experts can run a server, and they leave you feeling that the Internet is merely a library to be searched by the patient reader.

The Internet is much more than this. It's a platform for the communication and distribution of information. Everyone has something to say or to show; it may be as personal as a photo from a vacation or as important as a business catalog, but the impulse to communicate is a basic part of human nature. This book will show you how to transform that impulse into an Internet server: your own home on the World Wide Web.

Last Christmas I heard about people dropping out of medical school and law school to start companies that would put catalogs on the Web. Oddly, the folks enthusiastically telling me about this were accountants—very careful, very particular accountants who are not often given to excitement. With a small investment and good old-fashioned hard work, you have an opportunity to be part of the Web, but you must also be creative. A successful Web publisher has the following:

- Content with an audience.
- Attractive presentation.
- Swift, reliable access.
- A high level of interactivity.
- Reasonable security.
- A dynamic presence.

Web publishing allows you to go beyond the limits of print and conventional mail. You have the opportunity to be more than a billboard on the Information Highway, and this book will help you.

Hardware & Software Requirements

This book assumes you have a computer that runs Windows NT and has a direct connection either to the public Internet or to your internal TCP/IP network. You can use the tools and skills in this book to serve web documents off space leased on someone else's server, but if you want to run your own Internet server, you'll need the following:

- A Windows NT workstation or server that exceeds the minimum requirements suggested by Microsoft.
- An SVGA monitor, if you want to work with images.
- A sound card, if you want to work with audio.
- A CD-ROM drive.
- A full-time, direct connection to the public Internet or to your own internal TCP/IP network.

If you're creating a site for the public Internet, and you don't yet have an Internet service provider, you must get one. The process of finding an Internet service provider can be complex, and it's beyond the scope of this book. We recommend you investigate the options by talking to your local network providers. You can use your WWW client to look at a list of companies that provide Internet connectivity at http://www.yahoo.com/Business/Corporations/Internet_Access_Providers/.

The text of this book assumes that you have a basic understanding of Windows NT, although you don't have to be an NT expert. If you're not familiar with NT, you should read an introductory Windows NT book first.

What's Inside

Chapter 1, "What Is the Web?" provides a brief overview of hypertext and how it's used in the World Wide Web. It explains the relationship between Web servers, browsers, and URLs. This chapter also shows you the newsgroups and mailing lists you can use to keep up with the ever-changing Web.

Chapter 2, "The Basic Pieces," briefly describes the various technologies that go into the Web. It discusses the file formats that are common on the Internet, and how the Web uses MIME types to deal with them intelligently. The chapter ends with an introduction to HTML, the HyperText Markup Language.

Chapter 3, "Setting Up the Server," compares the most popular web server software and takes you through the process of installing and using the Alibaba Lite server from CSM, which is included on the Companion CD-ROM.

Chapter 4, "System Security," provides an overview of the simple precautions you'll need to take in order to secure your NT system, whether you're serving an intranet or the public Internet.

Chapter 5, "Importing Documents to the Web," shows how to convert your documents from several popular word processors and desktop publishing systems to HTML.

Chapter 6, "Checking Your Work," shows you how to use sound design principles and HTML validation utilities to ensure that your documents will look their best on every browser.

Chapter 7, "Images on the Web," is a brief look at using graphics effectively on the Web. It covers the commonly used graphics formats and ways to improve the appearance of your inline images. It explains advanced topics like transparency, interlacing, and clickable imagemaps.

Chapter 8, "True Multimedia: Adding Audio & Animation," gives a useful introduction to employing film and sound clips in your pages. Not only does it describe the various standards, but it also gets you started creating your own multimedia files and making links to them.

Chapter 9, "Simple Forms," reveals the secrets of interactive forms. It explains how to write a form in HTML and examines some of the commercial programs available to help you easily process the information browsers send you.

Chapter 10, "CGI & DLLs: Programming Your Server," covers the more advanced features of the Web. It shows you how to write CGI scripts to process forms and generate HTML on the fly, and offers some starting points for programming server extensions with the popular APIs now available with NT web servers.

Chapter 11, "Searching & Indexing," shows you how to make full-text indexes of your site and provide that index on your web site.

Chapter 12, "Fitting In: Joining the Virtual Community," describes how to attract people to your server and how to keep them coming back.

Chapter 13, "Future Directions," explains the newest technologies that are shaping the future of the World Wide Web. It covers the new features of HTML, VRML, the Virtual Reality Modeling Language, as well as real-time conferencing, HTTP-NG, electronic commerce, and other emerging Internet technologies.

Appendix A, "About the Online Companion," describes this informative tool and lets you know how to access it.

Appendix B, "About the Companion CD-ROM," describes the

contents of the CD-ROM included with your copy of *The Windows NT Web Server Book*. The Companion CD-ROM contains all the software you need to create your very own platform for interactive electronic publishing on the Internet.

To Protect & To Serve

After you begin using the Internet for distributing information, you may never want to go back to traditional media. The advantages become obvious:

- You can reach millions of people, both down the street and on the other side of the world.

- You can make updates and corrections immediately, which allows you to develop your material incrementally, making small changes without the overhead of reprinting.

- Most people use computers to compose their copy in the first place, so importing these documents to the Web is simple and convenient.

- Providing information on the Net is a two-way street. Messages don't flow only one way as they do with traditional media, but go back and forth between the client and server. This interactivity can provide the basis for dialogue between author and reader.

Companies can use this interaction to realistically evaluate the effectiveness of their advertising. Organizations and governments can use it to form virtual communities of people with similar interests and concerns. The Internet is more than a channel for reaching new audiences; it's also an opportunity to swap advice and opinions and to discover new friends and colleagues.

Of course, to discover the benefits of running a Web server you have to take the plunge and start serving. Chapter 1, "What Is the Web?" is an introduction to the concept of hypertext and how it works in the World Wide Web. If you're a long-time veteran of the Web, you can skip ahead to Chapter 2, "The Basic Pieces," which explains the basic technologies that make the Web work.

SECTION I

Gathering the Pieces

1

What Is the Web?

The World Wide Web is a (now massive) collection of clients and servers that support the WWW protocol, HTTP, on the Internet. At this very moment, more servers and clients all over the world are being put into use on the Web. Every online service is providing or has announced that it will soon provide WWW access. This chapter gives you a brief overview of the concepts of clients, servers, and protocols used to create the World Wide Web. In the process, we'll learn about the history and development of the WWW, as well as where to go to keep current.

Clients & Servers

If you've used the Web, you're already on your way to understanding the concepts of client, server, and protocol; they're harder to describe than to understand. A client is a program that wants something. A server is a program that provides something. A client can request things from many different servers. A server can provide things to many different clients. In general, a client usually initiates a conversation or session with a server. A server is

usually an automatic program that waits for client requests. A
client is usually acting at the request of a single user or at the
request of a program acting as if it were a person. A protocol is the
definition of the ways that clients may make requests of servers
and of how servers should be expected to answer those requests.
Figure 1-1 tells it all—two ovals connected by a double-ended
arrow.

Figure 1-1: *A simple client-server diagram.*

On the Web, it is the client's job to do the following:

◈ Help you form a request (which is usually initiated when
you click on a link).

◈ Send your request to a server.

◈ Inform you of the status of your request.

◈ Present the results of your request by properly decoding
inline images, rendering HTML documents, and transferring various files to their proper viewers.

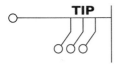
TIP

*A viewer is a program that can be called by your WWW client to
present certain kinds of files. For example, Acrobat files are not
presented by your WWW client, but by an Acrobat viewer. Movie
files might be viewed by a program such as QuickTime, on a
Microsoft Windows system, when they are referenced and downloaded by your WWW client.*

Common World Wide Web clients include Mosaic, Netscape,
and Lynx. (In this book, a WWW client is also called a *browser*.) In
general, WWW clients can also make requests of other kinds of
servers including Gopher, FTP, news, and mail.

A Web server's job is to do the following:

※ Receive requests.

※ Validate requests, including security screening.

※ Retrieve and properly form data in response to requests, which includes pre- and post-processing the data with CGI scripts and programs and marking files with the proper MIME types. (CGI scripts and MIME types will be explained in detail later in this book.)

※ Deliver information to the requesting client.

 The common Windows-based servers come from CSM, O'Reilly & Associates, the Internet Factory, and Netscape. A version of the CSM server (The CSM Alibaba WWW Server) is included on the Companion CD-ROM.

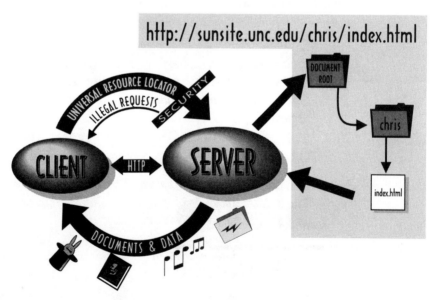

Figure 1-2: *The interaction of client, protocol, and server on the Web.*

The Web's HTTP protocol is said to be *stateless*, because the server immediately forgets about the interaction after it delivers the response to the client. (In a *stateful* protocol, the client and server would remember a good bit of information about each other and their various requests and responses.) The Web's protocol is easily implemented, because a stateless protocol is light (not much essential code or resources are required). Another appealing feature of stateless protocols is that you can move quickly and easily from server to server (at the client side) or from client to client (on the server side) without much cleanup or tracking. This ability to move quickly is ideal for hypertext (see "Hypertext," later in this chapter). Attempting to transact business in a stateless environment is pretty complex, however, and has so far been implemented in some fairly tricky ways as protocol workarounds. Much of the arcane programming that has occurred on the Web has been in an attempt to impose state on the stateless protocol.

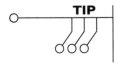

TIP

For those serious about transacting business in a totally electronic environment, secure Web servers are available. For more information on servers, see Chapter 3, "Setting Up the Server." Information on security in general can be found in Chapter 4, "System Security."

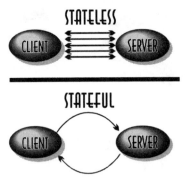

Figure 1-3: *Stateless and stateful relationships.*

The Internet and whatever is emerging from it are extremely widely distributed networks that support standard, or at least interoperable, protocols and allow for that interoperability to take place even across commercial and national domains. That is to say that no one owns the Internet or the WWW or their respective protocols. Different companies in different countries can and do create clients and servers independently, and the resulting products work together on the Web seamlessly (most of the time).

The great advantage of this approach is that the development field is fairly open, if not completely so. A group of undergraduate computer science majors can create a product and, eventually, a company that competes with products designed by software engineers from the world's largest computer companies, and the product of the undergrads can win on its own merits. The use of protocols, clients, and servers is also competitive and reasonably priced. You can become a publisher with only a small investment, and compete with some of the world's largest publishers and make your product accessible to millions of people all over the world. Granted, you'll have to be creative in your design, content, presentation, and advertising, but the point is that for the moment, there's a new concept of freedom of the press. And finally, you can actually afford to own a press yourself.

The Development of the World Wide Web

Since the publication of Vannevar Bush's essay "As We May Think," in the August 1945 issue of the *Atlantic Monthly*, the idea, but not the appropriate technology, of the electronic linking of documents has been hovering around the heads of information scientists, librarians, and even writers.

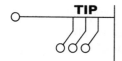

TIP

Bush's essay can be found on the WWW at http:// www.theAtlantic.com/atlantic/atlweb/flashbks/computer/bushf.htm.

Writers had been anticipating the linkage of ideas long before Bush's article. Aren't footnotes no more than primitive ink and paper hyperlinks to other works? Isn't Ezra Pound's use of brief references and borrowings from other authors a more subtle version of the same thing? T. S. Eliot's "The Waste Land," Robert Frost's *New Hampshire: A Poem with Grace Notes*, and Vladimir Nabokov's *Pale Fire* are other literary attempts to use what could easily be defined as hypertext in a paper environment. The point is that the need for something like hypertext has been in the air for quite some time.

Yet it was Bush who associated the idea with electronic technology. Bush foresaw that the new technologies that had emerged from the war effort could be applied to expand the way we think. Although his description of the Memex, with its odd recording and retrieval devices, seems as antiquated as his implicit social views—all scientists are male, all secretaries and clerical help are female—Bush's fundamental idea about how we think as we organize and use information has been the basis for what we today know as the World Wide Web and hypertext.

Hypertext

The term *hypertext*, invented by Ted Nelson in 1965, usually means text that is not constrained to be linear. That is to say that, while parts or even all of a hypertext document may be linear, parts or all of a document may be nonlinear. Hypertext escapes the bounds of linearity by means of links or references to other texts.

Hypermedia, of which hypertext is a limited subset, is media (texts, pictures, sound, video, whatever) linked to other media in a nonlinear fashion. You could think of hypertext as the salvation for those of us with short attention spans, with cluttered desks, who are not reading one book but are about halfway through six at the same time, who consider getting lost when traveling a diversion instead of a frustration. Of course, from a negative viewpoint, you could say that hypertext is a mirror of our more or less disorderly minds, desks, and lives.

The first hypertext implementations were by Douglas Engelbart, inventor of the mouse, and by Ted Nelson. Both Nelson's and Engelbart's implementations of hypertext were highly constrained by 1960s technology and by intricate design assumptions. Both projects were also more visionary than implementable. Nelson, for example, claimed that his project, Xanadu, proposed dealing with all copyright and accounting problems. Because of this robustness, Xanadu, according to Nelson, should be used for putting the entire world's literary corpus online.

In 1987, Jeff Conklin reviewed 18 different hypertext/hypermedia implementations in an IEEE publication. Interestingly enough, only 8 allowed concurrent multiple users and of those 8 only 4 allowed graphics and supplied graphical browsers. Few, if any, implementations came close to what we were to have less than four years later.

Xanadu's History

In 1967, Ted Nelson gave the name Xanadu to the project to implement his vision of distributed hypertext. A project Xanadu group was formed in 1979, with design work completed in 1981. But by 1987, Xanadu was still noted for "a crude front end . . . which runs on Sun workstations" (Conklin 1987). In 1988, things were looking up for Nelson and Xanadu when Xanadu was bought by Autodesk and Nelson was hired to continue the project there. By late 1988, the 1981 design was implemented but was quickly put aside in favor of a "MUCH FINER design" (quote from Nelson). By August 1992, Autodesk, having already spent several million dollars on Xanadu, decided to drop the project, leaving Nelson to shift for himself. As of this writing, Nelson's project has gone to the Far East and continues development in Australia, and Nelson is in Japan working with the Sapporo HyperLab. Like Samuel Coleridge's poem "Kubla Khan," Xanadu remains incomplete.

For the most current developments regarding Xanadu and Nelson, see http://xanadu.net/the.project.

Tim Berners-Lee, CERN & the WWW

In March 1989, at the European Particle Physics Laboratory, also known as CERN, Tim Berners-Lee proposed a project that would allow scientists to easily browse fellow researchers' papers. A later phase of the proposed project would allow scientists to create new documents on their servers. Tim was strongly influenced by Ted Nelson's self-published *Literary Machines 90.1* (Nelson 1980), but unlike Nelson, he was not at all concerned about the copyright of his materials, the royalties, or even tracking the usage as clients moved among servers. However grand the name, the World Wide Web was to be lean and mean. The first and second phases of Tim's proposed project each would require three months to implement. Tim wisely noted that the second phase, which might include collaborative authoring, annotations, graphics, and the like, should be considered open-ended. The proposed development team consisted of four software engineers and one programmer.

Tim's paper circulated at CERN and, after several rewrites, the project got underway in October 1990. By December 1990, a line-mode browser and a NeXTStep browser were implemented, and access was available to hypertext files, as well as to Usenet newsgroups within CERN.

To support his project, Tim proposed that a new language be developed for the transport and rendering of hypertext documents. This language was to be a subset of the already proven open language called Standard Generalized Markup Language, or SGML. Tim's new language would be known as HyperText Markup Language, or HTML.

The protocol for handling HTML and other WWW documents was to be called HyperText Transfer Protocol, or HTTP, which follows the Internet tradition of ending almost every protocol name with the letters *TP*. The server then is called a HyperText Transfer Protocol *daemon*, or an HTTPD, following the UNIX traditions of ending the name of any independent process with the letter *D* and using that spelling of "daemon." (In Windows, this kind of a program is called a *service*.)

HTTP uses an addressing convention called the Uniform Resource Locator, or URL (pronounced "you-are-el"), to locate any available data object on the Internet or on Internet-worked hosts. The *U* in URL is sometimes said to stand for "Universal" and, in fact, is referred to that way in several important documents. The basic idea behind the URL is that given certain information, you should be able to access any publicly available data on any machine on the Internet. That certain information consists of the following basic pieces of a URL:

- The access protocol to be used.
- The machine on which the data resides.
- The port from which to request the data.
- The path to that data.
- The name of the file containing that data.

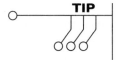

TIP

HTML, HTTP, and URLs will be more fully covered in the next chapter, "The Basic Pieces," and in the chapters that follow.

During August 1991, Tim's presentation and software were announced as available from CERN in Usenet newsgroups, notably alt.hypertext, comp.sys.next, comp.text.sgml, and comp.mail.multi-media. The cat was now out of the bag; unfortunately, the implementation of the software was most robust on an interesting but not widely used platform, the NeXT workstation.

Tim gave his WWW presentation at several conferences, including the Hypertext '91 conference in San Antonio, Texas, in December of that year. Among the other presenters at the conference were two people from Autodesk. Some have noticed that Autodesk ended their support for Xanadu not long after Tim's WWW presentation.

WWW was fully distributed throughout CERN by July 1992 and included Viola, a NeXTStep client that allowed drag-and-drop page building and linking, as well as the line-mode clients. (A line-mode client is a text-only browser usually written to operate in a simulated VT-100 environment—simulated, since VT-100s are no longer manufactured.) WWW was warmly accepted and was beginning to create a buzz on the Internet.

In January 1993, there were 50 known WWW servers in the world, including one at the University of North Carolina. Several browsers were released, including clients for the Macintosh and X Windows. When a new client was released the next month from the National Center for Supercomputing Applications (NCSA) at the University of Illinois at Urbana-Champaign, the WWW, as we now know it, began to take shape.

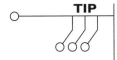

TIP   *For more about CERN see http://www.cern.ch/.*

NCSA Mosaic

If you're reading this, you've probably used Mosaic or one of the many other WWW clients, such as Netscape and Spyglass, that owe a heavy debt to that program. Until the introduction of Mosaic, one of the problems with the WWW was that there were no reliable clients or browsers for some of the most common computers and operating systems. CERN had focused mostly on initial implementation, document sharing, and linking. Tim and his development team were quick to meet the local demands of CERN and to meet their deadlines, which is no small matter. But CERN was quite a large NeXT shop, and they were more inter-ested in servers than in clients, despite the release of their Mac and X Windows browsers, which were somewhat unreliable and clunky. NCSA, on the other hand, had experience as cross-platform client developers. Their NCSA Telnet client is still widely used.

The NCSA Systems Development Group, headed by Joe Hardin, took on a project to create useful WWW browsers that would not only handle the WWW but, as Tim Berners-Lee had described, would support several other access protocols. This client was called Mosaic and was first released for X Windows in February 1993.

Later that month, Marc Andreessen posted a message to www-talk@cern.ch describing a simple extension to HTML. Marc proposed that images could be placed in the browser with a tag to be called <IMG>. What followed Marc's simple suggestion reveals a lot about the way that the WWW developed. A spirited exchange of messages ensued, including notes and points from Jim Davis, Jay Weber, and Tim Berners-Lee.

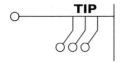

TIP

You can read it all on the WWW-talk archives at http://www.eit.com:80/goodies/lists/www.lists/www-talk.1993q1/.

For those who are believers in waiting for standards to be firm and well defined, reading this newsgroup archive should be instructive. One of the strongest arguments against implementing the <IMG> tag was that it should be incorporated in the "soon to be released" HTML version 2.0 standard. The NCSA team decided that it needed a quicker solution, however, and didn't wait for the standards debates to reach a consensus. As we write this book, the elements of HTML v3.0 are already being incorporated in new browsers, such as Netscape, and a debate over the relationship between standards and the speed of development is raging.

The NCSA team also gave careful consideration to the use of MIME types for identifying media formats, particularly the formats of sounds, pictures, movies, and the like. Using MIME types seemed like a logical move, since the Multimedia Internet Mail Extensions were already a long way toward being able to define and encode most known data types. MIME typing has the added advantage of being extendable and of having been proven to work. Even better, much of the code needed to handle MIME was already written and ready to be used by new applications—WWW clients and servers.

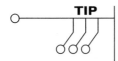

TIP

MIME types will be covered in the next chapter, "The Basic Pieces."

With the addition of the <IMG> tag, Mosaic became truly multimedia. Suddenly, the pages of hypertext began to look a little more familiar. Instead of dryly presenting scientific and scholarly information for the benefit of other scientists and scholars, the pages included photographs of people whom scientists had worked with for years but had never met. The authors of these pages had the opportunity to make their pages visually pleasing.

Until the creation of the <IMG> tag, HTML had been a very limited implementation of SGML. SGML is a language for defining the structure of a document, not necessarily its presentation. Now, you not only could have a very limited structure markup, but you had a very limited formatting language as well.

In December 1993, John Markoff wrote an article for the *New York Times* business section lauding Mosaic as the killer application of the Internet. The article included a screen shot of a Mosaic page, and everyone everywhere began to understand why being able to incorporate images into text on a widely distributed network was important. To many, the screen shot looked like a giant billboard glaring "your ad here." The WWW accounted for only 78 megabytes of Internet backbone traffic in December 1992 but for over 225,443 megabytes in December 1993. By November 1994, WWW traffic accounted for over 3,126,195 megabytes. The growth pattern was unmistakable. The number of known servers registered at CERN had grown to 1,500 by June 1994.

The Web had matured and was what the Internet had needed for so long. A decent graphical user interface to the anarchic, widely distributed World Wide Web had arrived and been recognized.

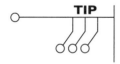

TIP

For more information about current usage statistics and general Internet developments, see the Internet Society pages at http://www.isoc.org/.

Netscape & the Browser Explosion

NCSA licensed their server technology to Spyglass, a commercial reseller, and their client software to a number of other vendors. Others realized that they, too, could write their own useful, special-purpose clients. Soon a surfeit of browsers was loose in the world, but of those, only two or three were free, including shareware or software free to educational institutions and not-for-profits. While these special versions could interoperate with most WWW servers, each had some small improvement that its developers hoped would set it apart. Over 20 WWW browsers were reviewed in an early 1995 issue of *Interactive Age*, but only a few had a measurable market share.

In March 1994, a mass migration from NCSA to Silicon Valley began. Among the first to leave was Marc Andreessen, who, along with Jim Clark, formerly of Silicon Graphics, founded what was at first called Mosaic Communications (before NCSA's lawyers called them). By October 1994, the company, renamed Netscape Communications, had hired many of the Mosaic, WWW, and Lynx developers. Netscape released its first browser and announced that it was working on a secure server to allow transactions over the Internet.

Netscape was clearly superior to the other browsers. The Netscape developers actually implemented many of the features that were still being discussed by the HTML standards group. Andreessen, Eric Bina, Rob McCool, and company replayed the drama surrounding the adoption and implementation of the <IMG> tag. While keeping a close eye on the direction in which the standards were moving and regularly participating in the Usenet newsgroups that discussed WWW issues, the Netscape developers, in the interest of producing an exceptional product, were willing to push beyond the limits of a developing standard, and they have been rewarded. By November 1994, Netscape accounted for about 20 percent of the accesses on several large servers, and by January 1995, it accounted for 80 percent. As of this writing, they offer their clients free to educational institutions and not-for-profits, both of which are still a large portion of the Internet, and Netscape browsers account for over 80 percent of the accesses on several large servers. You'll notice that many servers on the Internet have a notice telling you that to fully appreciate their pages, you need a client that supports the Netscape extensions to HTML.

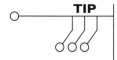

Check out Netscape's latest release and ordering information at http://www.netscape.com/.

The W3 Consortium

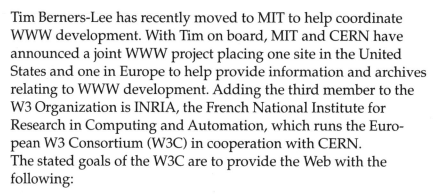

Tim Berners-Lee has recently moved to MIT to help coordinate WWW development. With Tim on board, MIT and CERN have announced a joint WWW project placing one site in the United States and one in Europe to help provide information and archives relating to WWW development. Adding the third member to the W3 Organization is INRIA, the French National Institute for Research in Computing and Automation, which runs the European W3 Consortium (W3C) in cooperation with CERN. The stated goals of the W3C are to provide the Web with the following:

- A repository of information, including specifications about the Web for developers and users.

- A reference code implementation to promote standards.

- Various prototype and sample applications to indicate how new technology can be used.

W3C is a membership organization. While there is no official membership list, several companies have indicated their intentions to join, including AT&T, Digital Equipment Corporation, Enterprise Integration Technologies, FTP Software, Hummingbird Communication, IBM, IXI, MCI, NCSA, Netscape Communications,

Novell, Open Market, O'Reilly & Associates, Spyglass, and Sun Microsystems. Expect to hear more from the W3C especially as privacy and security issues come more to the forefront of discussions about the WWW.

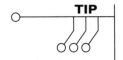

TIP

Check out the W3C pages for the latest standards developments and see why the Ws are green at http://www.w3.org/.

Internet Engineering Task Force (IETF)

The Internet Engineering Task Force oversees the general development of and the evolution of standards for the Internet. The IETF meets three times a year to set directions for the Internet. The various teams and research groups of the IETF produce the official Internet standards documents called Requests for Comments, or RFCs, as well as informative documents about the Internet and its history, culture, and ways and means. The latter documents are called For Your Information RFCs, or FYI RFCs.

According to the FYI RFC 1718, by G. Malkin, the IETF is the principal body engaged in the development of new Internet standard specifications. Its mission includes the following:

* Identifying, and proposing solutions to, pressing operational and technical problems in the Internet.

* Specifying the development or usage of protocols and the near-term architecture to solve such technical problems for the Internet.

* Making recommendations to the Internet Engineering Steering Group (IESG) regarding the standardization of protocols and protocol usage in the Internet.

* Facilitating technology transfer from the Internet Research Task Force (IRTF) to the wider Internet community.

* Providing a forum for the exchange of information among vendors, users, researchers, agency contractors, and network managers within the Internet community.

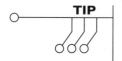

TIP

You can learn more about the IETF and, in particular, the "Tao of the IETF" at http://www.ietf.cnri.reston.va.us/home.html.

Keeping Current

The Web is growing very quickly. By the time this book is printed, the Web will have developed further and probably in ways that we cannot predict (although we'll make a few guesses at the end of the book). If you plan to be an active WWW provider, designer, or publisher, it's imperative that you try to keep up with the latest Web happenings. In the next few sections we'll look at some ways you can keep current with the state of the Web, and at some of the issues you should keep an eye on.

Web-Related Newsgroups

The WWW was created and expanded through worldwide cooperation and as a result of discussions that began in the Usenet newsgroup alt.hypertext and then spread to mailing lists and finally to newsgroups specifically about the Web. The existing Web was built on top of the earlier web of newsgroup postings and of e-mail that was generated by mailing lists. One of the best ways to stay current with Web developments is as the developers of the WWW began—by reading and participating in a number of newsgroups. Following are some of the newsgroups you might want to check into, the first three being the most important:

- comp.infosystems.www.providers   This group discusses issues related to providing information on the WWW. Much of the discussion concerns servers and server-side issues.

- comp.infosystems.www.announce   This newsgroup is where new pages, collections, products, and the like are announced. You can announce your latest developments for your service in this group as well.

- comp.infosystems.www.servers.ms-windows   Anyone involved in running a Windows-based Web site should subscribe to this group!

- alt.hypertext   The discussion in this newsgroup covers hypertext in general and, specifically, every known hypertext implementation. You can obtain lots of information about the WWW and HTML in this group.

- comp.internet.net-happenings   Gleason Sackman moderates this list of what's happening in the Internet-related world. This is the news gateway to his Net-happenings mailing list.

- bit.listserv.www-vm   This is a gateway of a Bitnet listserv that is concerned with the thankless task of managing a WWW server under VM, an IBM mainframe operating system.

- bionet.software.www   This group discusses the WWW as it is used in the biological sciences.

Web–Related Mailing Lists

You might also participate in the WWW–related mailing lists. Mailing lists deliver the discussion directly to your e-mail address, which some people consider more timely and more convenient than reading newsgroups. Others of us find ourselves drowning in mail as it is and prefer to read discussions in newsgroups. Currently, the mailing lists are more technical and a bit more focused than the newsgroups. If you're a developer with a keen interest in a certain area, the WWW mailing lists are for you.

WWW Mailing Lists at W3.org

- www-lib is the public mailing list discussing bug reports, patches, enhancements, and public contributions to the W3C reference library of common code (a.k.a. libwww).

- www-style contains technical discussions among those interested in or developing an application of Style Sheets for HTML (or some future World Wide Web markup language). Be sure that any mail you send to this list is about style sheets and style sheets only.

- www-speech contains discussion of the use and development of World Wide Web clients with speech-enabled interfaces.

- www-html@w3.org contains technical discussions regarding the design, development, and implementation of HTML. Issues relating to style sheets and the like are also covered. Participants stress that this list is for designers of the language, not for beginners.

- www-talk@w3.org contains technical discussion by and for those developing WWW–related software. Do not post questions about HTML; those should go to www-html. New user questions should go to the appropriate newsgroups, such as comp.infosystems.www.misc.

To subscribe to the WWW mailing list of your choice, send a mail message to listserv@w3.org. The message should contain a single line in the following format:

```
subscribe list-name your-name
```

For example, if Gregor Samsa wanted to become a subscriber to the www-talk list, he would send an e-mail message to listserv@w3.org that contained the following line:

```
subscribe www-talk Gregor Samsa
```

To participate in the list, he would send e-mail to www-talk@w3.org.

Any administrative requests, such as those that concern subscribing, unsubscribing, retrieving files from the archives, and so forth, should be sent to the listserv@w3.org address. To learn more about the listserv options, send the single-line message "help" to listserv@w3.org.

Other WWW–Related Mailing Lists

Following are some other Web-related mailing lists you might want to take a look at in addition to the W3.org lists discussed above:

※ www-security@nsmx.rutgers.edu is the official mailing list of the IETF HTTP Security Working Group. It's intended to be a forum on all aspects of security on the Web. Remember, this is a working group mailing list made up of people currently working on security products and policies; don't send new user or novice questions to this list. Read about it first at http://www-ns.rutgers.edu/www-security/ then subscribe if you are interested.

> subscribe www-security *your-email-address*

※ VRML@wired.com, the Virtual Reality Modeling Language mailing list, has been pretty quiet as of this writing, but it got off to a good start in late 1994 and may revive. The list is dedicated to discussing the implementation of virtual reality viewers in a platform-independent environment. To join, send the following single-line message to majordomo@wired.com:

> subscribe vrml *your-email-address*

※ http-wg is the mailing list of the HTTP working group. To subscribe, send the following single-line mail message to http-wg-request@cuckoo.hpl.hp.com:

> subscribe http-wg *your-full-name*

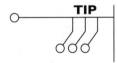

TIP

For additional mailing lists and archive information see http://www.w3.org/pub/WWW/Mail/Overview.html.

W3 Interactive Talk

W3 Interactive Talk, or WIT, was developed in 1994 as a means for those interested in various WWW topics to communicate entirely on the Web. WIT's stated intent is to be an improvement over newsgroups, in which old news evaporates into the ether in a few days, and mailing lists, which lack a reliable method of following a discussion thread. A short cruise of WIT will help you decide if it's actually much of an improvement. For us the jury is still out; we find ourselves returning to newsgroups and to the mailing list archives instead.

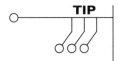
TIP

Take a look at W3 Interactive Talk at http://www.w3.org/hypertext/WWW/WIT/User/Overview.html.

Legal & Regulatory Issues

In addition to the continuing developments in the technology of the Web, there are certain pending legal and regulatory issues relating to the Internet and to electronic publishing that you'll want to be sure to stay on top of. First, despite the hype, the "Information Highway" is more of an "Information Railroad." That is, all the tracks on which this information travels are owned by various telephone companies, just as the rails on which rail freight is carried are owned and operated for the most part by railroad companies; highways, on the other hand, are owned and operated by and for the public through general taxes. When you pay for your connection to the Internet, you're most likely paying a telephone provider, either directly or indirectly. At present, you usually pay a flat rate for your connection to the Internet and your usage of that connection. The flat rate makes it easier to budget and easier to present to your bank, spouse, stockholders, board, or other funding sources. But it may not always be this way. You should keep an eye on upcoming legislation regarding the regulation and allowable rates for telephone companies and for Internet service providers.

Second, copyright law is in a state of flux, even as we write. No matter how the law changes, it will not be right or legal to publish materials to which others hold the copyright. Still, one of the main questions being asked at the moment is, what constitutes publishing, copying, and holding of information in the electronic environment? Remember that in the United States, you pay a hidden royalty for every blank video and audio tape you buy, and that royalty is distributed among a group of large copyright holders.

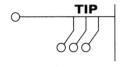

TIP *For current and reliable discussions of copyright on the Internet, see the Coalition for Networked Information's cni-copyright discussion group archives at gopher://gopher.cni.org:70/11/cniftp/forums/ cni-copyright.*

Third, the content of your server may be subject to some swiftly changing laws. A recently passed U.S. law would makes server administrators completely responsible for the contents of their servers. Since the laws concerning decency, free speech, libel, privacy, and fair use vary from community to community and from country to country, these areas of responsibility are difficult to determine. What's considered decent in San Francisco might not be considered decent in Tokyo, and vice versa. The questions of jurisdiction, even those concerning copyright, remain open.

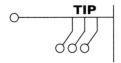

TIP *For more information on pending legislative activities in the United States, see the Electronic Frontier Foundation's Action Alerts at http://www.eff.org.*

Moving On

Now you have some idea of what the Web is and how it came into being. We've provided a number of references to Web sites where you can learn more about topics related to the Web, and references to places you can go to keep current with Web happenings.

In the next chapter, you'll begin learning about the basic pieces of the Web, including the Web's basic protocol and file format, HTTP and HTML, and the various multimedia and other file types commonly found on the Internet and the Web. You'll be on your way toward becoming an information provider—not merely a passive consumer.

2

The Basic Pieces

HyperText Transfer Protocol (HTTP) has been used since the inception of the World Wide Web initiative in 1990 (see Chapter 1, "What Is the Web?"). It's designed to provide a system that's fast enough to distribute multimedia information and flexible enough to use for very different purposes. Different ways of using the features HTTP makes available are explored in detail throughout this book. With the proper considerations, such as the power of your server, the capacity of your Internet connection, and so on, HTTP allows you to present almost anything you could want to a global audience. Sparing the technical details, it will be useful from the outset to understand how data is transmitted via HTTP on the World Wide Web. This chapter also examines other basic elements of the web server, with a brief introduction to HTML web page creation and details on how the web browser processes the multimedia information that your server will provide.

HyperText Transfer Protocol

As discussed in the previous chapter, HTTP is based on a client-server model of information distribution, or a "request/response paradigm," in the words of the Network Working Group's Internet Draft of HTTP specifications. This means that the information available on the World Wide Web is stored at central locations (servers) and is accessed by user request via a program located on a user's personal computer (the client). HTTP operates by sending messages from the client to the server and from the server to the client.

There are a number of different types of messages that a client can send to a server, but three types are most common: GET, HEAD, and POST. These messages are "requests" from the client to send different types of information. The GET request is sent to retrieve a Web page, for example. The client sends a request in the format GET *URL*, followed by a carriage return. This asks the server to return the document or file located at the specified URL. The response from the server consists of the body of the document, prefaced by information like the version of HTTP being used, the status of the request (e.g., OK, Not Found), and the MIME type of the document (see "MIME Typing," later in this chapter).

The HEAD request prompts the server to send all of the same information as the GET request except for the body of the document or file. In an HTML document, this includes all of the information specified in the <TITLE>, <META>, <LINK>, and <BASE HREF> tags (see "The Basics of HTML," later in this chapter). The HEAD request is used by programs called "robots," which request header information to verify that a URL is valid, to collect statistical information, and to perform other functions that don't require the body of the web page.

The POST request asks the server to accept information, whether in the form of a message posted to a newsgroup, a submission using a form (see Chapter 9, "Simple Forms"), or a submission to a database using a script interface between the web page and that interface (see Chapter 10, "CGI & DLLs: Programming Your Server").

This client-server model has a number of characteristics. First, information can be transmitted only by request, and therefore, it is not possible to "force" a message on the user as is done in, say, advertisements on television. Users have to be convinced to access a particular server to get information, and if they're not interested in what is presented, they're not compelled to stay.

Another important factor introduced by the client-server model is that virtually all information has to be provided from the server side of the equation. This means, perhaps obviously, that the server hardware should be sufficiently powerful to deliver all of the information that you make available, even to a large number of simultaneous users. For this reason, certain factors, such as the size of images on a page, the length of a single page, and the types of system calls made by a particular script, always need to be taken into consideration. The more effort required to load each page, the more heavily the server is taxed. The load on the server machine and the number of "hits" (requests from a client to a server) being taken by a server are factors that increase the amount of time it takes users to access your information.

An HTTP server (that is, the program that allows a machine to serve information to HTTP clients) fields requests from clients. For some servers, each time the server takes a request, it creates a new thread to serve that particular request. Generally, creating a large number of new threads is not a problem, because the threads respond to requests and finish extremely fast. However, since the majority of HTTP servers create threads that can only respond to requests one at a time, the server can be overloaded in situations of heavy usage and not be able to create threads quickly enough to keep up with the requests. This situation is one of three major causes of *lag time* (the amount of time it takes a page to appear in the client browser).

The one-at-a-time handling of requests is related to a second major cause of lag time, which is the *load*, or the amount of work that the CPU has to do at any one time. A machine taking a high number of hits must run simultaneous processes that compete for processor time. Both of these problems can be avoided or at least minimized by selectively promoting a site, by directing your promotions at particular populations among the Internet community (see "Choosing & Reaching Your Audience" in Chapter 12,

"Fitting In: Joining the Virtual Community"). It's also important to select HTTP server software that is appropriate to your needs (see Chapter 3, "Setting Up the Server") and to keep up with the latest version of servers, because improvements are made on a regular basis that help reduce the impact of these problems.

The third major cause of lag time in accessing a server is the amount of bandwidth. Every connection to the Internet has a certain upper limit to the amount of information it can transmit at one time, and it's very easy for a server to exceed that limit in low-capacity connections. The type of connection (for example, SLIP, T1, 56 kbps) over which you'll transmit your information should always be taken into consideration when you're deciding what to put up on the site. This is one of the ironic characteristics of a protocol as flexible as HTTP—it permits such a broad range of file types to be transmitted that it can tempt the provider into serving information that overreaches the hardware itself.

Having laid out the constraints of HTTP, it should be said that, by and large, most servers do not experience these problems in any serious way. HTTP is a very powerful protocol, capable of transmitting multimedia information to a client extremely fast.

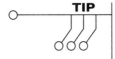

TIP

For full details and specifications of HTTP, look at various papers on this subject, available on the WWW at http://www.w3.org/ hypertext/WWW/Protocols/.

Files on the Web

Throughout this book, reference will be made to certain types of multimedia files. These files are in common usage across the Internet, some by default, some for particular qualities that make them easier to transmit, and some through active promotion. Most require some sort of viewer or helper application so they can be launched automatically by a browser.

File Formats

The following tables list the types of text, image, sound, animation, and compressed files commonly found on the Web.

Name	Extension(s)	MIME Type	Description
HyperText Markup Language (HTML)	.HTML, .HTM	text/html	The basis for the World Wide Web
Text	.TXT	text/plain	Plain ASCII text
Rich Text Format (RTF)	.RTF	application/ rtf	An interchangeable text file type that preserves some formatting
PostScript	.PS, .AI, .EPS	application/ postscript	PostScript files

Table 2-1: *Text types commonly found on the Web.*

Name	Extension(s)	MIME Type	Description
Graphics Inter-change Format (GIF)	.GIF	image/gif	The most common image format on the Web
Joint Photographic Experts Group	.JPEG, .JPG, .JPE	image/jpeg	A higher-resolution graphics format than GIF

Table 2-2: *Image types commonly found on the Web.*

Name	Extension(s)	MIME Type	Description
μ-law	.AU	audio/basic	Sun μ-law files, an 8kHz audio format
Wave file	.WAV	audio/x-wav	Microsoft's audio format
Audio Interchange File Format	.AIFF, .AIF, .AIFC	audio/x-aiff	Audio formats commonly used by Macintoshes
Macintosh Sound File	.SND	audio/basic	Macintosh sound resource file
Motion Picture Experts Group (MPEG) layer II	.MP2	audio/x-mpeg	Digital-quality audio usable by all platforms

Table 2-3: *Sound types commonly found on the Web.*

Name	Extension(s)	MIME Type	Description
QuickTime	.QT, .MOV	video/ quicktime	Macintosh proprietary animation format with sound capability
Motion Picture Experts Group (MPEG) layer I	.MPG, .MPEG, .MPE	video/mpeg	High-quality video compression
Microsoft Video	.AVI	video/ x-msvideo	Microsoft's proprietary audio/animation format

Table 2-4: *Animation types commonly found on the Web.*

Name	Extension	MIME Type	Description
Gnu ZIP	.GZ	application/ x-gzip	Gnu ZIP compression
Compress	.Z	application/ x-compress	Another type of compression, slightly more common than gzip
ZIP	.ZIP	application/ x-zip-compress	Widely used PC file compression
Tape archive	.TAR	application/ x-tar	UNIX format used to compile a number of files and directories into one file

Table 2-5: *Compression types commonly found on the Web.*

Different graphics formats are discussed in detail in Chapter 7, "Images on the Web," and audio and animation files are covered in Chapter 8, "True Multimedia: Adding Audio & Animation." Compression formats and HTML files are discussed later in this chapter.

MIME Typing

One of the most impressive aspects of the World Wide Web is how transparent the transmission of multimedia information can seem. A single link can bring up a text file, a document from across the world, a movie, or a recording. The reason for this seeming transparency is that the server, when sending a file of any type, can tell the client how to process that file. For example, the server tells the client whether to run the file through an audio tool or an animation program or to simply load it as part of a new Web page. To tell the client how to process the file, the server sends the file with an attachment specifying its type. This attachment is referred to as the file's Multipurpose Internet Mail Extensions, or MIME, type.

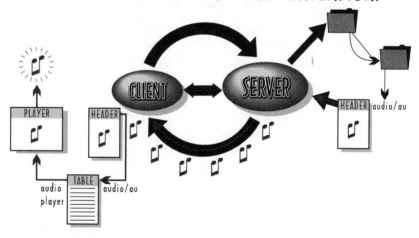

Figure 2-1: *MIME and the Web.*

This name comes from the original purpose of MIME typing, which was to allow for multimedia components to be sent with electronic mail messages by specifying their types in advance so that the mail program could display them as part of the message. MIME typing tells the browser what kind of file is being sent, so that the browser can then tell the user's computer how to display it. MIME types such as x-compressed, x-gzip, x-tar, and x-zip-compressed are understood to be compressed file types, and a browser saves files of these types to the user's drive.

Every HTTP server comes preconfigured to attach MIME types to certain files, but as you add new types of files, you'll want to specify their MIME types as well. You can add new MIME types to your server's setup through the appropriate setup dialog. Notice that some of the MIME types are preceded by an "x-". This prefix indicates that these types are not recognized by the Internet Assigned Numbers Authority (IANA), the agency responsible for setting file type standards on the Internet. This is the case with one of the more popular audio formats on the Web right now, MPEG layer II, which usually uses the extension .MP2 and is mapped to the MIME type audio/x-mpeg.

Once you've set the MIME type of a file, the users have to set their browsers to automatically launch a helper application upon receiving a file of that MIME type. As with the servers, most clients have a great deal of this preconfigured, but if you're using a non-standard multimedia format, it's a good idea to announce it on your Web pages and tell users that they need to configure their browsers accordingly. Every browser is configured differently, some with long text files called "mailcap" files, some with interactive menus. As long as you give users the MIME type and perhaps recommend an application, preferably freeware, that can display the file, users should be able to configure their browsers appropriately.

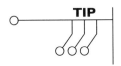

TIP

For further details on MIME types, check out "Introduction to MIME," at the URL http://www.cs.indiana.edu/docproject/mail/ mime.html, and the collection of documents available at CyberWeb, http://WWW.Stars.com/Vlib/Providers/MIME.html.

Compressing & Archiving

Transmitting files over the Web to be stored on the user's computer without being displayed is a very common practice because browsers are capable of using FTP in the same way that they use

HTTP. Since these files are identified with MIME types that are not "displayable" files, the user's browser automatically saves them to disk. To cut down on transmission time, most files are stored in compressed formats, to be uncompressed when they are on the user's computer. Three of the most common compression programs are gzip, compress, and pkzip. A fourth program, tar, is not a compression program per se, but can combine a large number of files into a single archive, called a tar file. This section provides a brief description of the tar, gzip, and pkzip programs and instructions for compressing and uncompressing files. (The compress program is not covered, since no Windows NT version of the UNIX compress program is commonly available.) Since the different compression programs have different functionalities, it's a good idea to be familiar with all of them. In general, if you're providing files on your server, the most efficient and transferable setup is to create a tar file and compress it using gzip for UNIX users, and to create a compressed ZIP archive with pkzip for Windows users.

For UNIX-Based Browsers

Typically, a UNIX (or UNIX-like operating system) user has a different set of tools for compression and archiving than Windows and Mac users. This section discusses what you need to do to prepare files for UNIX users to download.

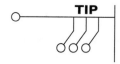

TIP

Note that tar and gzip both originated as UNIX programs. You must use a file system that can support long filenames when using UNIX-derived tools.

tar, or tape archive, is a program originated on the UNIX operating system used to compile a set of files into a single file for storage on tapes, as the name might suggest. Usually this program is used for backups, but the fact that it can compress full directory trees as easily as single files makes it useful for file storage as well. tar is an extremely versatile command, so we'll cover only four functions—creating, adding to, listing, and extracting tar files.

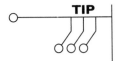

The Windows NT version of tar, along with some other utilities ported to Windows NT, is available at ftp://june.cs.washington.edu/ pub/ntemacs/utilities.

Extracting files from a tar file that someone else made is easy with the NT version of tar. Unfortunately, the process to create a tar archive with Windows NT is more difficult. As a Webmaster, however, you may eventually need to create directory tree archives for UNIX users as well as Mac and Windows users, so it is worth your time to understand the process. Creating a tar archive is a three-step process:

1. Create a list of files you want to archive. This is done by changing directory to the root of what you want to archive, then entering the following command:

   `dir /s /b > ` *`tarlist`*`.txt`

   This command creates a complete list of files to be archived, starting at the current directory location.

2. Unfortunately, the separator character in the paths in the tarlist.txt file is a single "\", which isn't well received by the tar program. Edit the tarlist.txt file with an editor that allows global replacements, and replace all the single "\" characters with two in a row: "\\".

3. To create the archive file, enter the following command:

   `tar -c -T ` *`tarlist`*`.txt -f ` *`outfile`*`.tar`

   This will take the list of files in *tarlist*.txt and archive them into the *outfile*.tar file.

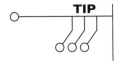

When the archive is extracted, the full pathname to the file will be included, since that is what was in the tarlist.txt file. If you want to include only the relative pathname, you should edit the tarfile.txt file and delete the path information up to the current directory, so the archive will include only the relative pathnames.

tar works silently and doesn't tell you which files are being archived. If you want to see the status of the archive as it progresses, enter the option v between the options c and f. This option gives you a verbose listing of the files as they are added to *outfile*.tar.

If you want to append a file to an existing archive, simply use the r option in place of the c option. Specify the name of the tar file that you want to add the file to and then the file or files to be added:

```
tar -r -f outfile.tar newfile.xyz
```

This command overwrites any file in the archive with the same name as the file being added.

If you want to update the tar file, changing files that have been updated and adding new files, you can use the u option, as follows:

```
tar -u -T tarlist.txt -f outfile.tar
```

This command overwrites older files (using the date and time of creation to judge which file is newer) and appends new files to the tar file.

To check the contents of a tar file, use the t option:

```
tar -t -f outfile.tar
```

This command gives you a listing of the files in the archive. You should note whether the files are prefaced with a directory name, such as subdir/README, rather than appearing just as README. If a directory name is in front of the file, tar automatically creates this directory when it extracts the files.

To extract the files from an archive, change to the directory in which you want the new files to appear, and enter the following command:

```
tar -x -f outfile.tar
```

While tar concatenates a large number of files into a single file, the tar file can be further compressed. gzip (Gnu ZIP) is an incredibly effective compression algorithm, reducing text files or source files containing code by as much as 70 percent, and it is a useful follow-up compression for tar files. Like tar, gzip is an extremely versatile program. By and large, you'll want to use it in two capacities: for compressing tar files or single files (such as binaries) and for uncompressing files with the extension .GZ or .Z.

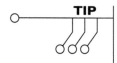

TIP

The Windows NT version of gzip is available from the same site as tar—ftp://june.cs.washington.edu/pub/ntemacs/utilities.

The format of the gzip command at its most basic is fairly simple. To compress a single file, such as our tar file *outfile*.tar from the previous section, enter the following command line:

```
gzip outfile.tar
```

gzip replaces the file *outfile*.tar with the file *outfile*.tar.gz, preserving information like the date of creation. gzip should only be used to compress a single file—to compress multiple files, put the files into an archive using tar and then use gzip to compress that archive.

To preserve the original file being compressed, you can specify a nondestructive compress, which creates a gzip-compressed file without overwriting the original. This option is specified with the -c option, as in the following example:

```
gzip -c outfile.tar > outfile.tar.gz
```

Since you're not replacing the original file, you need to specify what filename to write the output to, just as you would if compressing multiple files simultaneously.

There are a couple of options for uncompressing a gzip file. Both of the following commands produce the same output:

```
gzip -d outfile.tar.gz
gunzip outfile.tar.gz
```

For Windows–Based Browsers

pkzip is a widely used PC compression program. It's available as shareware from many Internet sites, and is supplied with a number of programs. There are also Windows-native compression programs that use the ZIP format, including WinZip and DragonZIP. To create a standard ZIP-compressed file of only the current directory with pkzip, use the following command:

```
pkzip -a outname *.*
```

The asterisks (*.*) indicate the filename(s) to be added to the ZIP file, and *outname* is the name of the ZIP file minus the .ZIP extension. If you want to add only specific files from a directory into a ZIP file, you can provide a list of filenames to be added on the command line.

To create an archive of files in the subdirectories as well as the current directory, add the recurse and pathname store options, as follows:

```
pkzip -a outname.zip -r -p *.*
```

You can get a complete list of options from pkzip by entering the following:

```
pkzip -?
```

To extract files from ZIP files, use the pkunzip command:

```
pkunzip filename.zip
```

To extract files keeping the pathnames that may be stored in the ZIP file, use the -d option:

```
pkunzip -d filename.zip
```

To refine this command a bit, you can specify that you do not want to extract certain files by using the -x option at the end of the command line:

```
pkunzip filename.zip -x README
```

Finally, if you're extracting an update or software patch and want only the files that have been updated to be overwritten by the files in the ZIP file, you can use the freshen or -f option, which replaces a file with a newer version:

```
pkunzip -f newfiles.zip
```

The Basics of HTML

The final basic piece of the Web that you'll need to understand before diving in is the actual language in which Web documents are written, called HyperText Markup Language, or HTML. The name may be somewhat deceptive, since HTML is not, properly speaking, a programming "language." HTML is simply a set of codes that are placed around and within text to allow it to be displayed a certain way by browsers and to be given certain attributes, such as a link to another file. For the server, it's irrelevant what type of computer or browser will be accessing the information that is coded in HTML. All browsers can interpret

HTML codes and use the codes to determine how the structure of the document is laid out—in other words, what the title is, what the headers are, where paragraph breaks are located, and so on. There is, then, no need to try to design pages for certain types of hardware or software.

Marking up a document for presentation on the Web is a remarkably simple process. Including graphics, audio files, or forms and linking to other multimedia resources or external files is somewhat more complicated but is by no means impossible to learn. The following sections provide a brief overview of some of the most common HTML coding, much of which will be elaborated upon later in this book. (Forms, for example, which can be some of the most useful parts of a web server, are discussed in Chapter 9, "Simple Forms," and Chapter 10, "CGI & DLLs: Programming Your Server.")

Locating the Documents

The first order of business is to create the HTML file itself. An HTML file is nothing more than a flat ASCII file with special commands enclosed in < > brackets. It can be named anything you want, but make sure that the file extension is .HTM or .HTML. This extension indicates to the server that the file is a hypertext document. After you've created the file, you'll put it in the area of your file system that is reserved for HTML pages. Your file's location and your machine's name or IP address provide that file's URL, or Uniform Resource Locator—the document's "address" on the World Wide Web.

URLs have the following standard format:

```
protocol://machine address:port/path/filename
```

The port specification is optional, and if none is entered, the browser defaults to the standard port for whatever service is specified as the protocol. For example, if you are using HTTP, the default port is 80. Following are some hypothetical examples of standard URLs:

```
http://www.shoop.com/users/dobbs.html
http://www.nra.org/ak47.gif
ftp://sunsite.unc.edu/
gopher://gopher.foo.bar.org
```

Other protocols in addition to the ones listed are news, mailto, and telnet. Telnet has essentially the same format, but you can specify a login name before the machine name by using a URL such as the following:

```
telnet://lynx@sunsite.unc.edu
```

For news and mailto, you simply enter the newsgroup to be read or the address to which you want to send mail:

```
news:comp.infosystems.www.announce
mailto:help@vmedia.com
```

In both cases, the mail server and news server used to execute these commands will be defined in the client.

For your site, all URLs will probably begin with HTTP, because that protocol can access HTML documents and multimedia files. If you want access to a site's home page, the URL is all you need to enter. To access some other page at the site, just add the file path and the filename. The path for documents you create will be relative to whatever top-level directory you specify in your HTTP server software (see Chapter 3, "Setting Up the Server"). If you've told your server that the top-level directory is \alibaba\htmldocs, a file located in \alibaba\htmldocs\users\homepages\ would have the path /users/homepages/. If the user doesn't know a document's filename, she or he can enter the file path and might be presented with an index page of available files in that directory, depending on how the server is configured.

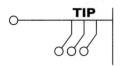

TIP

You may notice that under Windows, the file path separator is a backslash, "\", while the browsers use the forward slash, "/". This difference is understood by the Windows servers, so you don't need to worry about it.

Creating the Documents

Any HTML document should have certain features that mark it as HTML and that delineate its component parts. If for some reason you wanted to create a completely empty web page, it would look something like this:

```
<HTML>
<HEAD>
</HEAD>
<BODY>
</BODY>
</HTML>
```

Note that each tag has a second tag that is identical to it, except for the addition of a forward slash. The first tag is the opening tag, and the second, with the forward slash, closes out the first one. Anything you put in between these two tags is affected by the characteristics that are specified by the opening tag. Anything before the opening tag and after the closing tag is unaffected. One very common error in writing pages is to forget the closing tag, thereby giving everything the wrong characteristics.

The example page shown above would display as a blank screen on a browser, with no title (or rather, with the document's URL as the title). The first tag, <HTML>, indicates that the document is to be read as an HTML format file. The reason this tag is necessary is because in the near future, different versions of HTML, and possibly documents in other languages, will be read through web browsers. The <HTML> tag will tell the browser that the document is to be interpreted as HTML. The set of tags below (<HEAD> and </HEAD>) marks the area that serves as the header for the page. Anything in the header is located in between these two tags. The next set of tags, <BODY> and </BODY>, delineates—you guessed it—the body of the document. The information to be displayed on the browser should be placed in between this set of tags. The final tag marks the end of the document and should always be the last line of the file.

Title & Header Information

There's one tag that must be included in every <HEAD> section (that is, between the <HEAD> and </HEAD> tags), and that is the <TITLE> tag. The information between <TITLE> and </TITLE> is the title for the document and is displayed in the top of the browser window in most browsers. If you want this title to be the heading of the page as well, you should include it at the top of the body of the page. To make it more prominent, you can identify it as a "header," specifying the relative size of the font that you want displayed. The sizes range from 1 (largest) to 6 (smallest), and the tags are <H1> through <H6>. As always, when you open with a tag <H1>, be sure to close with the closing tag </H1>. To create a page with a title recognized by the browser and a large-font title across the top of the page, the code would look like this:

```
<HTML>

<HEAD>
<TITLE>ShoopSoft on the WWW</TITLE>
</HEAD>

<BODY>
<H1>The ShoopSoft Page</H1>
</BODY>

</HTML>
```

Three additional tags that may also be included in the header of the document give information about the document itself. The information defined in these tags, <META>, <LINK>, and <BASE>, may not actually be displayed on the browser, but it is useful for individuals looking at the source of your document, and it's used by programs that automatically gather information about web pages.

The <META> tag gives general information about the document, such as its expiration date (that is, when it should be considered obsolete), its owner, and how it was created. For example, the following tags define the owner of the document as "Bob" and the program used to create it as "tkHTML 2.3," and indicate that the document should expire at midnight on July 5, 1998.

```
<META HTTP-EQUIV="OWNER" CONTENT="Bob">
<META NAME="GENERATOR" CONTENT="tkHTML 2.3">
<META HTTP-EQUIV="EXPIRES">Tue, 05 Jul 1998 00:00:00 GMT
</META>
```

Note that the "generator" setting is specified using the NAME option, whereas the expiration date and owner are specified using the HTTP-EQUIV option. This is because the owner and expiration date are both variables recognized by the HTTP server when it sends or receives HEAD information (see "HyperText Transfer Protocol," earlier in this chapter). The HTTP-EQUIV option indicates that this is a variable that the server software should recognize. The generator information, though useful, is not understood or transmitted by the server, so it is specified using the NAME option, which means that this is a variable not necessarily recognized by server software.

The <LINK> tag is used to describe a document's relationship to other documents on the site. It identifies the relationship using the REL option, and identifies the document using the HREF option. So, for example, the following tag indicates that the document was "made" by a user who can be contacted at the URL mailto:webmaster@shoop.com.

```
<LINK REL="made" HREF="mailto:webmaster@shoop.com">
```

The <BASE HREF> tag is used to include the URL of the document in the source of the document itself, so that a user viewing the source out of the context of the web site can still locate it on the Internet. The syntax is simple—the following tag specifies the URL of the document as http://www.shoop.com/index.html.

```
<BASE HREF="http://www.shoop.com/index.html">
```

Formatting Text

Putting plain text on a page requires no special formatting. However, since browsers do not recognize spaces between lines or carriage returns in the code itself, you need to indicate where you want line breaks in the document. For a simple break, use the <BR> tag. To indicate that a section of text is to be interpreted as a paragraph, enclose the text inside the opening and closing paragraph tags, <P> and </P>. The <BR> or <P> tags are unnecessary inside a section of header text—a line is automatically inserted after a header closing tag.

You can format the plain text on a page in a number of ways. Enclosing text within the tags <B> and </B> makes it bold type, and enclosing text within <I> and </I> italicizes it. These tags are currently very common in HTML page design. You can also use the tags <EM>, for "emphasized" text, and <STRONG>, for text that is more strongly emphasized, than to use the more general <B>. Similarly, the tags <CITE>, for cited text, and <VAR>, which indicates a variable, are more useful than <I>, since they identify the text more exactly.

The layout of text on a web page can be modified using the list functions. The three most commonly used types of lists are the *unordered list*, designated with the <UL> tag, the *ordered list*, designated with the <OL> tag, and the *definition list*, designated with the <DL> tag. The major difference between these tags is that all items in the unordered list are bulleted, the items in the ordered list are numbered, and the items in the definition list are not bulleted or numbered.

An unordered list is created by opening the list with <UL>, marking each item in the list with the tag <LI>, and closing the list with </UL>. An ordered list is opened with the <OL> tag, and each item is also marked with the <LI> tag. The definition list is opened with <DL>, and each item in the list is marked with <DT>. Each item can then be defined or elaborated upon with text that follows the tag <DD>. After the last item, the list is closed with the tag </DL>. The list items themselves, <LI>, <DT>, and <DD>, do not require closing tags—they'll be automatically closed when another item is started, or when the list itself is closed. Any of the lists can be *nested*; that is, you can place a list inside a list, simply by opening another list with <UL>, <OL>, or <DL> before closing the first list.

The following is a sample page using the codes mentioned so far. Figure 2-2 provides a picture of how this page would look on a browser.

```
<HTML>

<HEAD>
<TITLE>ShoopSoft on the WWW</TITLE>
</HEAD>

<BODY>
<H1>The ShoopSoft Page</H1>
Welcome to the <B>ShoopSoft</B> page. This is our <I>very own
home page</I> on the World Wide Web.<P>
Here you can get information on the following services:
<UL>
<LI>Networking software
<LI>Custom hardware configurations
   <UL>
   <LI>Macintosh
   <LI>PC
   <LI>Workstations
   </UL>
<LI>HTML training seminars
</UL>

ShoopSoft's many virtues include:
<DL>
<DT>Reliability
   <DD>We guarantee quick response and 24/7
   accessibility.
<DT>Quality
   <DD>Our team has over 5 years of Internet
   experience.
<DT>Affordability
   <DD>Everything we do is free. Really.
</DL>

</BODY>

</HTML>
```

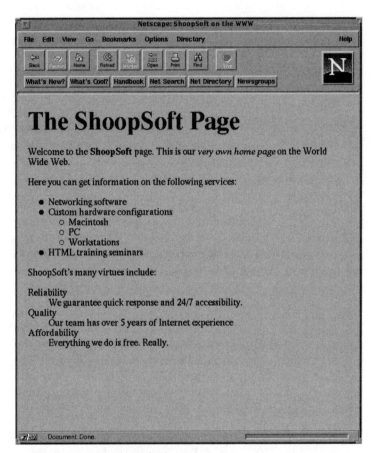

Figure 2-2: *A sample Web page.*

One of the added advantages of using a plain list like <DL>is that you can insert custom bullets into the list using the <IMG> tag, which we'll discuss later in this chapter. In brief, using the <IMG> tag within a definition list allows you to load an image in front of each list item. The tag also specifies an alternate character to display if the user's browser cannot load that image. The format for a two-item list using the <IMG> tag would be as follows:

```
<DL>
<DT><IMG ALT="**" SRC="dot.gif"> Item I
<DT><IMG ALT="**" SRC="dot.gif"> Item II
</DL>
```

Note that dot.gif in the example can be any filename or location you choose. Simply create an icon for your list, and enter that filename in place of dot.gif. Using this tag and custom-designed list bullets, you can give your pages a personalized feel with relatively little effort on your part.

Three other tags are commonly used for page formatting. <BLOCKQUOTE> (along with </BLOCKQUOTE>) indents a section of text to indicate that it is an extract—that it has been taken from some other source. Another commonly used tag is for preformatted text. It allows you to format text in your editor any way you choose and to display that formatted text. One of the limitations of HTML, for example, is that it cannot display more than one space between strings, so browsers cannot show text separated with a tab or display ASCII art. After formatting text the way you want it to appear on a browser, surround it with the tag set <PRE> and </PRE>, and it will display exactly as you have laid it out. Unfortunately, being "preformatted" means that formats like boldface and italics are not displayed and that the text will appear in the Courier font, which from a design standpoint is not a particularly appealing option. Finally, to divide your page with a horizontal line, use the <HR> tag. It creates a line that extends across the page, which is an attractive way of delineating sections and does not increase the time required for a page to load.

Hyperlinks

After you've added the text to your page and formatted it appropriately, you can integrate the page into your site and other sites using links to other pages and to different resources like multimedia files. The hyperlink is an extremely versatile tool in HTML. It can link to any type of resource you choose, so long as your server can specify a MIME type and the user has software that can display data of that type (see "MIME Typing," earlier in this chapter). If you wanted users to click on the words "our employ-ees' resumes" to access a new web page, for example, you'd insert a link similar to the following:

```
We're firing everyone. If you want to hire someone who works
here, then look at
<A HREF="resumes.html">our employees' resumes.
</A><P>
```

The <A HREF="..."> tag is closed with the </A> tag. The same is true of any tag that has parameters after the tag name. Just use the first word or character string of the opening tag with a slash to close it. The tag in the example above references a document at the same site. To link to a document at another site, simply insert the full URL of that site:

```
Learn more about the
<A HREF="http://www.w3.org/">World Wide Web</A>.<BR>
```

The most common links are to other HTML files, but you can use exactly the same format for linking to any other type of file:

```
Check out <A HREF="dobbs.gif">my photograph</A>,
<A HREF="/users/sounds/welcome.au">hear me say hi</A>, or
look at an MPEG movie of
<A HREF="http://www.fbi.gov/data/rp003x.mpeg">
me at a political rally</A>.<P>
```

It's a good idea when presenting something other than an image or a standard audio file (Macintosh sound resource, PC .WAV, or Sun .AU) to state what kind of resource it is, so that users can determine if they have the capability to play it on their machines.

Finally, HTML can be used to provide links to files, like binaries or source code, that are not to be displayed. Links are made exactly the same way as with multimedia files, but when users try to download the file, they're asked where to save that file and are responsible for uncompressing the file themselves (since you'll store all files for transfer in some sort of compressed format, as discussed in the "Compressing & Archiving" section, earlier in this chapter). A link such as the following references a file that has been compressed with tar and gzip:

```
Try our <A HREF="/users/data/bin/recipe093.tar.gz">new recipe
database</A> for FREE!<P>
```

You can use hyperlinks to go to a specific location in an HTML document. You create an "anchor" in that document and then specify the filename and the anchor in the link. To create the anchor in the document to be accessed, insert the tag <A NAME="*anchorname*">, where *anchorname* is replaced by whatever you want to call that anchor. Then, when building a link to the anchor on that page, reference it with the URL, the # symbol, and the anchorname, as follows:

```
<A HREF="/users/data/matthews/book.html#ch2">
```

If you want to go to an anchor within the same page, you can make a reference to *#anchorname* without any file information:

```
<H2>Table of Contents</H2>
<A HREF="#ch1">Chapter 1</A><BR>
<A HREF="#ch2">Chapter 2</A><BR>
```

Images

The use of images within a web page is a major element in creating a truly customized and impressive site. The use of images will be taken up extensively in Chapter 7, "Images on the Web"; this section will simply explain how to write the HTML code that puts the graphics on the page. The graphics format that all web browsers can display on the page itself is called a GIF (Graphics Interchange Format), and the default extension for GIF files is .GIF.

The tag for including images is <IMG>. A number of variables configure the <IMG> tag. The most basic format for including an image is <IMG SRC="*picture*.gif"> where *picture*.gif is replaced by the filename. As with the <A HREF> tag, you can specify the filename and draw an image from another server, simply by inserting the path or the full URL as the source filename. There is no closing tag for <IMG>.

Not all browsers can display graphics—in particular, the Lynx browser used on the older UNIX system cannot. Also, users of graphical browsers can elect to turn off automatic image downloading, which is usually done to speed up document loading over slow modem links. It's a good idea to specify an alternate character or set of characters to load. When not displaying images, browsers will, by default, look for an alternate character, which is specified with ALT. For example, in our custom bulleted list example earlier in the chapter, the list items were coded as follows:

```
<DT><IMG ALT="**" SRC="dot.gif"> Item I
<DT><IMG ALT="**" SRC="dot.gif"> Item II
```

If a browser could not display the image dot.gif, it would preface each list item with the character string ** instead. Specifying an alternate for images is considered to be good form because a significant number of users do not view images when accessing the Web.

Another way of customizing the layout of your page is to specify where you want the text beside a picture to be located. The ALIGN option aligns text beside the image with the top, middle, or bottom of that image. Simply put ALIGN=top, ALIGN=middle, or ALIGN=bottom inside the <IMG> tag. So, for example, to align the menu items listed in the previous example with the center of the list bullets, you could change the code for each to read as follows:

```
<IMG ALT="**" ALIGN=middle SRC="dot.gif">
```

Graphics can be linked to files in the same way that text is. One very common way of presenting graphics on the Web is to have a small version of a graphic linked to the full-size image. This is done in exactly the same manner as linking text, but in the place of the text, you insert the <IMG> tag:

```
<A HREF="/users/data/pics/clinton.gif"><IMG ALT="Clinton!"
SRC="clinton-icon.gif"></A>
```

The following example links both the image and the text to the URL:

```
<A HREF="http://www.netscape.com/"><IMG ALT="*" ALIGN=bottom
SRC="mozilla.gif">Netscape Home Page
</A>
```

HTML also currently recognizes an image that you've indicated as an *imagemap*, an image that has hyperlinks mapped to certain coordinates in the graphic. By clicking on the graphic in a certain place, the user is taken to the link that is connected to that area of the image. To specify that an image should be recognized as an imagemap, add ISMAP at the end of the <IMG> tag. The graphic itself also needs to be linked to an imagemap file. This process, and the rest of the process of creating imagemaps, is explained in the section "Clickable Imagemaps" in Chapter 7, "Images on the Web."

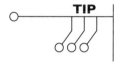

Many people find standard text editors perfectly adequate for writing HTML documents. Others prefer to use special programs that automatically write much of the HTML code using a menu-driven editor interface. If you find an HTML editor that you're comfortable with, by all means use it. However, you should always have some sort of reference to the HTML code itself and be familiar with it.

Netscape Extras

In 1994, Netscape Communications, Inc., introduced a new web browser that can display a number of tags not yet supported by other browsers currently in use. The new tags have been proposed as additions to the HTML standard and may be globally supported at a later date, but for now, many are unique to Netscape. There are several very nice features in the Netscape-enhanced tags, and if you don't mind the current limitations on who can see their effects, they're worth checking out. Some of the more interesting tags are described in the remainder of this section.

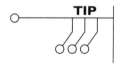

A full listing of the enhanced Netscape tags is available at the URLs http://www.netscape.com/assist/net_sites/html_extensions.html and http://www.netscape.com/assist/net_sites/html_extensions_3.html .

- **<HR>** Horizontal rule. The HR element (described in "Creating the Documents," earlier in this chapter) can be configured in several different ways. For example, entering <HR SIZE=number> lets you define the thickness of the line, and you can modify the length of the line using <HR WIDTH=number | percent>, specifying the length of the line in pixels or the percentage of the page width it extends across. Using the tag <HR ALIGN=left | right | center>, you can specify the alignment of the line if you've made it shorter than the width of the page.

- **<IMG>** Image. Most of the new Netscape extensions have to do with the <IMG> tag. We won't go into full detail in this chapter because all of the Netscape options are covered in Chapter 7, "Images on the Web."

- **<UL>** and **<OL>** Lists. The unordered list, or <UL>, generally has a standard order in which bullets are displayed as the nesting level of the list items increases, depending upon the browser. A new option, TYPE, has been added so that you can specify in advance the shape of that list's bullets as TYPE=disc, TYPE=circle, or TYPE=square. For the ordered list, or <OL>, the TYPE option specifies the type of character to be used for ordering the list. Entering TYPE=A designates the use of capital letters (A, B, C . . .); TYPE=a, lowercase letters; TYPE=I, Roman numerals; TYPE=i; small Roman numerals; and not specifying this option defaults to using numbers. The <OL> tag also has the new option START=, with which you can specify the starting value of the TYPE you've chosen. For example, setting START=4 would begin the list with D, d, IV, iv, or 4, depending on the TYPE specified.

- **<NOBR>** No break. Since web browsers, including Netscape, automatically wrap lines of text that are too long for the screen, lines occasionally lose the desired formatting. Text between <NOBR> and </NOBR> does not wrap around but continues off the side of the browser screen.

- **<WBR>** Word break. Using the <NOBR> tag, you can specify where you do want a line to wrap by using the <WBR> tag inside the no-break section. This is not the same as a line break tag; the word break tag tells the browser where a break could be placed only if needed.

- **<FONT SIZE=value>** Text font size. This tag allows the font size of a character or string to be increased or decreased. You can either specify a size in a range of 1 to 7 or use a plus sign (+) or minus sign (–) to indicate a relative change, which is based on the standard font size 3. To change the standard size, you can use the <BASEFONT=value> tag. If you set <BASEFONT=4>, for example, a + would increase the size to 5, and text without the font size change would appear as 4.

- **<BLINK>** Blinking text. This tag is fairly self-evident. Anything enclosed between <BLINK> and </BLINK> blinks. Since blinking text can be distracting, this tag should be used in moderation.

- **<CENTER>** Centered display. This tag allows any text or images to be centered on the page. Make sure to use the closing tag on this one so you won't center your entire page.

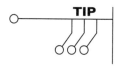

TIP

For an excellent introduction to writing HTML, check out HTML Publishing on the Internet for Windows, *also from Ventana.*

Moving On

This chapter has laid out the basics of what a web site entails. The HTTP protocol allows for a wide range of file types to be transmitted from the server to the client. These files must be defined as certain types if they are to be displayed by the user's browser as audio, video, or an image. If they aren't defined, they're saved to the user's hard drive, which is generally the desired result when sending programs, source code, and some text files. These files are compressed to save transmission time, using one or more of the major compression programs like tar, pkzip, or gzip. Finally, all of this information is laid out in the web page, which is created using a series of codes called HTML. This code allows you to create formatted text, include images, and create links to any files that you want the user to access.

Now that we've covered the basics of a web site, you can begin preparing to create your own site and pages. As noted previously, you need HTTP server software to serve your documents to clients. The next chapter will describe several types of servers. The rest of the book will be devoted to helping you develop the material on your server and make it accessible from your pages in as many ways as possible.

3

Setting Up the Server

Using Windows NT to serve the Web is becoming an increasingly popular alternative to using UNIX and UNIX-like servers, due in part to the relative simplicity of NT in terms of setup and site maintenance. Plus, the ease of programming a Windows NT system and the wide assortment of inexpensive tools for databases and data access offer an enticing alternative to the world of market-limited and fragmented UNIX tools. It would, at this time, be inaccurate to claim any fundamental advantages of using Windows NT over UNIX, and it's important to realize that the UNIX-based servers have had much longer to mature. The number of UNIX-based servers on the public Internet is far greater than the number of NT-based servers at the time of this writing. The NT market is growing dramatically, however, and the options for servers as this is written are many and growing. This chapter will discuss the features of some of the more popular NT-based web servers available. We'll also take a detailed look at using Alibaba, the server featured on the Companion CD-ROM.

Comparing Servers

There are many Windows NT web servers, and prices range from free to thousands of dollars. In most cases, you get what you pay for. (There are a number of servers written for Windows 3.1 that will also run on Windows NT, but these servers are not considered in this chapter because they cannot take advantage of the multithreading and security features of Windows NT.) Most of the NT-based servers are available in demonstration versions from their distributors, with 30- to 60-day timeout features. Several of these demo versions are included on the Companion CD-ROM. None of the servers mentioned in this chapter are available in source code form except by special agreement with the developer, and most are compiled for the Intel platform only.

Each of the servers discussed in this chapter has the basic features that allow it to function as a web server. Each server:

* Supports basic HTTP processing and functions as a basic web server.

* Operates as a Windows NT service.

* Determines MIME type based on file extension.

* Supports basic authentication.

Significant additional features for each server are described in the sections that follow.

Since the server market is still rapidly developing, some of the information will be out of date by the time you read this. And since specific features are sure to change rapidly, the following sections do not attempt to provide a comprehensive, feature-by-feature comparison of the servers. You should always check with the vendor of a particular product for the latest feature information and check with the newsgroups for the latest opinions from others in the NT server community.

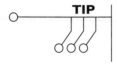
TIP

For an up-to-date feature comparison of web servers, see the list compiled by Paul Hoffman, available from http://www.proper.com/ www/servers-chart.html or http://195.227.249.2/www/ servers-chart.html.

Alibaba

The Alibaba server, from Computer Software Manufaktur (http://www.csm.co.at/), an Austrian company, is a middle-of-the-road server suitable for many public and internal web applications. It supports security through SSL, and features highly customizable access control. Alibaba is available for Windows 95 as well as Windows NT, and when running under NT can operate as a system service.

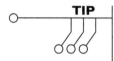

Both the SSL and S-HTTP secure protocols, as well as other security issues, will be discussed in Chapter 4, "System Security."

A special "lite edition" of Alibaba for Windows NT (for the Intel processor), licensed from the manufacturer, is included on the Companion CD-ROM. What makes this version special is that it is not a demo that will time out after a certain period; it is limited instead by the number of simultaneous IP connections that it will accept. This development edition server can be very useful for creating a web and testing it. The commercial version, and instructions for obtaining the unlock key, are also included on the Companion CD-ROM. (Note that, due to licensing restrictions, the secure SSL version of Alibaba is not included.)

Features

Alibaba has a rich feature set, which includes extensive logging capability; different responses to different clients; full security and screening based on IP address or username and password; a DLL-based CGI in addition to standard CGI and WinCGI, with ISAPI promised in the near future; the SSL security scheme (in the secure version, not included on the Companion CD-ROM); and a proxy server version. It supports server-side includes, integrates with the WAIS search engine, and can be remotely administered from other NT systems. Alibaba operates under Windows NT as a system service or application and under Windows 95 as an application. It also offers integration with the Windows ODBC interface through bundling with dbWeb (discussed in Chapter 9, "Simple Forms").

In addition, Alibaba allows you to create different virtual servers to support more than one unique web per single server system. Different IP addresses are mapped to different webs on the hard disk of the server system.

Programmability
Alibaba supports standard CGI, WinCGI, and a DLL-based CGI interface. These will be discussed in detail in Chapter 10. CSM has stated that they plan in the near future to support the ISAPI interface as defined by Microsoft and Process Software.

Administration
Alibaba has a Windows-based administration program that can administer Alibaba servers on local or remote systems. It has a property-page look, consistent with the Windows 95 interface, and gives complete control over all aspects of Alibaba's operation.

Since Alibaba is the featured server on the Companion CD-ROM, its use will be discussed in much greater detail later in this chapter (see "Using Alibaba").

Cost
Alibaba costs $450 for the Windows NT server and proxy server, and $799 for a bundle of the Windows NT server and dbWeb.

Commerce Builder

Built by Aristosoft (http://www.aristosoft.com/), Commerce Builder is a secure server—if you get a certificate for it—and it comes with a very complete set of server capabilities. It's currently the only server that supports S-HTTP (although others have promised to support S-HTTP in the near future). The Commerce Builder also has a proxy capability: it can act as a proxy server for others on your network.

Features

The proxy capability and support for multiple security types are rare among the current crop of Windows NT servers. Commerce Builder comes all ready for secure operation, although you need to supply a security certificate, as with any secure server. The Commerce Builder also sports a proxy server capability built into the basic server, which can cascade to other proxies, specify certain URLs that are not to be cached, and bar access to specified URLs. Extended logging is possible using the SMX feature (described below). One unique feature is Chat Room bundled with the web server. The Chat Room allows users to connect to your server and conduct a real-time chat simply by specifying port 8000 (or whatever you specify) instead of the default.

Programmability

Commerce Builder has defined a new way of creating a "super server-side include" capability called a Server Macro Expansion (SMX), where macros that replace server-side includes are placed into a special kind of HTML document. A fragment of a sample document with SMX syntax looks like this:

```
</ul>
<hr>
<h2>Complete SMX code for this page</h2>
<pre>%html-quote(%include(%fqppath(smx.htm),noexp))</pre>
</body>
```

The advantage of this approach is that the expressions can be nested and more flexible than SSIs, which rely on HTML comment tags. Unfortunately, since the documents start with %expand%, they will not parse properly in strict editors.

Commerce Builder also has standard CGI and WinCGI 1.2 programming support. You can use the freeware EMWAC WAIS text search tool with Commerce Builder to provide site-wide search capabilities to your users.

Administration

Administration for the Commerce Builder is performed through a Control Panel application. The application has a property-page feel, although the navigation is somewhat unusual. The Control Panel application can be used to administer a server remotely as well as locally.

Cost

In February 1996, Commerce Builder version 1.5 was selling for $795.

Common Gateway Interface

All the servers discussed in this chapter implement the Common Gateway Interface (CGI), an interface standard that allows you to write and run external programs that interact with the HTTP server and web browsers. CGI scripts can dynamically generate web pages and handle interactive forms. The standard is indispensable for web developers who wish to make their sites more than just flat pictures and text.

Most of the servers also support a variation on CGI called WinCGI. This modification allows Windows-based programs to be used as CGI programs.

Despite CGI's usefulness, CGI should only be used for functions which are employed relatively infrequently on your server, because CGI programs are slow when compared to API-based programs, which link directly to the server's code.

The details of CGI and API-based server extensions are explained in Chapter 10, "CGI & DLLs: Programming Your Server."

Communications Server & Commerce Server

Communications Server and Commerce Server, from Netscape (http://www.netscape.com), are the non-secure and secure servers that are capturing a large share of the server market both on Windows NT and Solaris (and other UNIX and UNIX-like systems). They are both true "industrial strength" server systems that also integrate with Netscape's other server support products. Netscape has products in addition to the web server, including a news server.

Features

Netscape's servers are full-featured, high-performance servers that can support any size commercial web site. They have a broad range of features including SSL secure protocols (with the Commerce Server), fine-grained access control down to the file level, the NSAPI application programming interface and CGI interfaces, and customizable error messages. The Netscape server operates only as a service under Windows NT, which makes debugging server extensions more difficult than it is for those servers that can also run as applications. The servers operate across a wide variety of host operating systems, including seven different kinds of UNIX and Windows NT on the Intel and Alpha operating systems.

Perhaps the most significant "feature" of the Netscape server, however, is the availability of additional software packages with which you can create a complete commercial web site. Unfortunately for Windows NT and many UNIX users, these additional server packages currently operate only on one or two kinds of UNIX.

Programmability

Netscape servers support standard CGI, plus a DLL interface called NSAPI. This is a very powerful interface, although less intuitive than the CGI replacement interfaces offered by other servers. The documentation is less than complete, although Netscape is big enough to have "developer support groups" (for a price, of course) and training classes of various types. Various sample programs are provided.

LiveWire

Netscape also offers a higher level of programmability with an extension called LiveWire, and access to databases with LiveWire Pro. These extensions, using the NSAPI as their foundation, let you embed Java-like code into HTML pages, which are then processed in real-time as they are sent to a browser. You can write code that is executed at the server or at the client, if the client is a Netscape browser. LiveWire programs are compiled before being used, and can be loaded and unloaded while the server is operating. In addition, LiveWire Pro provides database access to Sybase, Oracle, and Informix databases, and is packaged with a version of the Informix database.

The LiveWire system itself establishes the "state" of any client, using one of a number of techniques including cookies and URL modification, depending on your needs.

There is very little you won't be able to do with LiveWire and you should take a serious look at this capability, especially if you will be mixing UNIX and NT servers.

Using NSAPI, you can control almost any aspect of processing a client request, at many different points in the standard processing. Your server extensions are linked in to the server by adding entries in the Windows Registry. This is different from the server extension model that replaces CGI programs with DLLs, since the Netscape method allows you to become involved in the processing of any document, rather than just those accessed through a special path. Unfortunately, this also means the programming is much more complicated for "simple" tasks.

Administration

The Netscape servers are unique in that they use an administration interface that is controlled through the use of a web browser instead of a dedicated program. This means that you can administer the servers from anywhere you can reach them with a web browser.

Cost

Netscape's prices are $295 for the Communication Server and $995 for the Commerce Server, which includes the SSL encryption protocol. Other server packages are available ranging in price from $295 to $4000.

EMWAC HTTPd

The EMWAC HTTPd server was the first web server available for Windows NT. It was developed by the European Microsoft Windows Academic Center with funding from Microsoft. It is a nicely featured basic server product, and it's free. (Process Software has licensed the code and has created a much more advanced commercial server—see "Purveyor," later in this chapter.) The server is included on the Companion CD-ROM, so you can try it out right away.

Features

The list of features for the EMWAC server is basic (after all, you didn't pay for it). In particular, there are a few "standard" features that are not supported by the EMWAC server, including automatic response to If-Modified-Since. But if you simply want to serve up documents with no access controls and no fancy administration, then the EMWAC server might fit the bill.

Programmability

The only way to program the EMWAC server is through its standard CGI interface. Since the NT command shell is very limited, you'll want to go with the perl program tool to create CGI scripts.

Administration

Like its UNIX cousins, the EMWAC HTTPd is administered through text files that control its operation.

Cost

Free. What a deal!

FolkWeb

The FolkWeb Server, from ILAR Concepts (http://www.ilar.com) is a not-so-basic server that is distributed as shareware with a very basic price. This server is very powerful, boasting many useful features and interfaces. In addition, ILAR Concepts can use this server as a base for custom development for customers with special requirements. Of particular note is the direct support for ODBC databases.

Features

FolkWeb supports many features, including CGI, Windows CGI, and direct support of ODBC database connections. With FolkWeb, you can publish a database on the Web with no CGI programming at all: the FolkWeb ODBC interface takes care of it for you. The server also supports NCSA-style server-based imagemaps, and directory browsing for providing users direct access to the file directory listings. You can also map one document type to another, in case a particular client can't accept the preferred kind of file. (This is useful for JPEG-to-GIF substitution. If you're serving a JPEG, but a client doesn't allow it in the ACCEPT part of the HTTP protocol, the server checks its mapping table to see if a GIF replacement for the JPEG file is available.) FolkWeb is a multithreaded server with a new thread for each connection.

ILAR has promised support for server-side includes and S-HTTP or SSL in the next version of FolkWeb (2.0).

Programmability

FolkWeb is compliant with CGI 1.1 and Windows CGI 1.2, so you can add your own CGI programs. The server comes with sample programs in C++ to get you started.

Administration

The current version (1.01) has an administration tool with a property-sheet appearance. There's no need for any manual entries in the registry—the administration tool handles all this for you. They have announced that a remote server maintenance capability will be included in version 2.0.

Cost

The shareware license is $120.

Internet Information Server

The Internet Information Server is Microsoft's entry into the NT web server market and consists of three pieces: a web server, an FTP server, and a Gopher server. It was written just for Windows NT, so it is a very fast server, and is completely integrated with the Windows environment.

Features

This web server has several features not found in other servers, due to its close integration with Windows NT. First of all, it will operate only with Windows NT Server, and not with Windows NT Workstation. Its security mechanisms are integrated with the file system security provided with NTFS, and if you turn on user-level security, you must enter all the web users as users of the NT Server. This means that the user interface for adding users to the web server is the same as that for standard user maintenance.

In addition to basic authentication, the Microsoft server offers the use of Windows NT Challenge/Response security, but only to clients using the Microsoft browser. Logging can be done to an SQL database instead of a standard log file, if you want, and standard log files can be changed daily, weekly, monthly, or when they reach a particular size.

This server offers the unique feature of limiting the total network traffic for all Internet services provided by a system. This can be useful if you have an NT Server that is a file or print server in addition to a web server, and you don't want the web server to dominate use of the system. Internet Information Server also has integrated database access via ODBC and a powerful programming interface, discussed below and in Chapter 10, "CGI & DLLs: Programming Your Server." It is limited, however, to operating on port 80 only, as this parameter is not tunable.

Programmability

Microsoft and Process Software have defined a server API, known as the ISAPI. The ISAPI is halfway between the extensive server programmability offered by the Netscape API and the basic CGI replacement functions offered by other servers. The API defines two basic sets of functions: a CGI replacement DLL and a callback filter DLL. The filter DLL allows you to tinker with server operations at several points during request processing.

The CGI replacement DLL is very similar to CGI replacements included with other servers. It has good facilities for collecting and returning data from/to the clients, and supports easy ways to respond with common response headers. For more information about the ISAPI interfaces, please refer to Chapter 10.

Cost

Microsoft is making the Internet Information Server available for free download, and is also including it with the Windows NT Server Network Value Pack. It is available on disk for $99.

NaviServer

NaviServer 2.0 is offered as part of a complete authoring package from NaviSoft (http://www.naviservice.com), which is a division of America Online.

Features

NaviServer supports direct connections with the Illustra database; multi-homing; full integration with SQL databases and ODBC; an API of C- and Tcl-based interfaces that expose its core functions and provide primitives for manipulating the database; and SSL encryption support. It sports a "limited thread" model: instead of creating a new thread for every client request, there are three threads of execution for the server operation and two threads for the Illustra database.

Programmability

The NaviServer is highly programmable, through the use of its C and Tcl interfaces. For complete details about this unusual interface, you can check the online documentation from NaviSoft at http://naviserver.navisoft.com/index.htm.

Administration

The administration module for the server is accessed from any web browser, and through this interface you can control all the features of the server. Since the administration functions operate over the web itself, you can operate the administration program remotely. NaviServer uses the traditional .INI files for keeping track of its settings.

Cost

The price for NaviServer is $1495. (If that seems expensive, you'll be happy to know that the UNIX version sells for $5000!) This price includes a copy of the Illustra database.

Purveyor

Originally based on the EMWAC freeware server, Process Software's (http://www.process.com) Purveyor server moves well into the realm of commercially viable web servers, and beyond. It has a very rich feature set, integration with ODBC, and a programming API, in addition to the basic CGI interface.

Features

Purveyor server's many features include both SSL and S-HTTP security schemes, a proxy capability, and a very complete access control scheme, which is actually integrated directly with the Windows NT File Manager. It supports server-side includes, has a built-in search capability, and can be remotely administered from other NT systems, as well as non-NT systems. Purveyor functions under a number of operating systems, including NetWare, OpenVMS, and Windows 95, and offers built-in integration with the Windows ODBC interface through provided CGI programs. It also provides a forms-creation tool that helps you make search forms for the database (starting with the ODBC database) and allows you to specify which fields will be displayed and how the search form will be laid out.

Multiple virtual servers can be created for supporting more than one unique web per single server system. Different IP addresses are mapped to different webs on the hard disk of the server system.

Programmability

The Purveyor server supports CGI programs via the CGI standard mechanism, as well as the WinCGI interface. In addition, it features the ISAPI, which was jointly developed by Process Software and Microsoft. (See "Internet Information Server," earlier in this chapter, for a description of ISAPI.)

Administration

Purveyor uses three different tools for administering the server, depending on what you want to do and where you are. For all local server administration, there's a Control Panel application that has a property-page layout. All basic server functions are controlled from this application. Purveyor offers a very complete Access Control function for directories and files, and this control is integrated with the Windows File Manager application through extensions to the File Manager.

Cost

Purveyor lists for $495 for Windows NT and $295 for Windows 95.

Spry Web Server & SafetyWEB Server

The Spry/CompuServe web servers (Spry is a division of CompuServe) are high-performance, limited-thread servers, which do not create a new thread for each new incoming request. This allows the designers of the server code to manipulate the tasking performance for the server themselves, and can in theory offer very high performance when compared with servers that start a new thread for each incoming connection. (Naturally, programmers that work with thread-per-connection servers would dispute this idea.)

The Spry server has many built-in capabilities, and is a very capable server—particularly at the basic price of $495. Compu-Serve also offers a secure server called SafetyWEB, which offers SSL and S-HTTP, along with built-in search capabilities.

Features

Some of the more interesting features of the Spry server are file-level access control by user or group, server-side includes, a high degree of programmability, built-in proxy capability, logging to an ODBC database (in addition to logging to a file), remote adminis-tration, and real-time performance monitoring with the NT perfor-mance monitor. Some of the performance parameters that are reported in real-time include bytes received per second, bytes sent per second, current concurrent transactions, maximum concurrent transactions, total bytes received, total bytes sent, total transac-tions, and current transactions per second. The SafetyWEB server also includes secure protocols SSL and S-HTTP, plus a new feature proposed for HTTP known as Keep-Alive, which improves the efficiency of sending complete web pages by allowing all the elements on a single page—which is typically a collection of HTML and image files—to be sent during a single TCP/IP con-nection. The Spry servers are available for the Alpha platform in addition to the Intel processor platform.

Programmability

The Spry servers have two basic programming interfaces: the standard CGI interface and a Binary Gateway Interface (BGI). They've also stated their intentions to support the ISAPI.

The BGI, defined as a replacement for CGI, is based around the use of DLLs, where the DLL is preloaded and operates in the same memory space as the server. While this will offer very high perfor-mance, it also means that your design of the DLL can affect all aspects of server performance, and if your DLL crashes, so will the entire server!

The BGI works by having your DLL offer a defined interface to the server, with an entry point called BGIMain (W3BGI_HTTPRequest * pRequest). When a user of your server sends a request that invokes your BGI program, the server calls your DLL at this entry point. pRequest is a large structure that passes to the DLL all the entry points for server callbacks. With these server callbacks, your DLL can ascertain the information you need to handle the request, including all the information normally passed to a CGI program. As an example, the call your DLL would make to obtain the normal CGI-type environment information is as follows:

```
W3BGI_GetHTTPEnvDataFxn(
    struct _W3BGI_HTTPRequest * request,
    W3BGI_HTTPEnvData  variableRequested,
    size_t valueBufferSize,
    char * valueBuffer);
```

There are a number of other server callbacks that enable additional functionality in your DLL, including the following:

- W3BGI_SendFxn—Write directly to client.

- W3BGI_RecvFxn—Read directly from client.

- W3BGI_SendResponseHeaderFxn—Send response header (same as if web server were responding).

- W3BGI_GetRequestDataFxn—Get request data. Fetch name/value pairs from query string for Get requests. Fetch name/value pairs from query string and content string for Post requests.

- W3BGI_AuthenticateFxn—Authenticate user access to a given URI function.

When you've done your processing and are ready to send a page back to your client, you first send the header with W3BGI_SendResponseHeaderFxn and then send the content of the page with W3BGI_SendFxn.

Administration

The administration for the Spry/CompuServe servers is performed with two dedicated administration programs that can be run from anywhere on the network (as long as the user has system administrator privileges on the target system). One handles basic configuration functions, and the other handles server security.

Cost

The Spry Web Server is $495 and the SafetyWEB Server is $1295.

WebQuest

The WebQuest server, from Questar (http://www.questar.com), is a Windows NT–based server that was written specifically for Windows NT. The features of this server focus on administration, multiple domain management, extended SSI functions, and integration with ODBC databases for user queries and updates as well as event-logging. It is a multithreaded server, with a built-in process that monitors load history and intelligently maximizes the balance between resources and speed. WebQuest is also available for Windows 95.

An evaluation version of WebQuest is included on the Companion CD-ROM. This evaluation version is the complete server, with the modification that every page served will have a footer telling the reader that the page was served by the WebQuest WebServer demo.

Features

WebQuest supports multiple virtual servers for different IP addresses, using the "Multi-Domain Manager"; supports close integration with ODBC databases through the SSI+ interface; offers a graphical administration tool; has built-in support for SMTP mail, CERN-format imagemaps, and basic proxy server operation; and possesses the ability to add new IP addresses to your system through the administration tool. WebQuest also offers per-document, user login–based (not IP- or domain-based) access control, which is set up through the administration tool individually for each file requiring protection.

Programmability

In addition to the standard CGI interface, WebQuest offers an extended implementation of server-side includes (SSI) called SSI+, which offers some additional functions without requiring CGI programming. The tags supported in SSI+ include echo, include, fsize, flastmod, exec, config, odbc, email, if, goto label, and break. (Full documentation for these tags is included in the ssiplus.hlp help file, which is accessible when you install WebQuest from the Companion CD-ROM.)

The echo tag, for example, gives you the ability to send back to the user data entered on a form in addition to a known set of standard variables such as DOCUMENT_NAME, DATE_LOCAL, and SERVER_SOFTWARE. The include tag allows you to recursively insert the contents of another file into the data returned to the client. With the exec tag, you can call external command-line programs, and have their standard output results returned to the client. The odbc tag is customized with a number of attributes that allow you to query an ODBC database.

In version 2 of the server, Questar added additional SSI+ features, including direct calls to DLL programs and OLE2 objects, custom and third-party extensions to SSI, variables and variable manipulation, and conditional execution and branching.

Administration

The WebMeister administration application allows local administration of the WebQuest server, including all aspects of server operation and configuration. Of special note is the option that gives you a view of the web for the IP address you've specified. This tool shows you the web in three different display modes: a directory view, a view that checks all local hyperlinks, and a view that checks remote hyperlinks. This is a nice way to confirm the validity of links on your web right from the server administration tool.

Cost

WebQuest for Windows NT is priced at $495, and for Windows 95 at $249. These prices include 90 days of technical support, with a 12-month support contract available for $395.

WebSite

O'Reilly's WebSite (http://website.ora.com) was one of the first widely distributed commercial servers for Windows NT. The server itself was created by Robert Denny, the inventor of the now widely supported Windows CGI interface. EIT (Enterprise Integration Technologies) contributed a number of support programs as well as participating in the marketing of the server. WebSite can operate as a system service under Windows NT, or can be set to operate as an application program.

Features

WebSite is a highly functional web server with all the features you'd expect. There are several features that deserve special mention. One is the ability to multi-home the server: that is, if you've configured your NT system with multiple IP addresses, clients connecting to different IP addresses will home to a different web on the system. The programs bundled with the server are very useful in creating and maintaining a web site. WebView is a program that allows you to look at a graphical representation of your web site (or any web site, for that matter). The Mapedit program is an imagemap editor, which creates the files you need for clickable server-side imagemaps. There's also a program that does full text indexing for a WebSite web, and integrates seamlessly with the WebSite server. Two page-creation "Wizards" help you create a home page and a "what's new" page.

Programmability

At the time this was being written, WebSite supported standard CGI as well as WinCGI. The WebSite Application Programming Interface (WSAPI) will be released as part of the WebSite Professional product, which should be available as you read this.

Administration

WebSite comes with an administration tool, which can be used for remote server administration. It has a property-page layout. As you would expect, there's never a need to tinker with registry settings directly: all settings can be controlled through the administration tool.

Cost

WebSite lists for $499. Pricing for WebSite Professional was not set at the time this was written.

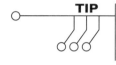

Due to the increasing popularity of Windows NT as a server platform, it's possible that other servers will appear by the time you read this. In particular, Spyglass is licensing their server on an OEM basis, and you should expect to see more servers based on Spyglass's code. Also, OpenMarket (http://www.openmarket.com), has a Windows NT–based server in beta at the time this is being written. Check to see what's available when you're ready to take the plunge and put up your NT-based server.

Using Alibaba

The lite edition of the Alibaba server included on the Companion CD-ROM is the same as the commercial product that you can upgrade to, with a single exception: the server will allow no more than four concurrent IP connections. While this is very suitable for development work, when you have only a single client running to test, it is not suitable for a live service, and you'll want to upgrade to a full server before going commercial—internally or externally.

To install the development version of the Alibaba web server, run the setup.exe program located in the Alibaba directory on the Companion CD-ROM. You have the option during installation to specify the destination directory for the Alibaba programs, as shown in Figure 3-1. The setup program copies all the files to the directory you specified, and installs Alibaba as a system server, but does *not* start the server. This allows you to make changes to the configurations for Alibaba before it starts the first time.

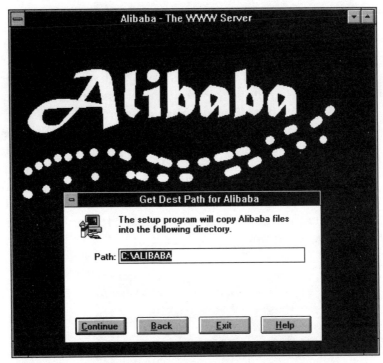

Figure 3-1: *The Alibaba setup screen.*

Just to get started, you can simply go to the Services application in the Control Panel and start the Alibaba service. By default, you can connect with your web browser to your own system on port 80, and see the default home page for Alibaba. If you specify the URL http://127.0.0.1/ALIBABA you'll see the built-in server documentation and demonstrations. You should spend some time navigating these pages to gain familiarity with the server and its capabilities.

Administering Alibaba

Alibaba comes with a Windows-based administration tool called Aliadmin. This tool allows users with administrator privileges to administer the server from any NT system on the same network. If you have the Microsoft Networks protocol turned on over TCP/IP (which you really shouldn't—see Chapter 4, "System Security"), you can administer your server from anywhere in the world.

When you first start the administration tool, you see the server selection dialog shown in Figure 3-2. If you're administering the server on the same system, leave the default of "local"; otherwise, enter the Microsoft Networks name for the system on which the server is running.

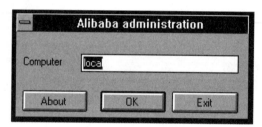

Figure 3-2: *Alibaba server selection dialog.*

Once you select the server, you'll see the Alibaba Administration property sheets, as shown in Figure 3-3. There are several pages on which you can enter configuration information. These pages are covered in detail in the sections that follow.

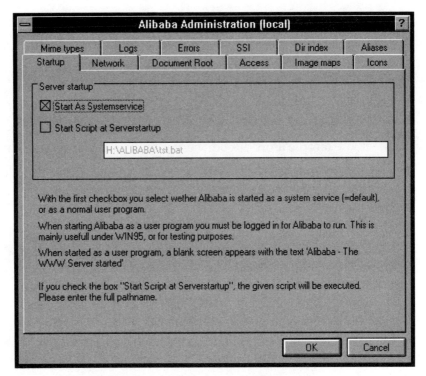

Figure 3-3: *Alibaba Administration property sheets.*

Startup

There are two options for starting the Alibaba service, as shown in Figure 3-3. Start As Systemservice will cause the Alibaba server to start up whenever the system starts, even if no one logs in to the NT system. This is the normal way to run the Alibaba server. If you're creating CGI scripts or extension DLLs for Alibaba, you'll want to deselect this option so that your debugger can start the server on demand. The second option, Start Script at Serverstartup, allows you to specify a batch file or executable to run whenever the server starts.

Network

The Network property page, shown in Figure 3-4, allows you to set parameters associated with the network operation of Alibaba. The Network Port To Use setting is the TCP/IP port number that the server will be addressed on. Typically, the port is 80, because web browsers will contact this port by default. However, you might want to have more than one server running on a system, for example a production server and a staging server. The production server, operating on port 80, would be open to the world, while the staging server, operating on another port of your choosing, would have access controls so only certain people could access it.

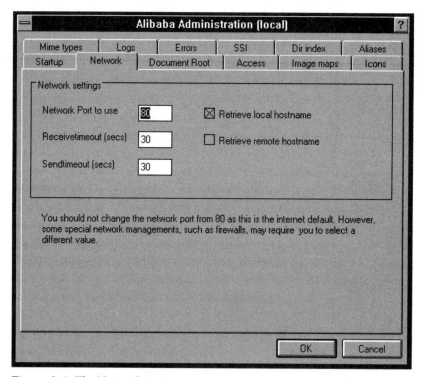

Figure 3-4: *The Network property page.*

The Receivetimeout and Sendtimeout values should be left alone unless you have a very slow link and are experiencing problems with timeouts.

The settings for retrieving local and remote hostnames give you the option to have Alibaba try to resolve the IP addresses of browsers contacting your system into text hostnames. You should leave the Retrieve Local Hostname option turned off most of the time, since it will delay processing if Alibaba needs to go out to distant DNS servers to resolve the IP addresses. One exception to this might be if you're conducting a special study of domains that are contacting your server, and want to have the domain names in the log files instead of just the host IP addresses.

Document Root

Alibaba supports multiple IP addresses to configure virtual servers on Windows NT. The Document Root property page, shown in Figure 3-5, allows you to establish the document root for the default server as well as other virtual servers. The setup program installs one virtual server in addition to the default, the server at IP address 127.0.0.1. Since 127.0.0.1 is a loopback address to your own machine, this lets you provide one web to normal browsers, but lets you have a different web available locally if you enter **http://127.0.0.1** in the browser's URL line. Alibaba sets this alternate web to be the server documentation by default.

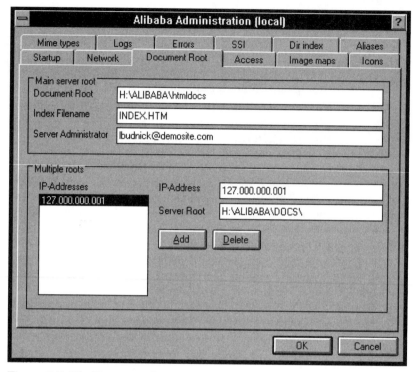

Figure 3-5: *The Document Root property page.*

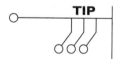
TIP
The addresses 127.0.0.1 and 127.000.000.001 are identical—the extra zeros are optional when the address is specified.

The Index Filename is the document that will be returned to a browser when no file is specified in the URL pathname. Typically this is INDEX.HTM, but you can make it anything you want. You should put your e-mail address into the Server Administrator field.

Access

The Access property page sets general security parameters for the server. (Specific access control parameters are set through the Alibaba Authorization Tool—see "Securing Your Web," later in this chapter.) The Access page is split into three parts: General, Index Ignore, and Client Types. The General page is shown in Figure 3-6. On this page you see the server-wide settings for the redirection filename, the file description filename, and the header and footer filenames. Unless you have a specific need to rename these files, you should not change them.

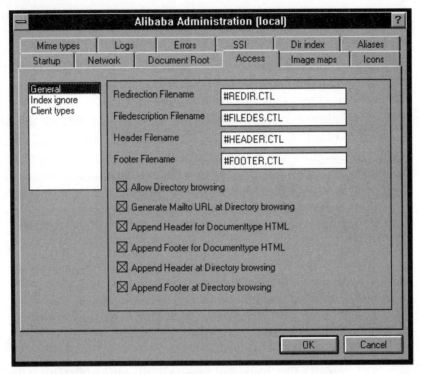

Figure 3-6: *The Access property page.*

The redirection file in each directory is controlled through the Authorization Tool, and allows you to specify filenames that are "virtual" on your system: when a browser attempts to load a redirected file, the system redirects the browser to the actual location, which may be on a completely different system. Hits on this virtual file are still logged, however, so you can keep track of how many times someone accesses the file. This would be useful if you have advertisers on the site and you want to keep track of how many referrals you send them. Note, however, that there may be fewer hits recorded on the remote site than you send them, since there are many proxy-caching servers on the Web these days, and many "hits" on a system are actually served by a proxy server instead of the real server.

The next three files are used when you allow browsers to look directly at the file directory listings, and are described in detail in the Alibaba manual, included in Microsoft Word format on the Companion CD-ROM. The six check boxes specify general options for directory browsing. Note that with the Authorization Tool, you can override the general settings for specific directories and files.

The Index Ignore page specifies which files are not shown to a user when browsing a directory. Typically these are the control files in the directory, which is the default setting. The Client Types page allows you to deny access to your site by any browsers except those you specify. Be *very* careful if you use this option! You could easily deny access to the majority of people trying to access your site. Probably the only time you would want to do this is if you had a special web set up just for browsers with certain extensions (say, browsers that supported Java), and the site would be useless without the extensions. You could then track down all the identification strings for the browsers that supported the extensions, and enter the strings in this page.

Imagemaps

Support for imagemaps is provided in two forms with Alibaba: CERN mapping and NCSA mapping. To decide which to use, you should find out what kind of mapping is supported by the tools you're using to create the imagemaps. On the Image Maps property page, the Reference File is the name of the file that maps the images to their imagemaps, and the Alias Name specifies a name that can be used in a URL that maps to the actual location of your imagemaps. By default, Alibaba uses the path /IMAGES to mean the imagemap directory.

Icons

When Alibaba creates a directory listing for a client, you can specify icons to be used to identify various file types. The Icons property page maps GIF image files to various filename extensions, as shown in Figure 3-7. There's also the option to display a short text description of the file, which appears to the right of the filename in the browser's window. For HTML files, Alibaba can actually pull the content of the <TITLE> tag out of the file, and display that text as the description. Also, you can create your own descriptions of particular files by creating a file description file, as mentioned in the "Access" section. The default icon is used when an unknown file type is encountered. You can add to the list if you have file types that are not shown in the list.

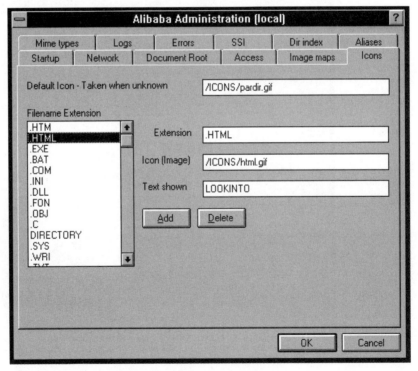

Figure 3-7: *The Icons property page.*

MIME Types

The HTTP protocol uses a convention to identify the type of information being sent to a browser that is based on the Internet MIME definitions. Figure 3-8 shows a few of the over 100 MIME types defined by default in the Alibaba server. Should you need to add your own types, you can do so with this page. MIME types are mapped to filename extensions, so that the server knows how to identify the files being sent to the browsers. As shown in Figure 3-8, all files that have the .HTML extension will be identified as text/html when they're sent.

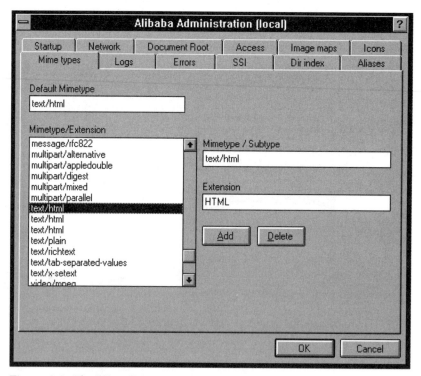

Figure 3-8: *The Mime Types property page.*

Logs

Alibaba supports two log types: the standard CERN logging format as well as an extended log format that allows you to log additional information about connections to your system. In addition, there's an error log format that contains information about errors occurring during the operation of the server. Log files are created on a daily basis, and new logs start at midnight.

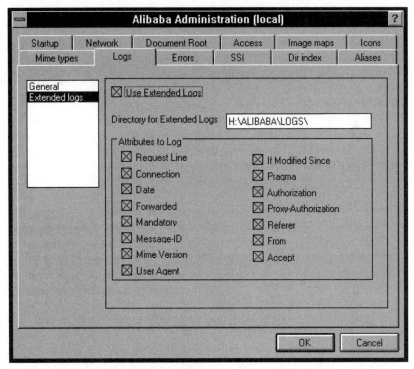

Figure 3-9: *The Logs property page.*

Figure 3-9 shows the options available for the extended log file. Extended logging is turned off by default, so if you want extended log files, you must activate them on this property page.

Errors

When servers receive requests for various documents, there are many times when error or informational messages must be returned to the browser instead of the document requested. The Errors property page allows you to customize the message returned to the browser along with the error code. For example, you may want to change the text of the default message for Error 401, shown in Figure 3-10, to something more useful for a particular site, such as the following:

```
<BODY><H1>Authorization required</H1>Please give us a call at
+1-617-555-1212 to obtain an account on this server!<P>
</BODY></HTML>
```

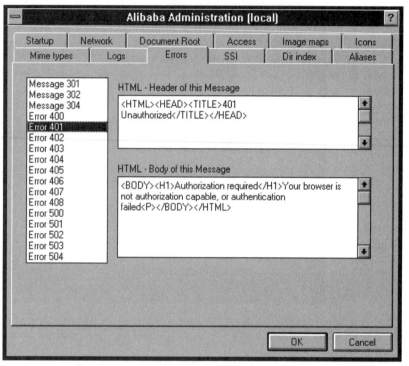

Figure 3-10: *The Errors property page.*

SSI

The SSI (server-side includes) property page allows you to set the filename extension for documents that should be interpreted as including server-side extensions. You can also make global changes to a few attributes of the SSI tags. Server-side includes are covered in more detail in Chapter 10, "CGI & DLLs: Programming Your Server."

Dir Index

This is another page that sets up parameters for displaying directories to clients. There are many options in the specification of up to five columns of information to be displayed to the user. Directory listings can be shown in a traditional or table-based format.

Aliases

Aliases are a very powerful feature of the Alibaba server. With an alias, you can change a requested URL into a physical path on your system. There are aliases for imagemaps (discussed earlier), CGI scripts for 16- and 32-bit programs, Windows CGI scripts, general paths, and DLL programs. The Aliases property page is shown in Figure 3-11.

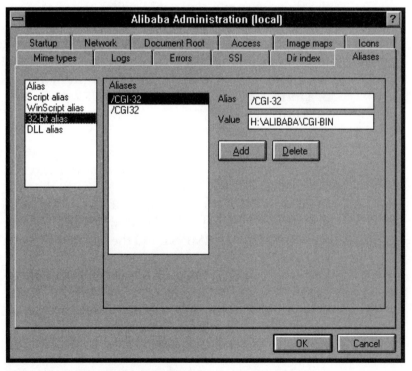

Figure 3-11: *The Aliases property page.*

Aliases are used to change a requested URL path into a path the server understands. For example, you could specify that the alias /DOCS should translate to C:\mydocs\basic-a\release1.0\ betaformat\hrml2.0. Now, if a user specifies the URL

```
http://yourhost/docs/index.htm
```

the server will translate that request into a request to return the document at C:\mydocs\basic-a\release1.0\betaformat\hrml2.0. This is clearly much friendlier than if the user had to enter the following URL:

```
http://yourhost/mydocs/basic-a/release1.0/betaformat/hrml2.0/
index.htm
```

Using an alias also allows you to move entire trees of information around on your web without changing the external URL. In the above example, you could switch to "release2.0" by changing the alias, and the user's URL would not need to change.

Aliases are also used to specify CGI script locations. By default, for example, Alibaba will translate the URL /CGI-32 to \ALIBABA\CGI-BIN. So when a user (from the Action attribute of a form, for example) specifies the URL /CGI-32/ COMMENTFORM.EXE, the program COMMENTFORM.EXE is actually found in \ALIBABA\CGI-BIN.

Another powerful use of an alias is to hide the actual name of a program from the user. In the Action attribute of a form, for example, instead of using the URL /CGI-BIN/ COMMENTFORM.EXE, you could simply use /COMMENT. Then, to the 32-bit alias list (assuming this is a 32-bit NT program) add the alias /COMMENT and the value C:\ALIBABA\ CGI-DLL\COMMENTFORM.EXE. Now, whenever the server gets a request for URL /COMMENT, it will actually execute the program COMMENTFORM.EXE.

Securing Your Web

Alibaba comes with a tool that administers user and site authorizations on your server. The Alibaba Authorization Tool, in the Alibaba program group, examines all your root paths and aliases and allows you to apply security to each group and directory in that group.

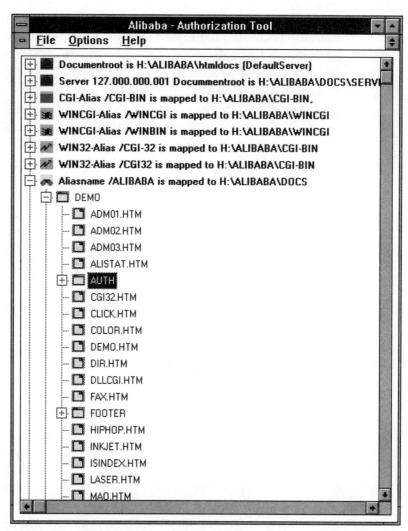

Figure 3-12: *The Alibaba Authorization Tool.*

Figure 3-12 shows the documentation web supplied with Alibaba, and the alias "Alibaba" opened up to examine the content of the web. If you double-click on a directory, you'll be shown a dialog that allows you to apply security to the directory based on user ID (basic authentication) and/or site ID. Alibaba has defined the concept of the "realm" into which you can group users and groups of users.

If you'll be using user-level web security, you should start by defining your own realm and users, since the default realm is shared by all Alibaba users. To create a realm, select File | Realm Admin from the Authorization Tool's menu, then click on the top New button. This will prompt you for a new realm name, and you should enter a name of your choice. Next, select the Demonstration Realm and delete it, so you don't accidentally use the demonstration accounts in your server.

Next, add the users who will be accessing your server, and if you want to, create groups that those users belong to. Groups are handy, because you can offer access to an entire group at a time—you don't need to specify individual users every time you assign access permissions to an alias or directory. The Authorization Tool offers you the choice of automatically generated passwords, which you can then take note of and provide to your users.

The other option for security is to restrict access by IP address. In this security model, you can allow or deny access to various IP addresses or domains.

Moving On

If there's one fact that will not change by the time you read this, it's that the market for Windows NT web servers is young and growing rapidly. Although UNIX servers are clearly the dominant choice for most web servers operating on the public Internet today, Windows NT servers are very popular on corporate intranets, and are becoming increasingly popular on the public Internet. Windows NT servers offer an easy way to create a web server, without the complexity and expense of setting up UNIX-based servers. As the Windows NT market matures, you should expect to see a sharp increase in the number of servers running Windows NT.

Once your web server is installed and running, you'll want to consider the issues surrounding securing your server, especially if you're providing a public service. In the next chapter, "System Security," you'll learn the basics of Windows NT and Internet security, and how to protect yourself from an occasionally unfriendly world.

4

System Security

Security is one of the hottest topics in computing for several reasons. One of the most important is the sensationalist coverage the mass media have given to cases involving computer security, such as the 1988 Internet Worm virus and the exploits of Kevin Mitnick, who was arrested in 1995 for breaking into a number of prominent Internet hosts. This coverage has tended to increase everyone's concern about computer security: regular users are worried that they might be victimized by computer criminals, while security experts consider these incidents major embarrassments.

It's good to be concerned about security, of course, but it's important to understand that a compromise is required. Increased security almost always comes at the expense of a reduction in the system's usefulness for legitimate users, and this is especially true for Internet servers. Each of the network services offers strangers some level of access to your computer; therefore, it's really impossible to be completely secure and still be a network server. Well-known hosts are especially tempting targets for hackers.

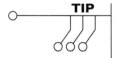

TIP

In the popular media, computer criminals are known as "hackers," which is a corruption of the word's original meaning—a hacker is anyone who enjoys working with computers and technology and stretching his or her technical capabilities. So when you read the term "hacker" in this chapter, please understand that we're not talking about our friends, just our enemies!

If you have experience with UNIX security problems, then the story with Windows NT security should come as good news: there are very few security issues with a well-maintained NT site. Part of this stems from the fact that NT was designed long after UNIX, and took advantage of the knowledge that had been gained in the intervening years. The other part is that Windows NT, by its nature, is not a multiuser system, so there are very few paths into an NT system. Also, many of the TCP/IP utilities that give UNIX and Solaris systems their richness of connectivity, such as NFS, SMTP mail, Telnet server, and remote commands, are typically missing from NT systems, and therefore pose no security threat. Finally, there is no "login shell" on Windows NT, so some of the most-used tricks of embedding shell commands into otherwise safe messages passed to an Internet server are not effective against NT. That said, there are still plenty of areas in Windows NT where security can be a problem.

The approach you take to system security will depend to a large extent on the kind of web server site you're running. If you have an "intranet" server that hosts browsers located inside a corporate firewall, or is completely insulated from the public Internet, your security concerns are significantly different from the concerns of the Webmaster responsible for security on a public Internet host. In this chapter, we'll examine three basic principles of computer security that you should pay attention to—isolation, simplification, and security administration—and we'll try to point out the different ways these principles apply to intranet and public Internet servers. In addition to actions you can take to protect your servers and networks, we'll also look at some of the secure protocols that can protect your user's information as it is being transmitted.

Isolation

The most secure system in the world is one that is turned off and locked in a safe. Unfortunately, this is not the best way to provide services to your users. System administrators must seek a balance between complete security (no network or modem connection and locking the machine in a vault) and being able to offer useful services without restriction. Both physical isolation and communications isolation come to play here. With a corporate intranet, there's a good chance that your biggest risks to security will come from inside your own company, and securing the room where you keep your servers will help to minimize the risks to physical intrusion. For a public Internet server, there's less chance that the general public (or the hacker from around the world) will waltz into your server room and reboot your server—the greater risk lies in the communications programs running on your server.

A good strategy to mitigate either type of risk is to put barriers between your server and those who would harm it or steal from it. Physical security is fairly obvious—you just need to be sure to do it. When it comes to communications security, there are many options and possibilities we'll discuss in this chapter.

The primary form of communications protection used at almost every web site is a *firewall*. A firewall is a special purpose computer that examines the packets of information going over the data lines into your company's network, and keeps out unwanted data. There are two basic types of firewalls: application gateways and screening routers. In general, the functions of a screening router are found in the same routers you use to connect to the Internet, and the functions of an application gateway are found in dedicated UNIX systems running special software. Recently, a few companies have announced support for Windows NT as well as UNIX, so you should check the Web for the most recent information. There are lots of names used to describe these devices, and there are a range of capabilities available, so you should evaluate your needs carefully and compare those needs to the features of the firewall device you are considering.

Screening Routers

A screening router protects your network by examining each packet that passes in and out of your network, and follows a set of rules that you define to decide which packets are allowed and which are rejected.

The decision about which packets to allow and which to deny is highly configurable, depending on the needs of the particular network. No one solution is right for everyone, since in general the more secure the firewall, the fewer legitimate services will pass through. Typically, you'll configure a screening router to permit only packets of the type that are specifically associated with a service you have decided to allow, and for which there is a destination in your network that you've evaluated for its security. Packets can be screened based on several attributes:

- The direction the packet is traveling: out to the Internet, or in to your network.

- The protocol to which it belongs, such as TCP, UDP, ICMP, IGMP, and so forth.

- The origination address (which can be faked by an intruder).

- The destination address.

- The IP port number of the destination.

- Whether the reply bit is set.

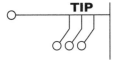
TIP

One hacker trick which has gotten lots of attention is faking the address of the sender (called IP spoofing), so that a screening router will allow the packet to pass, even though it is sent by a hacker instead of a trusted source. Although the origination address of a packet can be faked, the most common web protocols, HTTP and FTP, rely on a two-way communication to perform any useful work, so IP spoofing is not a major issue for web site operators.

Application Gateways

Although a screening router can provide a high degree of protection to your network, the capabilities of most routers are limited to examining individual packets with little, if any, knowledge of the higher level protocols passing through. An application gateway, on the other hand, understands the complete protocol (such as HTTP) and can look deep inside the packets to check out the content of the packet. Some application gateways even go so far as to terminate the protocol completely at the gateway and reoriginate the connection to the final destination. This kind of firewall can offer almost complete security to external threats, but may require modification to the basic Internet applications on your users' systems. When using the most secure application gateways, your Internet application doesn't actually contact the final destination, but rather contacts the firewall first. The firewall application takes the information passed to it by the client application, optionally verifies the identity of the client, then completes the connection by forwarding the connection request to the final destination.

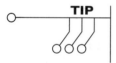

TIP

World Wide Web proxy servers are this kind of Application Gateway. To the browser inside your network, the proxy server looks like the "end point" that it's trying to connect to. To the ultimate end system, the proxy server looks like a browser. Some proxy servers are called "caching" proxies, since they take the additional step of storing pages retrieved from the World Wide Web in local storage. If a page is popular, and someone else from your internal network requests the same page within some period of time, then the proxy server will return its own copy and not make another request across the Web for the original copy. This saves time and network bandwidth. Some pages (such as the results from many search forms) should not be cached, and the HTTP protocol has mechanisms to deal with this.

Although application-level firewalls can provide very secure interfaces to the public Internet, you must watch loads and response times carefully. Users will become dissatisfied if response times increase too much, and may find ways around your firewall that open a back door to intruders.

Positioning Your Web Server

Now that you understand the basics of protecting your network from the Internet, you need to decide where to position your web server. It can go inside your firewall, outside your firewall, or it can straddle both the outside and inside networks.

Connecting your web server directly to the public Internet is a common solution, and is the easiest to accomplish. With this option, you should dedicate the function of the system to serving your web to the public, and not try to use the system for any other purpose. By dedicating your most exposed systems to serving public information, even if a system is compromised, you only lose what you wanted to be public in the first place. For example, if your system accepts credit card numbers for electronic commerce, you should never store those customer records on the public server. Rather, move them off the public server as quickly as possible and store them on well-protected systems.

If you choose to place your web server on the outside of your firewall, you will still need to provide access from the web server to the people inside the firewall that provide the content to that web server. You could configure your firewall system to allow internal users to connect to the externally connected web servers. Alternatively, you could connect the web server to both the internal and external networks. To connect a Windows NT server to two networks at the same time, use two network interface cards, each with a different IP address.

If you choose to connect your NT server to two networks, you must be sure that the web server is not providing a back door into your network. Windows NT installs with the default option of not routing packets from one network connection to another, but you can verify this by looking in the Registry at the key:

HKEY_LOCAL_MACHINE\SYSTEM\CurrentControlSet\Services\Tcpip\Parameters\IPEnableRouter. This will be set to 0 if the system is not routing packets.

You could also place your web server inside a screening router, and then configure the router to allow connections from the Internet through to your web server. Some companies that have opted for this solution have two levels of network protection: their production web servers are protected by a screening router, and they have application gateways between the production network and their internal networks. This solution offers the level of protection afforded by screening routers to the web servers, and offers the higher level of protection provided by the application gateways to the internal network.

Simplification

It's an accepted principle in the computer security world that the more complex the network operations on a system, the more likely it is that there's a security hole waiting to be found. The safest program is one that does nothing, and the programs most subject to security flaws are those that are the most complex. Also, reducing the number of networking programs running on a publicly accessible system will reduce the potential number of security holes.

Every program running on your web server should be scrutinized to ensure that it is required for operation of the web site, and if it isn't, remove it from the server.

FTP

FTP is a program commonly found on Internet servers. While the protocol itself is not particularly insecure, the basic operation of FTP creates a situation where your users are entering their login and password information over a nonencrypted path. If anyone has access to the dataline over which this information is sent, he or she can easily sniff out all the login and password information for your system.

The only way to completely avoid this problem is to allow only anonymous FTP logins. This prevents real login and password information from passing over the network. It also prevents you from offering any services to trusted persons that differ from what you offer the general public, however. One possible middle ground is to allow FTP access to regular users only from the inside of your company, but never use this capability from the public Internet. This way, the only security risk comes from people inside the company.

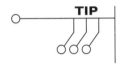

If you find that there are files you want to share, but only with specific persons, and not with the general public, you may be forced to allow non-anonymous logins. If so, please refer to the "Security Administration" section for some tips on how to minimize your security risks.

The SMB Protocol

The basic networking protocol for Windows systems is the Server Message Block (SMB) protocol. SMB can run over a number of networking protocols, including NetBEUI and IP. Unless you need to have file-sharing services available over the Internet, you should always disable the capability of running SMB protocols over IP. (NetBEUI typically cannot pass through routers, so leaving the SMB protocol running over NetBEUI poses no security risk for the Internet server.)

It's fairly simple to disconnect the SMB protocol from TCP/IP, but it does require you to tinker with protocol bindings. In the Control Panel, start the Network Setup application, and then click on the Bindings button. A list of networks will be displayed. Find any binding that connects the Server, Workstation, or NetBIOS with TCP/IP, and disable the binding.

NFS Services

Although Network File System (NFS) services are a great way to share file systems across a network, there are plenty of security issues surrounding the use of NFS. NFS programs don't come with the base Windows NT system, so there's nothing to worry about if you haven't specifically added NFS support to your servers. For public web servers, the security risks of running the NFS protocol outweigh the advantages.

Security Administration

Up to this point in the chapter, we've been talking about technical security issues. But as important as strict technical issues are, issues of policy and administration are just as important. This section will help you understand how to establish administration policies that can help keep your web server secure.

Secure the Web Server Services

You should carefully configure your web server to avoid any security holes both in the server itself and particularly in the CGI programs you write to support server operations. All the commercial servers can be configured to offer security by user name or by IP address, and you should seriously consider implementing one or both of them. Server security configuration is covered in more detail in Chapter 3, "Setting Up the Server," and CGI security concerns are discussed in Chapter 10, "CGI & DLLs: Programming Your Server."

Secure Other Applications

There are a number of applications other than those supplied with Windows NT that can provide services to the Internet, including POP3 and SMTP servers, Telnet servers, WAIS and Gopher servers, and custom IP-based services. Unless you really need them—

don't run them! Every application adds security risks, since each adds complexity and yet more network code. In particular, there's almost no reason to run a Telnet service from Windows NT that is open to the general public. Once you have determined that an application is required, however, you must secure that application. Every application you run can open security holes that the Internet hacker might exploit. You should evaluate each and every application to make absolutely sure you are running that application in the most secure way possible, and stay up-to-date with any security precautions the software vendor may have to offer. For other services, be sure to follow the security precautions for the particular product with great care.

NT Accounts

If you're running a web server on a corporate intranet—a network that is mostly disconnected from the public Internet—then you may wind up sharing the web server system with other general purpose applications, or you may find the need to have a number of people allowed access in order to maintain the web. If so, you need to get into basic Windows NT security for user logins and passwords. You may also have user accounts on a publicly accessible system if non-anonymous logins must be used.

Even though Windows NT is not a multiuser system in the sense that users use the power of the central server to control their screen displays, as is done under UNIX with the X Windows system, NT does have a clear understanding of "user accounts" and a very strict security model for those accounts. Users of an NT system, while not relying on the "shell" services of a UNIX system, can in fact take advantage of services available from an NT system such as file services and print spooling. (The protocol used by Windows NT is called a Server Message Block, or SMB, protocol, and can operate over a number of underlying transport protocols.)

Every user who needs to access resources from a Windows NT system should have an individual account, set up through NT's User Manager. Since every user has a single login/password combination, the security of the login depends on the strength of the password. Windows NT allows the administrator to specify several parameters that can affect the strength of the password. There's always a trade-off, however: if you make the security parameters too tough, users will wind up writing their passwords down near their systems, which opens the door to internal security problems. Since the threat of security breaches from internal sources far overshadows that from external sources, this is not an insignificant problem. The parameters that can be adjusted are as follows:

- *Minimum and maximum password age.* These determine how often a user must change the password, and, once changed, how soon before it can be changed again.

- *Minimum password length.* This is the minimum number of characters that make up a password. You can easily see how longer passwords are much tougher to crack, since the number of combinations is the nth factorial of the number of characters available to use in the password. You should always require at least 8 characters, and 10 would not be unreasonable.

- *Password uniqueness.* It's human nature to want to create easy passwords, and once they're memorized, to use favorite passwords over and over. This parameter allows you to force a certain number of unique passwords to be used before allowing reuse of an old password.

- *Account lockout.* Even the best password can be broken if a hacker has the ability to try endless combinations. This parameter sets the number of times a connection can be attempted before the account is locked out, and then how long the lockout will remain in force.

In addition to the automated checks that can be placed on the selection of a password, there are a number of procedural recommendations for choosing passwords that you should ask all users who have a password on any computer system to follow:

- Don't use your login name in any form (by itself, doubled, reversed, etc.).

- Don't use any part of your full name in any form.

- Don't use a nickname or any other well-known made-up word.

- Don't use anyone else's name, including the names of spouses, children, friends, and coworkers.

- Don't use the name of a computer.

- Don't use any easily gleaned bit of personal information, such as a birthday, Social Security number, or license number.

- Don't use any single word that appears in a dictionary, English or foreign.

- Don't use a word from a dictionary, preceded or followed by a single number.

- Don't use any word or name derived from science fiction or fantasy. All cracking dictionaries include "hobbit," "Tolkien," "Heinlein," and other similar words—avoid them like the plague.

- Don't use the same number or letter repeated several times.

- Don't use the same password on publicly accessible systems and internal systems.

- Do use a mixture of uppercase and lowercase letters.

- Do use numbers and nonalphanumeric symbols.

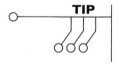
TIP *However, do choose a password that's easy to remember, so you won't be tempted to write it down.*

The other half of the login process is the user ID, and that can be made more difficult to guess as well by at least disabling the Guest account, which is normally present on every NT system. You should also make the Administrator account password particularly difficult, since that account cannot be disabled, and that's another account every hacker will try.

Each account login is associated with one or more groups, which define the rights for that login. The standard groups include Administrators, Backup Operators, Guests, Power Users, Replicator, and Users. Each group has permissions to perform a certain set of tasks, such as the following:

- Access this computer from the network.
- Act as part of the operating system.
- Add workstations to the domain.
- Back up files and directories.
- Change the system time.
- Debug programs.
- Force shutdown from a remote system.
- Log on as a service.
- Shut down system.
- Take ownership of files or other objects.

In Windows NT 3.51 there are 27 different security attributes that can be assigned to groups and/or individual users. You should learn enough about these various groups and security attributes so that you assign only the minimum necessary permissions to a group or individual.

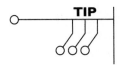

TIP

Despite all that has been written about Internet security, the biggest threats to your computer systems come from within. Either through malice or ignorance, you and others inside your own company are the biggest risk to your own systems. Careful administration and rigorous security policies can minimize these risks.

NT File Permissions & Ownership

Securing the file system is something that comes almost naturally for UNIX users and administrators, but is a new idea for those migrating from Windows 3.1 or Windows 95. You should always take positive action to keep users from accessing any part of the file system they don't need to see.

The Windows NT file system can be thought of as an upside-down tree. At the top of the file system is a series of root directories, one for each file system (drive C, drive D, etc.). Inside the root directory resides a number of directories and files. These branches from the root can also contain directories and files, and so on.

Each of the files and directories is identified in a structure on the disk, which contains all the information about the files and directories. You can view the information about a file or directory with the File Manager Security menu options. From this menu, you can view the permissions on a file or directory, the owner of the file or directory, and the types of audits that are active on any particular file or directory. Windows NT provides you with the ability to audit use of the file system. Audits consist of log entries for success, failure, or both, of any of the following actions on the file or directory:

- Read
- Write
- Execute
- Delete
- Change Permissions
- Take Ownership

This gives the system administrator a great deal of power in tracking all actions in a file system. By default, all auditing is turned off, so if you want to track these actions, you must turn on the audits yourself.

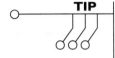

TIP

Security and audits only apply to the NT File System (NTFS) and not to the legacy DOS FAT file system. You should use the NTFS for all partitions on your hard disk except the boot partition. The boot partition should never be made available for any type of nonlocal access except by an administrator. You can make the boot file system NTFS as well, but this limits the effectiveness of traditional file-system diagnostic tools, which you may need in the case of a system emergency.

Every directory and file on an NTFS system has several attributes, most of which are visible through the File Manager. For a directory, permissions are split into directory permissions and permissions that apply by default to files within that directory. There are six distinct permission attributes for files and directories: Read, Write, Execute, Delete, Change Permissions, and Take Ownership. These permissions can be assigned to arbitrary groups and users, depending on what your security needs are. (In contrast, UNIX and Solaris systems offer three attributes: Read, Write, and Execute, and these are applied to the owner, a single group to which the owner belongs, and everyone else—the "world.") To make this manageable, there are a number of "prepackaged" options that can be assigned at the directory level in addition to creating your own custom combinations. These preset permissions are shown in Table 4-1. In this table, "not specified" means that the permissions for the files in the directory are not specified by this option, and users will have no access to the files unless granted in another way. The permission "execute" for a directory means that a user can change directory into the directory.

Attribute	Directory Rights	File Permissions
List	Read and execute	Not specified
Read	Read and execute	Read and execute
Add	Write and execute	Not specified
Add & Read	Read, write, and execute	Read and execute
Change	Read, write, execute, and delete	Read, write, execute, and delete
Full Control	All	All

Table 4-1: *File and Directory Attributes.*

One of the features of this file system that is very different from most UNIX systems is that the administrator can *take* ownership of any file, but no one, including the administrator, can *give* ownership to anyone else. This prevents a fraudulent administrator from tinkering with the file system and then covering his or her tracks.

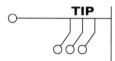
TIP

The best defense against data loss due to system hackers or an accident is a good backup policy. Not only will a reliable set of backups allow you to restore files that have been maliciously deleted or accidentally lost, but the log files archived on the backups may be your only evidence of the hacker's activities. A good backup policy should make a full backup of the system at least once, and ideally twice, a month. You should do an incremental backup of files that have changed several times a week; once a day is ideal. For reliable backups, you should always keep multiple sets of working backup tapes, which you rotate through, round-robin fashion. If you always use the same set of tapes for backups, you may find that your most recent set is corrupted, and you have no recourse. Tape is cheap, especially compared to irreplaceable data.

Secure Protocols for the Web

There are several options for providing secure connections between web clients and web servers. The basic intent of any secure protocol is to protect the confidentiality of user data. In addition, the secure protocols may verify the identity of the server and possibly client, through the use of authenticated certificates.

The two leading security protocols today are Secure HTTP (S-HTTP) and Secure Sockets Layer (SSL). Both Secure HTTP and SSL use encryption to protect secure information. Encryption is, simply put, the process of encoding information so that only parties who understand the code can read that information. Secure HTTP and SSL are different in one basic way: Secure HTTP is an application protocol, meaning it can be used only for HTTP transactions, whereas SSL is a protocol that can be implemented with any application protocol: HTTP, FTP, Gopher, Telnet, and others. S-HTTP and SSL can easily coexist on a single system, so both protocols may wind up being popular on the Internet. In the following sections, we'll examine both Secure HTTP and SSL, and we'll take a look at a couple of additional privacy methods common on the Internet.

Secure HTTP

Secure HTTP is a variation of HTTP, the standard protocol used on the World Wide Web. It is implemented in the same way that HTTP is implemented on current browsers and servers, but Secure HTTP provides the ability for both servers and clients to send encrypted information. Secure HTTP is capable of communicating with both secure and insecure servers and clients (the security functions are disabled when Secure HTTP communicates with the latter).

One of the more important features of Secure HTTP is that it doesn't require the client to use a public key. Secure HTTP supports three types of protection: encryption, which is discussed in detail in this section; authentication, which verifies that a message has not been changed since it was sent and that the name of the sender is accurate; and signature, which is the inclusion of a unique digital signature identifying the sender of the message.

The signature on a document is a certificate that verifies the identity of a particular individual or organization. The certificate is unique and is distributed by data security organizations, such as Verisign. Verisign is a spin-off from RSA Data Security, one of the pioneers of electronic cryptography, and has an arrangement with most secure server makers to provide certificates for their web-hosting software. The certificate is attached to a document, and this signature verifies the source of a document.

Authentication Certificates

Although many protocols can provide privacy, when a user is interacting with a server on the Internet, an important issue is the "officialness" of a web server. Particularly when sending sensitive information, such as credit card information, a user wants some assurance that the web server to which the information is being sent is not a hacker! One way to provide this assurance is through the use of a hierarchy of trust. At the top of this hierarchy is an organization that everyone trusts. This organization issues signed certificates to a number of certificate-issuing authorities. (Of course, with digital information the "signature" is electronic rather than written. To find out more about digital signatures and certificates, look at RSA Data Security's home page at http://www.rsa.com/.) The certificate-issuing authorities in turn provide certificates to web server operators, with which they can prove they have been "authenticated" by a trusted authority. The process of getting a certificate from a trusted authority involves a number of nonelectronic steps, sometimes including personal interviews or visits. This is all done to assure the end user that the operators of a server are who they say they are.

If you wish to operate a secure server, you'll need to obtain a certificate from a recognized certificate authority. For many operators, this can be accomplished by working through Verisign (http://www.verisign.com/).

The process of authentication uses a message transmitted between a server and a client called a Message Authentication Code, or MAC. The MAC is not encrypted using the public and private keys as described previously, but instead is encrypted with what is called a "shared secret" that, for example, can be in the form of a password. The server creates a MAC by encrypting both the message itself and the timestamp of when that message was transmitted. The shared secret is used to encrypt the MAC so that only a provider who knows the shared secret can create that particular MAC. A user or client who wants to verify the integrity of a document can use that same shared secret (which has to be communicated to the user via some secure means) and check it against the MAC. Essentially, this process eliminates the need to have a third party verify that a message is authentic. A user says, "I don't believe you sent this," and the sender replies, "Check the MAC with this password: shoop!3." When the password and the MAC match up, the document is considered valid.

The most vital element of protecting a document, however, is encryption. Encrypting information allows it to be sent securely without any danger of its being intercepted by a third party. Information can be encrypted in one of two ways, either by assigning a key when a session is started and transmitting that key between the server and the client, or by using a prearranged key that is selected using information in a document header.

With the first method, the server either uses a client's public key or, if that client does not have a public key, generates a temporary key for that session. This session key is generated in the following way: a text string is generated by the client software, and the client sends the text string, encrypted with the server's public key, to the server, saying, "This is my session key." The server then encrypts secure information using that session key and sends it to the client, and the client uses the same session key to decrypt the message.

In the second method, the server sends a code naming a particular key and tells the client, "Select this key out of the keys you already understand, and use it to decrypt the following information." This method is useful for repeated transactions between a particular client and server.

Both methods should be transparent both for the user and for the server administrator. The software will choose the most appropriate method.

Secure HTTP, like regular HTTP, communicates by sending text messages between clients and servers. In regular HTTP, these text messages include header information, the HTML documents themselves, and information about files, such as their MIME types. In Secure HTTP, these text messages establish a secure session between a client and a server before the server sends the document itself.

A client starts a secure session by sending a request for a secure document, and the server replies that the document being sent is a secure document. This reply is followed by header information about the document being sent. Two header lines are mandatory: the first line names the type of encryption being used, and the second contains MIME type information for the document. The Secure HTTP Internet Draft recommends the MIME type application/http for secure documents. Other optional header lines can contain information about prearranged keys, MACs, and specific settings for different encryption types.

This information, and another set of transactions between the server and the client called the "negotiations," allow encrypted information to be successfully received and decrypted. The negotiation headers describe the capabilities of the client to the server, telling the server what encryption formats can and cannot be understood, for example. After all of this information is transferred, the content is sent, encrypted in whatever format is named in the first mandatory header line. The content is optionally followed by a digital signature to verify the source of a document.

Using these methods, Secure HTTP allows clients and servers to perform a range of functions not possible with regular HTTP, including verifying a document's validity and ensuring the secure transmission of information. This standard will probably be adopted by most servers and browsers in the near future. SSL, which was developed by Netscape Communications for its client and server software, presents an alternative model to Secure HTTP.

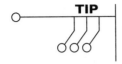

For a description of Secure HTTP, look at EIT's information pages at the URL http://www.eit.com/projects/s-http/index.html. To see how it is being implemented, check out the Secure NCSA HTTPD home page at http://www.commerce.net/software/Shttpd/.

SSL

SSL was developed by Netscape Communications and integrated into the Netscape Web browser and the Commerce Server, which is Netscape's commercially available server software. Many other server makers also support SSL. To use SSL, a server first has to have a certificate, that is, a verification of the identity of the individual or organization that is accepting secure transactions.

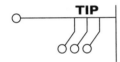

For information about acquiring an RSA certificate for use with SSL servers, see Verisign's Web pages at the URL http://www.verisign.com/netscape/.

During the process of acquiring a certificate, the server software generates a public and private key code. The server's public key will be used to generate a session key in the same way that Secure HTTP does. The client generates a session key and uses the server's public key to encrypt and send that session key to the server. The user does not have to have his or her own public key, because SSL generates a temporary session key on the fly.

SSL and Secure HTTP have similar uses, even though the syntax of the messages sent between the server and client is different. SSL has the same security capabilities as Secure HTTP—authentication, encryption, and signature. Because SSL operates at a lower protocol layer than S-HTTP, these features can be used in any TCP/IP protocol, not just HTTP.

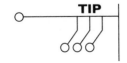

Full details about the SSL protocol are available from Netscape at the URL http://www.netscape.com/info/security-doc.html.

PCT

Private Communications Technology, or PCT, offered by Microsoft (http://www.microsoft.com/windows/ie/pct.htm), is based on SSL. It addresses some of the weaknesses in SSL, and is designed to be fairly compatible with SSL. According to Microsoft, PCT has fixed some of the "problems" with SSL, and reduces the number of messages that the client and server must exchange. (Corporations being practical, Microsoft is also including SSL protocol support in their Internet Information Server, and Netscape is continuing to improve their SSL protocol.)

PGP, PEM & Other Privacy Methods

There are other methods used to secure Internet communications besides SSL, S-HTTP, and PCT. Most of them are designed for the encryption of electronic mail, and focus on the protection and authentication of messages. Pretty Good Privacy (PGP) and Privacy Enhanced Mail (PEM) are well-known and well-accepted in the Internet community. Some browsers and servers support PGP and PEM, but since they're based on RSA-licensed encryption technology, and the United States has placed extremely restrictive rules on exporting these technologies, folks outside the United States have a tough time finding browsers that can handle PGP and PEM. MOSS is a variety of PEM modified to support MIME.

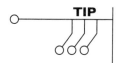
TIP

For more information about computer security, check out the Web site at http://www.alw.nih.gov/Security/.

Moving On

This chapter has provided just a brief introduction into the complex area of system security. Keeping a busy site secure from a determined, knowledgeable attacker is extremely difficult. Fortunately, most attackers are neither knowledgeable nor particularly experienced. In the final analysis, the essence of good security is vigilance. No configuration is perfectly secure, but if you take basic precautions and are constantly on the lookout for problems, you can make your system relatively secure and avoid being an easy target. An actively maintained site tends to be a secure site.

Once you've set up your server and have the knowledge and tools to keep it secure, it's time to start populating your site with compelling content. Many organizations have already developed a large store of documents that they want to put online. It's usually unnecessary to convert such documents by hand from their native formats into the Web's HTML format. The next chapter will show you how to automatically convert documents from popular word processing and desktop publishing environments into HTML.

SECTION II

Adding Content

5

Importing Documents to the Web

If you have more than a few pages of information to put on your web site, it's unlikely that you'll be creating information only for the web in HTML format. Instead, you'll probably have a body of documents in some other format, or you'll be creating new work with the intention of creating multiple output formats. Common sources of documents for web servers might be product documentation and descriptions, advertisements, design and requirements documentation, reports, letters, and memos. The formats may vary from plain flat-ASCII text files to highly structured SGML. Furthermore, it's unlikely that HTML is the only destination format for many documents—most of the time you'll be creating source documents to be used in a variety of publication formats, including the web, paper, and perhaps other online services. These days, even the idea of a common HTML format is becoming elusive, due to the competitive extensions added by Netscape and the slippery nature of "proposed standards."

Major corporations have addressed these issues by developing "industrial strength" document management systems, while others pick a standard document authoring platform that can export to all the needed output formats. The choices that you'll make for creating and converting documents are highly dependent on the format and quantity of documents you want to publish on the web. While truly large-scale document conversion and management is beyond the scope of this book—and probably out of reach of most mere mortals' budgets—you should not overlook the capability of your solution to scale up to the demands you might place on it. You should also keep in mind the limiting consequences of developing single-purpose conversion and management tools.

There are a number of automated procedures you can use that will automatically convert non-HTML documents into HTML. In this chapter we'll review in detail two freely available programs for converting plain ASCII text and Rich Text Format documents into HTML, plus provide an overview of some of the commercial tools available to help you in text conversions.

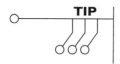

TIP

If you really want to get into development of documents for Web publication, you might wish to check out HTML Publishing on the Internet for Windows (also from Ventana), which focuses on the publishing and creative aspects of the Web.

Text to HTML

ASCII, or the standard character set, is the name for the file format of text files that have been saved as Text Only, scanned in from a printed page, or created in a program like xvi (the NT version of the UNIX vi program), which does not attach formatting information. If you're converting unformatted ASCII text to a web document, you'll almost inevitably need to mark up much of the document manually or import the document into an HTML editor (see Chapter 2, "The Basic Pieces"). However, a perl script called txt2html.pl is capable of doing some of the markup for you. txt2html.pl goes through the text and identifies certain text elements that should be marked up with specific HTML tags. Since the script contains options that are, to a limited degree, configurable, you can tell the program in the command line what to look for. Running the script from the command line requires you to redirect your text file to stdin for txt2html.pl and to redirect that output to the new HTML document, as in the following example:

```
perl txt2html.pl < textfile.txt > webpage.html
```

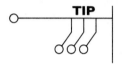

To run txt2html.pl, you must have perl installed on your NT system. Perl is included on the Companion CD-ROM, along with directions for using it. Perl, which has its roots on UNIX systems, is an extremely valuable script-processing program. It is used for many scripting applications on the Web, and is used frequently to create CGI programs.

This command creates a marked-up version of *textfile*.txt with the name *webpage*.html. txt2html.pl contains a number of formatting tricks, which may be more useful in composing documents than in translating them but do provide some flexibility. For example, to create a head with an <H2> tag, in the text file you can enter the head with a row of equal signs beneath it, as follows:

```
This is header 2 text.
==================
```

txt2html.pl replaces those two lines with the following line:

```
<H2>This is header 2 text.</H2>
```

You can invoke the <H3> tag by entering a row of dashes directly underneath the head. This should not be confused with entering a row of dashes with no text or characters directly above it, which generates a horizontal rule tag (<HR>).

txt2html.pl is also capable of translating lists that include simple tabs and symbols (such as dashes, asterisks, letters, or numbers) into ordered or unordered lists, depending on the bullet type. For example, consider the following section of a text file:

```
ShoopSoft's many virtues include:
  * Reliability
    - We guarantee quick response and 24/7
      accessibility.
  * Quality
    1. Our team has over 5 years of Internet
       experience.
    2. We have a money-back guarantee of
       satisfaction.
  * Affordability
    - Everything we do is free.  Really.
```

txt2html.pl translates this text into HTML as follows:

```
<HTML>
<HEAD>
</HEAD>
<BODY>
<p>
ShoopSoft's many virtues include:<BR>
<UL>
<LI> Reliability
<UL>
<LI> We guarantee quick response and 24/7 accessibility.
</UL>
<LI> Quality
<OL>
<LI> Our team has over 5 years of Internet experience.
<LI> We have a money-back guarantee of satisfaction.
</OL>
<LI> Affordability
<UL>
<LI> Everything we do is free.  Really.
</UL>
</UL>
</BODY>
</HTML>
```

Notice that txt2html.pl is capable of distinguishing between an ordered list (marked with numbers) and an unordered list (marked with asterisks, as in the subordinate items under item 1). You should separate the nested lists with tabs, but it's not necessary to change the type of text bullet that you use in order for txt2html.pl to recognize the nested list as a new list, so long as it is indented from the list level above it.

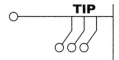

TIP

To obtain information about txt2html.pl and to check for new updates, see the developer's WWW page at the URL http://www.cs.wustl.edu/~seth/txt2html/.

To configure txt2html.pl, you can either change the defaults in the program itself or select options from the command line. In all of the command-line options, you can either use an abbreviation for the option, such as -s, or the full name of the option, such as -shortline. In the following descriptions of command-line options in txt2html.pl, you can replace *n* with the numerical value of the variable you're setting.

The -s option allows you to set the maximum length for a short line that you want to preserve as a short line. In other words, if a line contains fewer than a certain number of characters, txt2html.pl inserts a line break at the end of the line to preserve its formatting.

`[-s n ] | [-shortline n]`

To mark a certain amount of text as preformatted (<PRE>), you can simply enter a certain number of spaces before that text. Using the -p option, you can define the number of spaces txt2html.pl should locate before switching to preformatting mode.

`[-p n] | [-prewhite n]`

Similarly, if your file contains text that "looks" preformatted (such as a chart with columns separated by spaces or tabs, a table with columns, etc.), txt2html.pl marks it as preformatted after finding a specified number of lines of this preformatted-looking text. The -pb option lets you designate the number of lines that txt2html.pl should encounter before inserting the <PRE> tag.

```
[-pb n] | [-prebegin n]
```

For example, if you set the value of -pb to 2, then the following listing, standing alone, would not be marked as preformatted, because it consists of only one line of preformatted-looking text:

```
Bill Jones        118 Phillips Trace Road     Kalamazoo   MI
```

However, a listing like the one below *would* be marked as preformatted:

```
Bill Jones        118 Phillips Trace Road     Kalamazoo   MI
J.R. Dobbs        P.O. Box 1                   Quantico    VA
```

Finding the required number of preformatted lines—in this case, two—causes txt2html.pl to insert the opening tag for preformatted text, <PRE>.

After you've defined how to begin a section of preformatted text with the -pb option, you can also define how to end the section. Using the -pe option, you can set the number of lines that do *not* look like they should be preformatted. After finding that number of lines, txt2html.pl inserts the </PRE> closing tag at the end of the preformatted-looking section.

```
[-pe n] | [-preend n]
```

As an example, if the -pe option were given a value of 2, then the following section of text would all be marked as preformatted:

```
Bill Jones        118 Phillips Trace Road   Kalamazoo MI
J.R. Dobbs        P.O. Box 1                 Quantico VA

The above clients should receive mailings. The following
clients should not:
Raymond Williams Route 3, Box 10            Birmingham  AL
Desmond Dekker   101 Q. Elizabeth           Kingston Jamaica
```

However, if the value of the -pe option were reduced to 1, then the above paragraph would only mark the addresses as preformatted, and leave the single line of text separating the addresses as regular text.

TIP

It's useful to set -pe to a higher value if you want to include some lines of text that don't look like preformatted text inside a section of preformatted text.

The -e/+e option removes the standard headers that frame a complete HTML document, such as <HTML>, <HEAD>, and <BODY>. Removing these headers makes it easier to insert the text into an existing HTML document. Since the default is for every document to contain these tags, if you're planning on using txt2html.pl to insert text into other HTML documents, you'll want to change the value of the default in the script itself (line 186).

```
[-e/+e] | [-extract / -noextract]
```

To create a horizontal rule (<HR>) in a document, you can enter a line of dashes. Use the -r option to set the number of dashes that txt2html.pl should find before replacing them with the <HR> tag.

```
[-r n] | [-hrule n]
```

txt2html.pl formats a line composed of all capital letters any way that you specify with the -ct option, discussed below. To tell txt2html.pl what kind of line you want to have recognized as all capitals, you can set the -c option to indicate the number of capital letters at the beginning of a line necessary for the line to be treated as all caps.

```
[-c n] | [-caps n]
```

For example, if you set the -c option to a value of 5, then the following line would not be treated as "all caps," since it begins with only three capital letters, and so would not be marked up with the tag that you set with the -ct option:

```
HEY! Check out this site: http://www.shoop.com
```

If you set the value of -c to 2, however, then the line above would be recognized as a line of "all caps." This might be confusing, since you know that it is not actually all capital letters, but what you're doing is telling txt2html.pl how many capital letters in a row it will need to find before treating the line as something special. This "special treatment" means that, after encountering the specified number of capital letters, txt2html.pl marks that entire line with the tags you set with the -ct option.

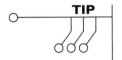

TIP *If you have lines of text that have a number of capital letters but that you do not want specially marked up, then you should set the -c option to a fairly high number.*

After telling txt2html.pl what is to be treated as a line of all capitals, you can set the HTML tag with which that line is to be marked up. Set the -ct option to the HTML tag surrounded by quotes, and txt2html.pl marks up all capitals-only lines accordingly.

```
[-ct "tag"] | [-capstag "tag"]
```

This option is one that you might want to set in the program itself. Change the entry on line 144 of the script to set the default for this option. The default for capitals is for them to be marked as <STRONG>. To continue with the example above, let's assume that we've set the -c option to 2. Thus any line beginning with more than two capital letters in a row will be marked up with whatever tag has been set in the -ct option. Assuming we have not changed the default value of the -ct option from "<STRONG>" then the line in the example above would be translated into the following:

```
<STRONG>HEY! Check out this site: http://www.shoop.com
</STRONG>
```

You can use the append option to include a file at the end of any documents translated.

```
[-a file] | [-append file]
```

If you include a file with HTML codes in it, they are interpreted as HTML codes and not as text. If your e-mail address in your signature file is surrounded by brackets, for example, the brackets are interpreted as indicators of an HTML tag. If you want an HTML browser to actually display characters such as the ampersand, quotation marks, or brackets, you need to use the corresponding HTML entities, the codes that tell a browser to display these special characters. For example, the string ">" tells the browser to insert a greater-than symbol, and the string "<" tells the browser to insert a less-than symbol, as in the following line:

```
This page has been created by &gt;&gt;SHOOPSOFT&lt;&lt;
Enterprises.
```

On an HTML browser, this line would appear as follows:

```
This page has been created by >>SHOOPSOFT<< Enterprises.
```

Any HTML markup, such as a hyperlink to a home page or a mailto tag, included in the file you want to append to your translated documents would be correctly interpreted by the browser. For example, if you wanted to include a link to your home page at the bottom of a translated document, you could enter the HTML tags and text "as is":

```
This document is part of <A HREF="http://www.shoop.com/bob/
index.html">Bob's Pages</A>.
```

This line would be interpreted as containing a hyperlink.

The +a option turns off the append option if it is turned on in the script itself. By default, the append option is turned off, but if you change the default in the script, you can use the +a option to turn it back off.

```
[+a] | [-noappend]
```

The -t option allows you to specify the title of your document. By default, the document is left untitled. Make sure to enclose the document title in quotation marks.

```
[-t "title"] | [-title "title"]
```

The -tw option sets the number of spaces that are equivalent to a tab. This option is most useful when creating nested lists, since txt2html.pl uses the tabs to determine where to place lists in an HTML document. The default is set to eight spaces, which might be too many for some word processors. Again, you might want to consider setting this variable in the program itself (line 177).

```
[-tw n] | [-tabwidth n]
```

The -iw, or indent width, option determines the number of
spaces to indent a nested list in the HTML document. Since a
browser automatically determines where to place nested lists, this
option is necessary only for the formatting of the source itself, to
make it more readable as HTML code. The default is set to two
spaces.

`[-iw n] | [-indent n]`

In plain ASCII text, it is common practice to "underline" a word
by putting an underscore before and after that word. Use the -ul
option, shown below, to determine how many underscores are
necessary for txt2html.pl to treat a word as underlined and to
enclose it in <U> </U> tags. The default is set to one character,
which seems to work fine.

`[-ul n] | [-underlinelong n]`

Using txt2html.pl can help you translate your documents into
the most basic HTML format, but as mentioned at the outset, for
attractive customized documents, you're better off formatting by
hand or using an advanced editor. One other possibility is saving
your documents in Rich Text Format, which is a file format that
preserves all of the formatting codes of a document. A document
saved in Rich Text Format, or RTF, can be converted with an
extremely powerful and versatile program called rtftohtml and,
with some configuring, will end up being as attractive as the
output from any editing you do manually. By and large, though,
txt2html.pl, rtftohtml, and other converters are best used to convert a sizable body of documents, rather than an individual
document or small group of documents, simply because of the
amount of time involved in properly configuring any conversion
program.

Island InTEXT

One very useful multipurpose web creation tool, and perhaps the best noncustom ASCII converter, is Island InTEXT. This program is part of a larger software product suite that includes products that can index and parse documents for a variety of output formats. It's actually unfair to the program to discuss it only in context of ASCII file conversions, since it is really a much more comprehensive program than that. A great strength of this program is that it can accept a complete set of documents in a variety of input formats, and create a complete web of HTML documents based on that.

At the time this was written, supported input formats included Microsoft Word, WordPerfect, Ami Pro, WinCim, Windows Write, and plain ASCII. Most users of word processors pay little attention to defining structure in their documents, and because of that, they have some trouble when converting to HTML. Island InTEXT overcomes this limitation to some extent by analyzing the content of a document, and introducing structure based on the layout and context.

In addition to the capabilities of this low-cost Windows program, Island sells libraries that can be used in the background to produce a very sophisticated searching and indexing system for a web (or other) server.

RTF to HTML

RTF, or "Rich Text Format," is a file format that lies somewhere between pure ASCII and a binary word processor format. RTF saves the formatting of a document in ASCII codes that can be interpreted by other word processing programs and allows a wide range of word processed documents to be translated into other formats. Rich Text Format documents contain both the text of a document and all of the formatting codes that are used in that document, and these codes can be interpreted by many word processors and other applications. For example, the following is the first sentence of this section, saved in Rich Text Format:

```
par \pard\plain \s15\sa240\tx360 \f4 RTF, or \ldblquote Rich
Text Format,\rdblquote is a file format that lies somewhere
between pure ASCII and a binary word processor format.
```

You can see a number of the RTF codes embedded in the sentence, such as those telling the word processor to insert double quotes (\ldblquote, \rdblquote) around the string "Rich Text Format."

It is possible to convert from RTF into HTML with a freeware program called rtftohtml, included on the Companion CD-ROM. The program is usable without modification, with a number of prespecified codes that cover the majority of styles used in standard word processors. It works particularly well with the standard document styles of Microsoft's Word for Windows. If you're using specially configured styles, however, you can add them to the rtftohtml file that contains translation rules. By configuring rtftohtml to work with your in-house word processor, you can quickly translate your documents into custom-formatted HTML documents.

A number of formatting styles in rtftohtml are predefined. rtftohtml converts any text that you write using the font Courier into typewriter-style text (<TT>) on the HTML page. Tables are not yet supported in this translator, and are converted into preformatted text (<PRE>).

rtftohtml can be incredibly intuitive in its conversions. For example, if you have a table of contents at the beginning of your document, rtftohtml makes it a separate file and creates hyperlinks between that document and the chapters and sections to which it refers. rtftohtml will make all of the entries already in your table of contents into hyperlinks, pointing to the appropriate locations in your document. In addition, any paragraph headings that use the header tags <H1> through <H6> will be inserted into your table of contents as new entries, and this text will also be linked to the appropriate location. Similarly, rtftohtml moves any footnotes in your document to a separate file and hyperlinks the footnote markers in the main document to the appropriate footnote text in the separate file.

As when using any conversion features, you need to make sure that you're using the correct styles so that rtftohtml will recognize them. If rtftohtml encounters a format it doesn't recognize, it generates an error message and leaves the text unchanged (including it as regular text). For the most part, rtftohtml will correctly interpret any styles that come with your word processor. Make sure that you use a different style for each new format that you want to see in an HTML document. If you create any new styles, or if your documents use custom styles, then you'll need to add these styles to the configuration file for rtftohtml (see "Defining New Styles," later in this chapter). You can also check this file to see what styles rtftohtml already understands.

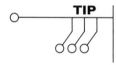

TIP

Don't forget, if you're going to use the rtftohtml converter, you must always save your word processor documents as RTF. Also, if you are using Microsoft Word for Windows, you should turn off the "smart quotes" feature, so that only straight double-quotes are used in your documents.

Graphics

When rtftohtml finds a graphic embedded in the RTF document, it does two things. First, it creates a hyperlink to that graphic in the HTML document at the location where it found the graphic in the word processor file. Since this link is an <A HREF> link, rtftohtml does not embed the graphic itself in the HTML document. (It's possible to change this feature, using the -i command-line option, so that all graphics are referenced with an <IMG SRC> tag, which *does* embed the graphic. See "Command-Line Options," later in this chapter.)

In addition to creating the link, rtftohtml actually exports any included graphics and saves them as separate files. The file name is the name of the RTF document, the number of the graphic, and an extension that indicates the format that the graphic is in. For example, converting a file called CATALOG.RTF that contains three embedded Microsoft Windows bitmapped images creates the graphics files CATALOG1.WMF, CATALOG2.WMF, and CATALOG3.WMF. The three formats that rtftohtml is capable of creating are Windows bitmap (.BMP), Windows metafile (.WMF), and Macintosh PICT (.PICT). The file type depends on the format that rtftohtml exports to, but in our experience converting from RTF generated by Word for Windows, only the Windows metafile format (WMF) is created.

The link created in the first step, either <A HREF> or <IMG SRC>, is made to a GIF file (CATALOG1.GIF, in the example). This means that you have to use a separate program to convert the extracted bitmap, metafile, or PICT to a GIF. You can convert the graphics files with Paint Shop Pro, included on the Companion CD-ROM. Paint Shop Pro can convert files in either of two ways. If you want to look at the images you're converting while you convert them (to resize them or add comments, for example), you can open each file into Paint Shop Pro, then save it in GIF format. If you have a number of files to convert, and don't want to open them individually, you can use Paint Shop Pro's Batch Convert feature, available under the File menu.

Since rtftohtml automatically uses the .GIF file extension for inline images, the files created by the scripts described in this chapter will automatically work in the HTML documents.

Command-Line Options

Assuming that you have no updates to the translation rules file, you can run rtftohtml using the following command-line options:

```
rtftohtml [-i] [ -V] [-o filename] [-P extension] [-T]
[-G][file]
```

The options are described in the following table.

Option	Description
-i	Indicates that embedded graphics should be linked to the main document using an <IMG> tag. The default is to use the <A HREF>-style link.
-V	Prints the current version to the screen.

-o *filename*	Indicates that the output file name should be *filename*.
-P *extension*	Uses *extension* as the extension for any links to graphics files. The default is .GIF.
-T	Indicates that no table of contents file is to be generated.
-G	Indicates that no graphics files should be written. The hypertext links to the graphics files are still generated. This is a performance-enhancing feature for when you are retranslating a document and haven't changed the graphics.
file	The name of the file to be processed. If no *file* is given as a parameter, standard input is used and the body of the document is written to standard output (unless overridden by the -o option). If a *file* is given, the output is written to the filename *file* with .HTML as the extension. (If .RTF appears as an extension on *file*, it is stripped before the .HTML is appended. This means you'll never see textfile.RTF.HTML.)

Table 5-1: *Command-line options for rtftohtml.*

Defining New Styles

While the translation file that comes with rtftohtml has a number of styles already configured, you'll probably want to add more to allow for cleaner translations of your pages. By modifying this configuration file you can create a very powerful and versatile pairing between your existing word processing setup and your HTML pages. You need to modify two sections of the configuration file, called html-trans, when you add a new style. Essentially, these tables define what sort of input to match with the appropriate HTML tag and how the HTML tag should be inserted into the HTML document. The tables are labeled .PTag, .TTag, .TMatch, and .PMatch, in order of their appearance in the html-trans file.

.PTag

The paragraph tag, or .PTag, table will probably require very little modification. This table controls how various paragraph formatting tags are exported into the new HTML document. Suppose you wanted to add the Netscape extension <CENTER> as a new paragraph tag. You would add the following line to the .PTag table:

```
"center","<center>/n","</center>/n","/t","/t","<p>/n",
1,1,0,1,0
```

The html-trans file contains an abbreviation for each of these items. The following is a brief definition of what each item indicates to rtftohtml:

❋ The first item gives the name of the style itself. This is defined in the paragraph match, or .PMatch, table.

❋ The second and third items are the opening and closing tags for the HTML markup. Note that both are followed by the "/n" string. This string causes a new line to be inserted after the tags are written to the new HTML file. Note that if you're using a tag that does not require a close tag, such as the horizontal rule <HR>, you can enter a null string by just putting two quotation marks in place of the third option.

❋ The fourth and fifth items are the replacement strings for tab characters. The fourth is the replacement tag for the first tab in every paragraph, the fifth for tabs anywhere else. In this case, they are both replaced with the "/t" command string, which places a string of spaces into the new HTML document.

❋ The sixth item gives the paragraph marker to be used inside any text with this format. It should be set either to <BR>, for a line break, or <P>, for a paragraph break. The "/n" string, again, causes a new line to be inserted after the tag is written to the HTML source file, for easier reading.

❋ The next four items are binary switches that turn options on or off. If the value is 0, the option is turned off; if it is 1, the option is on. The seventh option, if turned off, will not allow any text formatting markup (such as <STRONG>,

<EM>, <TT>, etc.) inside this tag. For example, if bold text is placed inside text defined as a header (using the <H1> through <H6> tags), it will confuse browsers. The eighth option allows nesting, such as when you want a list and a subordinate list within that list. The ninth option, if turned on, will cause rtftohtml to delete all of the text up to the first tab in a paragraph. This is useful if your text document has an ASCII character like * as a list bullet, since you will not actually want that character as a part of the list item. It would be deleted and replaced with a tag like <LI> if this value were turned on. The tenth option automatically inserts a new line in the HTML source document when a line exceeds 80 characters. This new line is only visible in the source document itself, and will not be displayed as a new line when the document is viewed by a browser. This option is simply to make it easier to read the HTML source code itself, since it has no effect on the way the document will appear on the web. The only exception is in the case of the preformatted text tag <PRE>, which tells the browser to display the layout of the text exactly as it appears in the source code. If you're using the <PRE> tag in this line of your .PTag table, then make sure that this value is set to 0.

◈ Finally, the last option determines the level at which an item should be listed in the table of contents. The default is that a paragraph marked <H1> gets top-level listing, <H2> is a subhead of that, and so on down to <H6>. Simply set this final option to 1 if you want the style in question to be given a table of contents entry.

.TTag
The text tag, or .TTag, table is straightforward. It is composed of the name of the tag, the opening tag, and the closing tag. If, for example, you wanted to add the Netscape tag <BLINK> as a new style, you would add the following line to the .TTag table:

```
"blink","<BLINK>","</BLINK>"
```

.TMatch

In contrast to the .TTag table, the text matching, or .TMatch, table is probably the most difficult to grasp, but also one of the most versatile. This table converts combinations of text formatting styles to HTML tags. For example, this table drives the conversion of text that is labeled as "Courier" font to the HTML <TT> style. It is composed of five options. The first two are the font and font size, which you can use to select the style based only on those characteristics. This is how rtftohtml knows to translate all Courier fonts into <TT>, or typewriter, style in the HTML document. You can enter a null string ("") for the font and/or a 0 for the font size to configure rtftohtml to ignore either or both in matching the text to a particular style. Following is the line that rtftohtml uses to translate Courier fonts into typewriter-style text:

```
"Courier",0,00000000000000,00000000000000,"tt"
```

The third and fourth items, the long strings of zeros, are the match and the mask options. The match option determines exactly what formatting (i.e., bold, italic, hidden, etc.) to look for in the original text by using a string of binary switches, with each switch corresponding to a particular formatting type. The mask option uses the same binary switches as the match option. The difference is that where the match option specifies the formatting settings to be matched, the mask option specifies the formatting types to be considered. For example, using the mask option, you could tell rtftohtml to look at the settings for bold, underline, and hidden. In the match option, you could determine what those should be set to in order for a match to be returned. This makes it possible to tell rtftohtml, "If an RTF string is bold and underlined, but not hidden, mark it up with the HTML strong style," for example.

You should think of the match and mask options as charts, with each column of the chart representing a different formatting type, as shown in the following table.

Sub	Sup	DbU	DtU	WU	U	Hid	AC	SC	Sh	Out	ST	Ita	Bld
0	0	0	0	0	1	0	0	0	0	0	0	0	0
0	0	0	0	0	0	1	0	0	0	0	0	0	1

Table 5-2: *Sample match/mask settings for underlined text and for bold, hidden text.*

The characters in the top row of the chart represent in order: Subscript, Superscript, Double Underline, Dotted Underline, Word Underline, Underline, Hidden, AllCaps, SmallCaps, Shadow, Outline, StrikeThrough, Italics, and Bold. This chart contains two examples of formatting selection. The first is Underline; thus, all of the formatting options except for Underline are turned off with a 0 value. The second is a Bold, Hidden string; thus those two options are turned on with a 1. Using this configuration method, you can select any of those formatting types in the match and mask options of the .TMatch table.

Here's a more concrete example of how the match and mask options work. rtftohtml is preconfigured so that any text that is italic and underlined is a citation to be marked up with the <CITE> tag, and any text that is italic and not underlined is simply to be italicized with the <I> tag. This configuration is specified with the following two lines:

```
"",0,00000000000010,00000100000010,"i"
"",0,00000100000010,00000100000010,"cite"
```

Note that in both lines, the mask option is set to look at the underline column, but in the match option, one has underline turned on, and one does not. This configuration is what allows rtftohtml to look to see if a variable is *not* selected and match it according to what it finds. By and large, most of your match and mask options will be the same, but if you want to define a new type style that matches on the basis of a format style that is *not* in use, simply put a 1 in the appropriate column in the mask option and a 0 in the corresponding column of the match option.

The fifth and final option in a .TMatch table is the HTML style that you want to match this particular text type to. Simply enter the name of one of the styles that you have defined in the .TTag table, and rtftohtml will tag any matched text in the .TMatch table from the original document with that style when creating the new HTML document.

.PMatch

The paragraph match, or .PMatch, table is what matches certain styles that you have configured in your word processor to a particular HTML tag. A .PMatch entry contains only three variables: the style name from your word processor, the "nesting level," and the HTML style name as specified in the .PTag table. You specify the nesting level of a style only if you want to make a nested list, using one of the list tags (such as <DL>, <OL>, or <UL>). If you've defined two styles in your word processor, one for lists and one for a list within a list, say "List Level 1" and "List Level 2," you could match those styles with an entry like the following:

```
"List Level 1",1,"ul"
"List Level 2",2,"ul"
```

This entry makes any text written with the style "List Level 2" a subset of one of the list items in "List Level 1," or some other option with the nesting level set to 1.

The most standard type of entry that you'll make, however, will be matching one word processor style to an HTML style. In the previous example of creating a style for the Netscape tag <CENTER>, you could configure your word processor to output a style called "Centered Text" and create a .PMatch entry as follows:

```
"Centered Text",0,"center"
```

This entry would match your centered text to the style that is configured in the .PTag table described earlier.

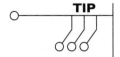

TIP

For more information on rtftohtml, see the RTFTOHTML Users Guide, *starting with the table of contents at the URL http://www.sunpack.com/RTF/rtftohtml_overview.html.*

Word Processor Converters

While it is possible to save your documents as Rich Text Format in almost any word processing package and then use the program rtftohtml to convert them to HTML, as explained previously, a number of add-ons for commercial packages are available on the World Wide Web or via anonymous FTP for people who prefer a more direct route from their word processors to HTML. You should check out the guidance offered in *HTML Publishing on the Internet for Windows*, also available from Ventana, if you'll be creating a lot of original Web material. You can also check with the maker of your word processor package and ask about available HTML converters. All the major word processors have some kind of HTML export capability.

SGML on the Web

If you have a large repository of SGML documents that you want to publish on the web, then you probably already know how to do it using commercial translation tools, such as provided by Omnimark. At the moment, there are no freeware tools available for Windows that down-convert SGML documents with their own structure to the HTML format. But if you're willing to require web users to view your documents with an external viewer, you can put your SGML documents directly on the web.

SoftQuad's free Panorama SGML viewer accepts an SGML file and a file called a style sheet, which describes to the viewer how to interpret the SGML codes. To create a Panorama-compatible web document from an existing SGML document, you need to purchase the "professional" version of Panorama. This product, which currently retails for $139, allows you to take an existing SGML document and create the style sheet that describes how the Panorama viewer will display your document. Web users with the free Panorama viewer installed on their systems can then load your document and associated style sheet in order to view your SGML document.

Creating Your Own Converters

HTML is a reasonably simple markup language that only uses printable ASCII characters for the representation of all text and control codes. If you have an internal legacy document format that no one else understands, or are working with a standard data stream that is not popular with the freeware community, you may want to create your own converter to HTML. You can create scripts in perl, a UNIX-based tool that has been ported to the NT environment. You can also create a standard executable program written in C (for example) that parses your input stream and writes out HTML, or an instance of an SGML document. Or you can choose to go with Omnimark, which is specifically designed to assist with legacy document conversion—but this isn't cheap.

An important consideration is whether you want to convert directly from your internal file format to HTML, or go through another, more useful format first. Since HTML will continue to evolve, and is really useful only for web publications, the best solution might be to convert your documents into SGML with a DTD you create, and then use a commercial tool to down-convert to HTML. This gives you the flexibility to also create printed documentation from the same source, as well as use other tools to convert to other online formats as you find it necessary. Since the second stage of conversion is from SGML, it's likely that there will be commercial tools available to convert into the desired destination format.

Moving On

A number of possibilities exist for converting your documents from their current format into HTML. Almost every application is capable of producing ASCII text format and RTF output, and efficient translators that are easy to customize to your document type are available for both ASCII and RTF. There are a number of application-specific add-ons and converters that can be used to quickly bring documents into HTML as well. Even with the wide range of possibilities that these applications present, manual markup should always remain an option, especially if you have only a document or two to convert. Every program requires time to configure, and if you need it for only a few conversions, you might actually save time (and get valuable experience in authoring HTML) by simply running through the text of the document and entering tags manually.

Once you've used the authoring information in Chapter 2, "The Basic Pieces," and the document conversion tools explained in this chapter, you should be ready to move beyond text into the wide world of multimedia. In Chapter 6, "Checking Your Work," we explain how to check your pages and links for HTML style and accuracy and how to check the sites and files that you're linked to. In the chapters that follow, we explore the possibilities of including multimedia files in your web documents and on your site. These chapters will explain everything from putting a graphic on your home page to including full animation in your site, and how to go about it most efficiently and impressively. Combining carefully created text with high-quality graphics and audio is what distinguishes an excellent WWW site, and the upcoming chapters show you just how to accomplish it.

6

Checking Your Work

As you'll no doubt discover upon launching your World Wide Web server, the primary source of feedback about broken links and ineffective sites will come directly from your site's users. In some basic sense, all Web pages are perennially "under construction," or perhaps, in beta test. In the near future, however, as the Internet and the Web become more important in commercial transactions, personal interactions, and information distribution, the unfinished quality of a Web site—a broken link here, an HTML error there—will no longer be an expectation on the part of the user. Soon, if not already, a Web site will be an organization's primary point of interaction with users on the Internet, and the quality of that site will determine the kind of impressions that visitors to the site will receive about that organization. An error on a Web page will be no less noticeable than a typo in a magazine advertisement—and no less damaging.

Aside from the standard errors that are inevitably made when creating a new Web site, working in HTML presents special complications. Like the Web itself, HTML is a constantly evolving and changing structure. Every effort is made, when HTML is changed in some way, to ensure that older versions of correct

HTML continue to be understood by Web browsers and HTML editors. Unfortunately, what is "correct" and "incorrect" has become blurred somewhat in general usage, since several browsers support a number of "incorrect" types. This means that tags that are perfectly valid HTML will be phased out as the language becomes more strict and more specific (and simultaneously more refined). To keep abreast of these changes and to ensure a site's integrity in the face of them, it is vital that you check your site thoroughly for valid HTML syntax and style.

This chapter will outline a number of elements of good HTML style that will help make your documents attractive, useful, and easy to maintain. We'll also present some automated alternatives to manually checking the syntax and style of your HTML, as well as the integrity of your links. This type of validation work can help you avoid discovering, one visit too late, that your site has embarrassed you on what may become one of the most public, and global, forms of mass media.

HTML Style

By responsibly designing your pages according to the set of accepted standards broadly referred to as "HTML style," you'll ensure long life and limited maintenance for your web site, and you'll have more time to improve the site because you are spending less time fixing it. By following HTML style as closely as you can, you'll be saving yourself and the people who maintain your site a great deal of time and effort as HTML standards evolve. Furthermore, now that automated information-gathering programs wander the Web in search of content for indexing, a malformed HTML document is overlooked in popular indexes. Since these robots and wanderers can read only correct HTML, in a general way, the accuracy with which you create your documents will determine your accessibility. Keeping style in mind throughout the web-authoring process will allow your site to remain high quality, both aesthetically and technically, as the web grows and changes.

Structural Markup vs. Page Design

As mentioned briefly in Chapter 2, "The Basic Pieces," HTML is not a programming language per se. It is a markup language, based on the Standard Generalized Markup Language (SGML) standard, although many complain that it has not followed the principles of SGML as much as it should. This has an important implication for developing web documents: the configuration of the display of a markup language is *not* up to the author. In a printed book, the author and editor clearly define the layout and presentation. However, the HTML markup language defines only how a string of information, such as a section of text, is different than other strings of information. It provides, as the name suggests, markup codes. These codes are passed on to an interpreter, such as a web browser, that specifies the information's format. Thus HTML defines the structure of a document rather than its design. Essentially, you should create HTML documents as if each user will be reading the source code and determining what to do with it on his or her own. Treat HTML not as a graphics or page design system but as a set of instructions that specifies how text is to be read and defines its relationship to the rest of the document.

Using HTML to mark structure means avoiding a number of pitfalls. Primary among these is the temptation to use markup tags for "effect"—in other words, using the eccentricities of certain browsers to create a specific type of display or layout. One example of this is using header text to emphasize certain sentences, instead of for titles of sections and subsections of a document. This practice will seldom create the same effect on different browsers and platforms, and the emphasized text will incorrectly appear as part of the document's table of contents in those programs that automatically generate tables of contents from header text. If you design your pages with a single browser in mind—for example, by overemphasizing the use of Netscape's new HTML extensions—your pages run the risk of becoming obsolete when new browsers come online and new HTML specifications are adopted.

Cross-Platform Testing

One effective way to avoid the potential problems of designing for a single browser is to check all of your pages on a range of browsers, making sure that the design is acceptable on all of them. More important, you should look at how different machines—Macs, PCs, and workstations running UNIX—display pages, since moving from platform to platform often results in very different types of displays even when you use the same browser. This test alone may not be enough, however, since users can configure their browsers differently with regard to image loading, colors, and fonts. Your best bet to ensure that the widest variety of browsers will display your pages attractively and, by extension, to ensure that users will find your pages useful, is to treat HTML as a language for marking structure, and not as a language for specifying the design of your pages.

As browsers develop, more specific ways to display certain tags are created and used, which is why it is a good idea to use tags that are not only technically accurate, but as structurally specific as possible. In other words, use the <CITE> and <ADDRESS> tags for citations and addresses instead of the <I> (italicized text) tag, even though on most browsers the <I> tag currently produces output seemingly identical to the <CITE> and <ADDRESS> tags. The paragraph tag <P> without a closing tag </P> also produces seemingly identical output to using the <P> tag alone; it appears to simply create a paragraph break but is actually a marker that contains the structure of a full paragraph. It may at times seem easier to use more design-intensive approaches or shortcuts to coding, but you'll appreciate the benefits that using specific markup tags for different parts of a document will bring as the Web evolves.

Standard Page Elements

To create pages that conform to HTML style standards and, more important, that are broadly usable and appealing, you should keep a number of considerations in mind. Among these considerations are certain standard types of header and footer information that should be included in your documents, text alternatives to graphical elements of your pages, for users who are unable, or choose not, to view graphics, and link text that is useful and appropriate rather than silly or distracting.

Header Information

One of your first considerations should be, as noted earlier, the specific types of HTML markup that you use. Three tags you should consider using add information to the document that the user doesn't necessarily see. The <META>, <LINK>, and <BASE> tags, located in the header of a document (between the <HEAD> and </HEAD> tags), contain information about your document that is similar to information provided by the comments in a well-written computer program or script. These tags contain information about the authors of the document, about its relationship to other documents, and about the document itself. This information is not displayed on the screen itself but is available to users who view the source of your documents, and it can be read by information-gathering programs that read Web files over the Internet.

You can use the <META> tag to name certain variables in a document, such as the author and the program that was used to generate the document. The latter may be important to specify if you're using an HTML editor that generates nonconforming code, and you want to insure that the document is always edited with the same program. The following is an example of <META> tags being used to define document characteristics:

```
<META NAME="GENERATOR" CONTENT="tkHTML 2.3">
<META NAME="AUTHOR" CONTENT="webmaster@shoop.com">
<META HTTP-EQUIV="OWNER" CONTENT="Bob">
```

Some HTML authoring software, such as Microsoft's Internet Assistant, automatically generates a <META> tag.

There are two types of <META> definitions: HTTP-EQUIV and NAME. The <META> attribute HTTP-EQUIV setting links the information in the CONTENTS setting to an HTTP response header, as described in Chapter 2, "The Basic Pieces." However, if you don't know the exact name of the HTTP response header that you want to identify, you're better off using the NAME setting, because it simply creates a variable name.

Another useful <META> definition is the identification of an expiration date for documents. To set this date, you can use the <META> tag as follows:

```
<META HTTP-EQUIV="EXPIRES">Tue, 04 Dec 1993 23:59:00 GMT
</META>
```

The <LINK> tag indicates the relationship of the HTML document to other documents and objects (for example, images and mailto links) on the site. You should use a different <LINK> tag for each object that you want to link to. For example, the following set of <LINK> tags would define information about a document:

```
<LINK HREF="mailto:webmaster@shoop.com" REL="made">
<LINK HREF="http://www.shoop.com/pricing/section2.html"
REL="next">
<LINK HREF="http://www.shoop.com/pricing/index.html"
REL="previous">
```

In the first tag, the author is defined as webmaster@shoop.com, and the contact URL is a mailto link to this address. Alternatively, this URL could have provided a link to the author's home page. Browsers can use this link information to show where comments can be sent to the author or to display more information about the author. The second <LINK> tag defines the next document to be accessed if the documents are being read in order, and the third defines the previous document in the hierarchy.

A number of other relationship definitions are possible, all of which take the following format:

```
<LINK HREF=URL REL="relationship">
```

Other relationships that you can define with the <LINK> tag are "parent," which indicates that the specified URL is one level up in the HTML document hierarchy, and "bookmark," which defines the specified URL as a bookmark, or "frequently used page," at that site.

The <BASE> tag allows you to put the URL of the file into the text of the document itself, so that if a file is saved or exported out of the context of the web site, its original location is preserved. The format of a <BASE> tag takes the following form:

```
<BASE HREF="http://www.domain.com/path/filename.html">
```

A significant disadvantage of the <BASE> tag is that you cannot relocate the root of your web, or even a subtree, without editing each and every file that contains the <BASE> tag.

As noted at the beginning of this section, these three header tags do not currently produce any output on browsers, but they provide valuable information to robots, to users viewing the source, and to document maintainers. Since future releases of browsers will incorporate these tags into dynamically generated toolbars and links, specifying them in advance of their implementation by browsers gives your site a leg up in the development of the Web.

Footer Information

Information that should be included on every page, preferably at the bottom, includes the name of the author of a page or Webmaster of the site with a mailto link or a link to that person's home page; a link to the home page of the site; a "last revised" date (in standard format, such as 9 December 1994, since readers worldwide will have access to the document); and if applicable, a statement of copyright, including the name of the person or institution holding the copyright, and perhaps a link to a copyright or legal disclaimer page. A sample footer, with a horizontal rule above it to delineate it from the body of the page, would look something like the following:

```
<HR>
<A HREF="mailto:webmaster@shoop.com">F. Nietzsche
</A>, ShoopSoft Webmaster, <ADDRESS>webmaster@shoop.com
</ADDRESS>. Last Revised: 9 Dec 94.<BR>
All contents copyright 1994, ShoopSoft Enterprises<BR>
<A HREF="http://www.shoop.com/">Return to the ShoopSoft Home
Page</A><P>
</BODY>
</HTML>
```

Note that the final tags mark the end of the document—first the end of the body, then the end of the document itself. No other text or markup should be entered after these two tags.

Alternatives to Graphics

Another HTML style consideration that you should keep in mind is that images are always optional on browsers. Users on low-speed connections generally choose to turn image loading off, and if they are forced to use the images on a page for navigation, they'll be frustrated by the increase in the time each page takes to load. This means that button bars, imagemaps, and other graphics-dependent navigational tools, even something as simple as a gray button marked "Previous" that returns the user to the previous page, are not always visible to a user. For users not viewing graphics, or unable to view graphics (as in the case of text-based browsers), you should include two types of text options. The first is an ALT setting in your image tag, such as the following:

```
<IMG ALT="Previous Page" SRC="pics/previous.gif">
```

This setting enables text-only browsers to automatically load the alternate text instead of leaving a meaningless string like [IMAGE] in its place.

For the best readability, you should duplicate any links made to a graphic or icon in text. For example, if a page contains a row of buttons for navigation, you might want to put a row of text links to those same pages beneath the row of buttons, giving the user the option of using either buttons or text links. In addition, make sure that you list all of the links in an imagemap in close proximity to the imagemap, because without the coordinate information, the HTTP server generates a server error when a user clicks on the imagemap when image loading is turned off.

Appropriate Link Text

Hyperlinked text is always emphasized in some manner on a browser, and to most users, these links are intuitive. The combination of emphasis and obvious usage makes a link such as the following somewhat unnecessary and silly looking:

```
you'll find info on monkeys <A HREF="monkeys.html">here</A>
```

Using "here" or "click here" as the text for a link is bad form; it distracts the user from the information in the document and makes the document appear as a sort of interface and not as a source of information. Hyperlinked text should be as transparent as possible and not call attention to itself with link text. A better design, one that integrates the linked text and the information, would take the following form:

```
we also have <A HREF="monkeys.html">info on monkeys</A>
```

Absolute & Relative URLs

An ongoing debate in the web authoring community is over whether to use absolute URLs or relative URLs when creating hyperlinks between documents on the same server. In brief, an absolute URL takes the following form:

```
<A HREF="/users/shoop/docs/pricing.html">
```

When you omit the host and protocol parts of a URL, the client assumes that the resource being referenced is on the same server as the document. When the pathname lacks the initial forward slash (/), the client further assumes that the URL is relative to the document's directory. Thus a relative URL would take this form:

```
<A HREF="docs/pricing.html">
```

To date, no unequivocal resolution has been reached in favor of either type of URL. In some ways, the debate is rather trivial, because both absolute and relative URLs affect server and browser performance to the same degree. However, each type of link does afford some design advantages.

An advantage of using relative URLs is the portability of a body of documents linked together relatively. If, for some reason, you need to move an entire HTML hierarchy, either to another machine or simply to another directory, a relatively linked body of documents requires minimal updating because the links are expressed in terms of their relationship to that document. Using relative URLs also allows a user to download an entire HTML hierarchy to another machine, either to be viewed locally or to provide a mirror of the same information at a different site, with minimal changes. This design technique is especially useful for large documents that are divided into separate pages, because a user can obtain the entire body of documents and browse the documents as local files without having to connect to your site—saving time for the user and CPU and bandwidth for the server.

Absolute URLs, however, provide a consistent structure to the HTML hierarchy. More importantly, they allow for a more consistent method of accessing documents that might be higher on a directory tree or in a different directory tree altogether. For example, if you wanted to provide a link from a document in /html/users/bob/sermons/ to the document in /html/users/shoop/pricing/services.html, a relative link would have to express this path as follows:

```
<A HREF="../../shoop/pricing/services.html">outrageously low
prices</A>
```

An absolute link would have a more intuitive format:

```
<A HREF="/users/shoop/pricing/services.html">outrageously low
prices
</A>
```

An absolute URL also allows users looking at the source to easily identify the location of particular documents that are linked to a web page.

In either case, it's a good idea to employ a standard method of hyperlinks, at least between clearly defined sections of your web documents. For example, you might want to use absolute links for your menu system, to provide easier definition of horizontal and vertical movements across documents, but relative links within particular sections, such as catalogs or paginated text information.

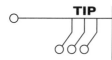
TIP

For a collection of style guides and authoring information, look at the compilation of links at the URL http://coombs.anu.edu.au/SpecialProj/QLTY/QltyHome.html. One of the best style manuals in this collection, from the Yale Medical School, is located at the URL http://info.med.yale.edu/caim/StyleManual_Top.HTML and should be consulted often throughout the authoring and design process.

Validation Programs

It's a lot to ask of any one HTML author that she or he check each document and tag for the appropriate style specifications. There are, though, many reasons for doing so, as noted in the beginning of this chapter. Since not everyone is familiar with the nuances of HTML, especially HTML v3.0, it's a good idea to find some help. Automated document checkers, or validation programs, parse your documents according to style and accuracy standards. These programs are capable of giving your HTML documents a thorough going-over, checking style, and alerting you to a stylistic faux pas or a link that just doesn't work. Validation programs are comprehensive and sometimes more rigorous than is necessary for the majority of existing browser software. However, you should bring your documents in line with the recommendations of these programs, since the HTML standard will become more tightly enforced as browsers and editors themselves conform more closely to HTML. In this section, we give you the details of two of these programs. One checks for content and style and the other checks for valid links. Using these programs will cut down greatly on the time that you need to spend manually checking your pages, and they'll catch errors that might not even be apparent at first glance.

Checking Content & Style With htmlchek

As discussed earlier, both the style and the syntax of HTML are important factors in determining a document's validity on the Web. Obviously, it is more important to ensure that the syntax of the coding is correct because incorrect coding causes a number of browsers to generate errors. However, as the Web moves further toward a unified standard, those practices of coding that are currently classified as style, such as the use of certain tags within other tags or the use of tags that define the structure of a document but don't affect its appearance (such as <HTML> and <BODY>) will become syntactical requirements for browsers and editors. Included on the Companion CD-ROM is a perl script called htmlchek.pl that checks both style and syntax in a single run-through of a document.

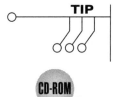

TIP

To run this program, you must have perl installed on your NT system. Perl is included on the Companion CD-ROM, along with directions for using it. Perl, which began on UNIX systems, is an extremely valuable script-processing program. It is used for many scripting applications on the Web, and is used frequently to create CGI programs.

To run htmlchek as is, without any special configurations, you enter a simple command line from the command prompt similar to the following:

```
perl htmlchek.pl webfiles.html > errors.txt
```

You can specify multiple filenames or use wildcards on the command line to check multiple files.

The output file that htmlchek creates is divided into two parts. The first section gives you an outline of the warning and error messages that are generated by the program, according to the sorts of errors that you've instructed the program to look for. There's a difference between warning messages (which contain the string "Warning!") and error messages (which contain the string "ERROR!"). Warning messages are usually generated by style errors, which do not necessarily prevent the document from displaying correctly on a browser but may cause problems later. Error messages indicate errors in the HTML markup itself and cause an inaccurate display when your document is viewed. The second section of the output file lists all of the tag types that you've used in a particular document and all of the options that you specified for these tags. Using the optional cross-reference checking function, you can specify a third type of output, listing all references to other files that are made in all of the HTML documents through the use of HREF tags. To use this feature, the referenced files must be part of the list of files you are checking. For example, if an HTML file references another HTML file called "test.htm," then "test.htm" must also be in the list of files to be checked by htmlchek in order for the reference to be resolved.

In addition, you can configure it in a wide variety of ways using command-line options or a configuration file. In the next several sections we'll look at the various configuration options.

Configuring Your Output

Three options control the way htmlchek generates error and warning messages. You enable these options with a setting of 1 and disable them with a setting of 0, as in this sample:

```
perl htmlchek.pl inline=1 webfiles.html > errors.txt
```

- **inline=1**   By default, htmlchek generates error messages with references to the filenames and line numbers where the errors are located. To include the actual text of that line in the error messages, set the option inline=1.

- **nowswarn=1**   Since extra white space can generate errors on some browsers, htmlchek generates a warning when it encounters extra white space. Since some documents legitimately contain white space, however, you might want to turn these warnings off just to save yourself some time. Setting nowswarn=1 disables the white space warnings.

- **sugar=1**   This option adds a prefix of *"filename: linenumber:"* to each error message, making it easier to quickly read the messages and making the output compatible with some editors that can interpret it, such as emacs.

Tag Definition Options

Four options allow you to define a new tag to be accepted by htmlchek. Using one of these options tells htmlchek how to treat the new tag: whether the tag requires a closing tag, whether a closing tag is optional, if no closing tag should be used, or when a closing tag is not only required but also when no other identical tags can be enclosed in that element (for example, no <A HREF>...</A> set can include another <A HREF> tag). All of these options are tag lists, defined by listing the tags and separating them with commas.

- **nonpair=**   Defining a tag as nonpair tells htmlchek that no closing tag should be used. Tags already defined as nonpair are <BR> and <HR>.

- **loosepair=**   The option loosepair defines the closing tag as optional. For example, the <LI> tag in lists can optionally have an </LI> at the end of the item in HTML v2.0, but it is not required.

- **strictpair=** A strictly paired tag (strictpair) must have a closing tag to be accurate. A common example is the accidental omission of </STRONG> at the end of a <STRONG> tag, which formats all the text after that tag in boldface. The majority of HTML tags are strictly paired.

- **nonrecurpair=** This type of tag is both strictly paired and cannot contain any identical tags, as in the <A HREF> example cited previously.

The following is an example of a tag definition option:

```
strictpair=b,i,em,strong,p
```

Since the first four extensions are already defined as strictly paired, this configuration line would be redundant. Defining the paragraph tag as strictly paired would change it from the default loosepair. In all tag lists, the case is not important—tags can be either uppercase or lowercase.

Other Tag Options

htmlchek also allows you to modify tags that have already been defined. These modifications allow you to configure htmlchek to your particular style of authoring. In some cases, the recommendations that htmlchek makes by default should be considered advance notices of changes in HTML.

The following command-line options take tag listings as arguments, just like the tag definition options discussed in the previous section:

- **lowlevelpair=** This option, followed by a list of tags, defines strictly paired tags as low-level markup, or in other words, tags that are allowed to contain other tags that are also low-level pairs. That is, any pair of tags defined as a low-level pair can contain any other pair of tags defined as a low-level pair. For example, a set of low-level markup tags that are already understood by htmlchek are the <A> </A> and <EM> </EM>, meaning that the the use of emphasized text inside a hyperlink, as in the following example, will not cause htmlchek to return an error.

```
<A HREF="http://www.shoop.com/">Check out the
<EM>ShoopSoft Home Page</EM></A>
```

Tags that are not low-level markup include lists, headers, and paragraph markers. If these tags contain one another—for example, a header tag containing a list—htmlchek will warn you that this is incorrect HTML syntax. Another common error is a header inside a hyperlink, as in the following:

```
<A HREF="http://www.shoop.com/pricing/"><H2>Pricing
Info</H2></A>
```

The above example will generate an error on many browsers, because a pair of tags that is not low-level (<H2> </H2>) has been included inside a pair of tags that is low-level (<A> </A>). The same effect could be legally achieved by using the following markup syntax:

```
<H2><A HREF="http://www.shoop.com/pricing/">Pricing
Info</A></H2>
```

That syntax works because a low-level pair can be safely included inside a pair that is not low-level. Unless you know that a pair of tags is low-level, however, you should not define it as low-level because if the tags turn out not to be low-level, including them inside of low-level markup tags will confuse browsers and may generate errors on your pages.

◈ **lowlevelnonpair=** This option produces the same effect as lowlevelpair for tags that are not strictly paired, such as <BR>, the line break tag.

◈ **nonblock=** The nonblock option also allows a strictly paired tag to contain low-level markup. However, if an option is defined as nonblock, it cannot contain any other elements that are also included as nonblock. For example, the address tag (<ADDRESS>) cannot contain a header tag because both are defined as nonblock.

◈ **deprecated=** By specifying a tag in this option, you mark it "deprecated" (obsolete but still supported). You might want to include tags like <B> and <I>, the bold and italics tags, in this category, as these tags may become deprecated in future versions of HTML, so that you can replace them with more specific tags like <STRONG> or <VAR>.

Three settings define allowed or required options in the following format for certain tags:

```
tag,option:tag,option...
```

* **tagopts=** This setting allows tags to have additional options, as in the optional settings for the paragraph tag for alignment and line wrapping. The following line would allow both of these options and their configurations (for example, ALIGN=center) to be accepted by htmlchek:

  ```
  tagopts=p,align:p,nowrap
  ```

* **novalopts=** To allow a tag option without any setting, such as the image option ISMAP for imagemapping, it should be listed in the same format as a tagopts setting, as in the following example:

  ```
  novalopts=img,ismap
  ```

* **reqopts=** Pairing a tag with an option in the reqopts listing causes htmlchek to generate a warning whenever that option is not included. An example of how this option is useful for future planning involves the WIDTH and HEIGHT specifications for inline images, which are currently supported only by Netscape but will be part of the new HTML specification. The following setting tells htmlchek to warn you of any place where the dimensions of an inline image are not defined using the WIDTH and HEIGHT settings:

  ```
  reqopts=img,width:img,height
  ```

The final tag option supported by htmlchek uses a numbering system to determine the strictness of the program in generating a warning. The dlstrict setting determines how strictly htmlchek checks the definition list, defined by the <DL> tag. (Definition lists are explained in detail in Chapter 2, "The Basic Pieces.") A setting of dlstrict=1, which is the default for htmlchek, allows the tags <DD> and <DT>, the tags for the text of a definition and for a term that is being defined, to be placed anywhere inside a definition list. A setting of dlstrict=2 requires that the two tags coexist, but the definition term can indirectly precede the definition itself.

The strictest setting is dlstrict=3, which requires that every tag that marks the text of a definition, <DD>, be immediately preceded by the definition term itself, indicated with the tag <DT>.

Parsing Options

Two settings control the way that an HTML document is parsed with regard to the less-than (<) and greater-than (>) characters. The metachar option is similar to the dlstrict option in that you use a 1 to 3 setting to specify the strictness, except in the case of the metachar option, 1 is the most strict and 3 is the least strict. Setting the option metachar=3 will allow either the less-than or greater-than character inside a comment (such as <!—<HR>—>) to pass without warning. But including these characters inside a comment can sometimes confuse browsers. The stricter setting metachar=2 does not allow these characters inside comments. It allows a comment to extend over more than a single line, however, which can generate an error on the strictest of browsers. The strictest setting, metachar=1, does not allow comments to extend past a single line.

The other parsing option is more of a style setting. If you set nogtwarn=1, htmlchek warns you of any loose less-than or greater-than characters in the text of your document. You should simply replace these characters with the correct ISO Latin-1 entity ">" for the greater-than character and "<" for the less-than character.

Language Extensions

By default, htmlchek checks your documents according to the HTML v2.0 standards currently in place. However, you can have it check according to the Netscape extensions as well. In your command line or configuration file, you can specify:

```
netscape=1
```

Cross-Reference Checking

Cross-reference checking, that is, checking the references that you have linked into your document, should be the last step of the document-checking process using htmlchek. While htmlchek is not capable of actually going to sites that are linked to your pages and checking if the links are valid, it does collect all of the links to off-site resources in a single file for you. It also lists unreferenced locations in your documents, such as an <A NAME="Section_1"> anchor without any link to it. Optionally, you can use htmlchek to generate a "dependency map," that is, a full listing of the files that reference resources, so that you can check those resources as well.

Seven command-line options control cross-reference checking: four control the output, and three determine the input by defining how to resolve the URL of links. The first two options are necessary for cross-reference checking to be stored in output files, one for each document:

* **xref=1**   This option turns on cross-reference checking in the first place, and, unless you enable the next option, refsfile, error messages are sent to the screen as the program runs.

* **refsfile="*prefixname*"**   This option creates reference files with three suffixes. The first, *prefixname*.href, lists the references using the HREF option (that is, <BASE>, <A HREF>, etc.); the second, *prefixname*.src, lists all of the inline images (<IMG SRC>), and the third, *prefixname*.name, lists all of the destination locations that are specified in the HTML documents.

* **map=1**   The optional dependency map is generated using the map=1 option, which generates a file called *prefixname*.map. You must also include xref=1 in the command line or configuration file for the option to work.

◈ **append=1**   htmlchek automatically overwrites any old reference files. To prevent this, you can use the command-line option append=1 to append entries to the files that contain reference information.

Three options determine the URL prefix of documents to be checked.

◈ **dirprefix="*pathname*"**   By specifying this option, you give htmlchek the information it needs to complete relative URLs in your documents. Enter the beginning of any relative URLs that you're using, such as dirprefix="http:// www.shoop.com/" or dirprefix="/users/bob/". You can enter the protocol type or simply specify the full path.

◈ **usebase=1**   This option directs htmlchek to obtain the URL from the <BASE> tag rather than from the name of the file and a directory prefix. This option requires that <BASE> be the first tag in the header of your document.

◈ **subtract="*pathname*"**   Specify this option if you're running htmlchekon files outside the current directory. For example, if you're running htmlchek from /html/stats/ htmlchek/ to check files in /html/users/bob/, you'd enter a command line similar to the following:

```
perl htmlchek.pl xref=1 refsfile="bob-check"
    subtract="/html/users/bob/"
    dirprefix="http://www.shoop.com/users/bob/"
    /html/users/bob/*.html > outfile.check
```

This command line would strip off the directory name /html/users/bob/, and whenever htmlchek encountered a relative URL, it would preface it with the following:

```
http://www.shoop.com/users/bob/
```

htmlchek would not return "file not found" errors by trying to search for relative URLs in the working directory.

One of the limitations of cross-reference checking is that it can work only within a single directory tree. If, for example, you wanted to check the references that exist in the trees /html/users/bob/ and /html/pricing/, you could not do so from one command line. The easiest way around this limitation is to run multiple command lines with the same refsfile=*"prefixname,"* using the append=1 option in the second (and any subsequent) command line, as in the following example of two command lines run in sequence:

```
perl htmlchek.pl xref=1 refsfile="output"
    subtract="/html/users/bob/"
    dirprefix="http://www.shoop.com/users/bob/"
    /html/users/bob/*.html > outfile-bob.check
perl htmlchek.pl xref=1 refsfile="output" append=1
    subtract="/html/pricing/"
    dirprefix="http://www.shoop.com/pricing/"
    /html/pricing/*.html > outfile-pricing.check
```

These command lines would create three cross-reference checking files, output.href, output.src, and output.name, containing the information from both the /html/users/bob/ and /html/pricing/ directory trees, and two separate main output files, outfile-bob.check and outfile-pricing.check.

To produce a single main output file as well as a single set of cross-reference checking output files, change the redirect command in the second command line to append to the output file specified in the first command line, as follows:

```
perl htmlchek.pl xref=1 refsfile="output"
    subtract="/html/users/bob/"
    dirprefix="http://www.shoop.com/users/bob/"
    /html/users/bob/*.html > outfile-all.check
perl htmlchek.pl xref=1 refsfile="output" append=1
    subtract="/html/pricing/"
    dirprefix="http://www.shoop.com/pricing/"
    /html/pricing/*.html >> outfile-all.check
```

Using Configuration Files

After getting a sense of how extensive a single command line must be for htmlchek to thoroughly check your HTML documents, you may want to use configuration files for checking sets of documents. In a configuration file, you specify the configuration options much as you do in a command line, placing a separate option on each line. The configuration file should have the extension .CFG. Since a configuration file specifies only the language definition options, you can't configure certain options there. Specifically, you have to define the append, dirprefix, refsfile, sugar, and usebase options on the command line and not in the configuration file. To use a configuration file, enter the option configfile="*filename*" (or cf="*filename*") in the command line.

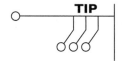

TIP

For extensive documentation of htmlchek, see the Users Guide *at the URL http://uts.cc.utexas.edu/~churchh/htmlchekprog.html.*

Checking Your Links With Checker for Windows

While htmlchek checks your HTML documents in a number of ways, Checker is capable of following external links and checking their integrity, which htmlchek cannot do. This program follows each link, relative or absolute and internal or external on a single page, resolves the hostname, and checks to confirm that the document in question actually exists. Checker does not check an entire web, it checks only a single page at a time. Checker is easy to use and requires only that you put entries for your local server into the configuration file, checker.cfg. You must edit this file directly, using a text editor such as the notepad program which comes with Windows.

The configuration options that you specify on the command line can be stored in a configuration file, which can save you the work of re-entering the options each time that you run the program itself. Two options that you can pass to Checker affect the way that it checks particular documents:

- **-base-address**   This is the base address for the server you want to check. If you add this entry, Checker will prefix all absolute URLs on your web with this base address. (See "Absolute & Relative URLs," earlier in this chapter.)

- **-current-address**   This is the URL path up to the current directory of the page you are checking, and is different from the base-address if you are not checking pages in the root directory of your server. This option determines the host and directory information that Checker puts at the beginning of a relative URL. For example, if your web page contains a reference to a file such as <A HREF="pics/pipe.gif"> and you specify a -current-address value of http://church.bob.org/users/bob, Checker looks for the existence of http://church.bob.org/users/bob/pics/pipe.gif.

One limitation of Checker is that it has to be run on the same machine as the document that is being checked. This doesn't mean that all of the files referenced with Anchor tags in the document have to be on that machine, so long as you have specified the -base-address option correctly, but that the HTML document itself needs to be on the same machine that Checker is on.

Checker comes with a setup program, which will install the program files and create a program group and icon to start the program. Once the program is installed, edit the configuration file with a text editor to enter the URL of your own server. The server must be running when you use Checker. When you first start Checker, it will appear as in Figure 6-1.

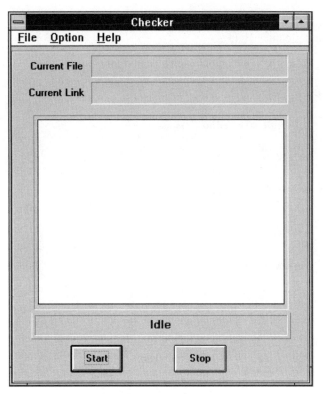

Figure 6-1: *Checker's initial screen.*

Open the file you want to check with the File | Open menu item.
Start the checking process by clicking on the Start button, and then
be patient while Checker does its job. Once the check is complete,
you'll see a result similar to what is shown in Figure 6-2.

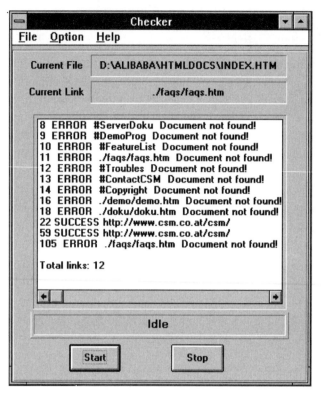

Figure 6-2: *A completed check.*

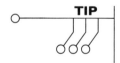

TIP

*The Checker home page is located at the URL http://
www.ugrad.cs.ubc.ca/spider/q7f192/branch/checker.html.*

Many of the new integrated web authoring tools, such as
Microsoft's Front Page, include the ability to check links on the
web you are editing. For more information about Microsoft's
Front Page, check out the URL http://www.microsoft.com/
msoffice/frontpage/index.htm.

Moving On

HTML authoring can be a more difficult process than might be apparent from the simplicity of the codes themselves. Since the Web and the HTML standard are constantly evolving, page design and authoring must follow a rigorous standard so that pages do not become obsolete. Primary in these design considerations should be the types of tags that you use. You should take special care to use each tag in the correct context and sequence and as specifically as possible in delimiting the structure of an HTML document. A number of tags that are not necessarily apparent to the browser, or that seem extraneous, such as tags that contain authoring information on each page, are features that will make your site appear more standardized and easier to maintain. A number of programs can help automate the process of validating both the HTML and the links between documents and files on the web. Using syntax, style, and link checkers in conjunction with manual checkups will ensure that your documents have the integrity that is necessary to create a useful and long-lived site.

After taking care of the basics of server setup and web page authoring and after checking your work, you should consider creating an aesthetically interesting and innovative site. Using other features of HTML, such as the forms and CGI scripts, you can create a high level of interactivity on your site. Also, the ease with which web browsers handle multimedia—images, sounds, animation, and so on—means that you should give them a prominent place in your site design. The following chapters are devoted to helping you develop a high level of innovation for your site using these impressive features of the World Wide Web.

7

Images on the Web

Many factors caused the great explosion of growth in the World Wide Web in 1993, but probably the single most significant was the release of Mosaic for the X Windowing System version 0.10 from the National Center for Supercomputing Applications (NCSA).

Not only did the programmers at NCSA create an easier-to-use and more intuitive interface for Mosaic, but they also took the liberty of enabling it to display pictures, right in the midst of text. This feature made Mosaic attractive to the many thousands of people on the Internet who had never heard of the World Wide Web and, more importantly, made the Internet interesting to millions who had never heard of it before.

Inline images have made the WWW useful for advertisers who want to include pictures of their products and graphics of their trademarked logos, as well as for scientists who want to share figures and diagrams with their colleagues. Inline images have also sparked the imagination of artists, who use WWW servers as centers of collaboration, and they have inspired teachers to develop entire courses of study and virtual museums on the Web. All of these would've been difficult or impossible without the ability to easily embed images into Web pages.

Comparing Links & Inlines

You can integrate images into your web pages in two ways: by linking them to your pages with hyperlinks (*linked* images) or by placing them directly on the page (*inline* images). Linked images use the hypermedia and MIME-typing capabilities of the WWW client (see Chapter 2, "The Basic Pieces") to let the user click on a hyperlink and download an image. You can include such a hyperlink with the HTML anchor code, like this:

```
Here's a <A HREF="/pics/linked-image.gif">picture.</A>
```

The word *picture* is a hyperlink, and the user can activate it to download the image. After the client downloads the image, the client usually executes a "helper application" to display it. The Netscape family of clients handles this process differently, by displaying images from invoked links inside the browser window.

Graphical browsers display inline images right on the page. This useful ability allows the author of the page to add illustrations, logos, and diagrams in the context of the surrounding text. Adding an inline image is very simple; the <IMG> tag signals the browser that a graphic should be inserted, like this:

```
<IMG SRC="vmedia.gif" ALT="Ventana Online Logo"> This inline
represents the Ventana Online Visitor's Center.
```

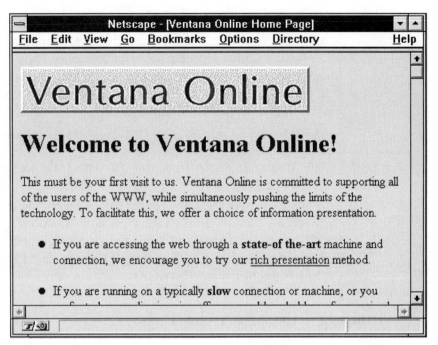

Figure 7-1: *An inline image.*

When it encounters the <IMG> tag, the client retrieves the URL that follows the SRC element. Note that the <IMG> tag is stand-alone; there is no equivalent closing tag. If you omit the host and protocol parts of the URL, the client assumes this image is on the same server as the document, and when it encounters a URL whose pathname lacks the initial forward slash (/), the client assumes the URL is relative to the document's directory.

If the user is running a client that cannot display inline images, or more commonly, if the user has elected not to download inline images in order to save time, the client displays the text assigned to the ALT tag. If there is no ALT tag for an <IMG> tag, Netscape users will see the default image icon with no text label instead. Always provide an ALT specification with any inline image; you can either use it to describe what the picture illustrates or leave it blank (ALT="") so people using text-only clients won't see the distracting "[IMAGE]".

Inline images are often used in combination with hyperlinked images. For example, a page could include a small, icon-sized inline image with a larger, photograph-quality copy of the same image hyperlinked to it for people who want a better look. To do this, simply include an ordinary hyperlink anchor around the <IMG> tag, as in the following markup:

```
<A HREF="/pics/urizen.jpg"><IMG SRC="/pics/urizen.gif"
ALT="image
from Urizen"></A> In this etching from <cite>Urizen</cite>,
you can see the inter-relation of Blake's poetry and art.
```

This creates a hypertext anchor for the inline image itself, which the user can click to get the larger version. As noted previously, if the client cannot display inlines, the hyperlink is anchored to the text specified with the ALT setting. If there is no ALT specification, the link is anchored to "[IMAGE]".

Placing Inlines on the Page

HTML gives the author of a page a certain amount of flexibility in specifying how inline images are displayed. Unfortunately, this flexibility falls far short of the capabilities professional designers are accustomed to, but with a little practice, you'll be able to understand and utilize these basic capabilities to create effective pages.

Common HTML

The most commonly implemented version of HTML is version 2.0, which is the first version to support inline images. As a default in HTML v2.0, the client aligns the bottom of the image with the bottom of the text. You can change this default by adding the ALIGN setting. If you add ALIGN=top to the <IMG> tag, the top of the image is aligned with the top of the tallest item in the line, including other pictures, and *not* with the top of the text as you might expect. ALIGN=middle aligns the middle of the image with the bottom of the text, not with the middle of the text. ALIGN= bottom gives you the default placement.

Netscape Extensions

The release of Netscape has included some HTML extensions that increase the options for the alignment of images. These extensions aren't part of the HTML v2.0 specification and not all browsers recognize them. (Browsers that do not recognize the Netscape extensions implement the default ALIGN=bottom placement instead.)

It's difficult to predict when or even whether all clients will implement these HTML extensions. Although they are becoming commonly used, they aren't part of any formal standard developed by the HTML Working Group. An established Internet tradition favors the adoption of the first practical and implemented solution to a problem as an "official" standard. All of the HTML extensions that the authors of Netscape provided either add functionality to HTML as a page layout language or fix poorly designed features in the original HTML. Since the primary authors of Netscape are also the original implementers of inline images in NCSA Mosaic, their additions to HTML in this area carry considerable weight.

The first of these additions is the use of ALIGN=texttop to correct the strange behavior of ALIGN=top. When you use ALIGN=texttop, Netscape aligns the top of the image with the top of the text, rather than with the top of the tallest element on the line. Likewise, ALIGN=absmiddle aligns the middle of the image with the middle of the text, rather than with the bottom of the text. To allow you to align the bottom of the image with the bottom of the lowest element in the line (including other images), Netscape also adds ALIGN=absbottom. The last of these variations on top, middle, and bottom alignment is ALIGN=baseline, which does the same as ALIGN=bottom.

Two additional Netscape extensions to ALIGN are the left and right settings. When you specify ALIGN=left, your image is displayed in the next available space in the left-hand margin and text is wrapped around it, if necessary. ALIGN=right has the same effect, but Netscape places the picture in the right-hand margin.

This effect is commonly known as "floating" the image. Table 7-1 lists all the Netscape ALIGN extensions.

ALIGN tag	Function
ALIGN=texttop	Aligns the top of the image with the top of the text.
ALIGN=absmiddle	Aligns the middle of the image with the middle of the text.
ALIGN=absbottom	Aligns the bottom of the image with the lowest element on the line.
ALIGN=baseline	Does the same as ALIGN=bottom.
ALIGN=left	Drops the image into the left-hand margin and wraps the text around it.
ALIGN=right	Drops the image into the right-hand margin and wraps the text around it.

Table 7-1: *Netscape ALIGN extensions.*

The <BR> tag, which tells the client to insert a carriage return and break the line, has been extended for use with floating images. As you can see in Figure 7-2 and the following HTML markup, the <BR CLEAR=left> tag indicates to the client to break the line and move far enough down the page to avoid wrapping subsequent lines of text around images in the left margin:

```
<IMG SRC="dbweb.gif" ALIGN=left ALT="dbWeb Logo">dbWeb
offers a no-programming way to get your databases on the
Web!<BR CLEAR=left>
<P>By wrapping text on the right side of the image, you can
create a caption clearly associated with a particular image.
</P>
```

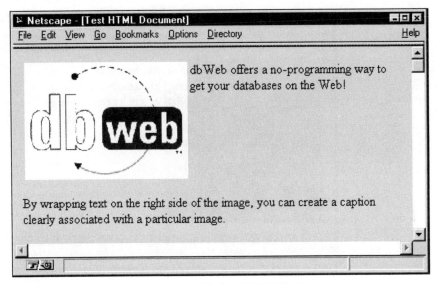

Figure 7-2: *Use of left alignment with the <BR CLEAR> tag.*

In the same way, the CLEAR=right setting spaces the subsequent text to avoid obscuring any images that are right-aligned. You can avoid images on both sides by using the CLEAR=all setting.

Netscape also adds two more settings, HSPACE and VSPACE, for the <IMG> tag. These settings are especially useful with floating images. Although Netscape honors these settings for use with all inline images, they are most often used with ALIGN=left and ALIGN=right. They allow you to specify the horizontal and vertical spacing, in pixels, between the floating image and the text that wraps around it. You can see this effect in Figure 7-3, which is a page from an imaginary computer company's catalog. The alignment and spacing of the text and image was created with the following ALIGN=left setting:

```
<P>
Ventana has a Web site at http://www.vmedia.com.
Check it out.
<IMG SRC="frontend.gif" ALT="" HSPACE=5 VSPACE=5 ALIGN=left>
There is a modem-friendly low-graphics mode as well as
a rich presentation method for those with high speed
connections.</P>
```

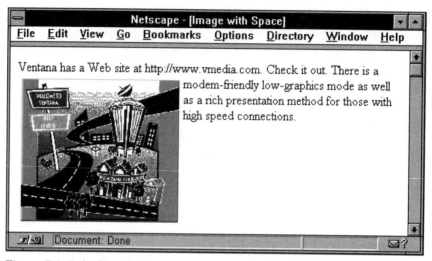

Figure 7-3: *Left-aligned image with horizontal and vertical space.*

Figure 7-4 shows the same text and image with no white space. You can see that the additional white space in Figure 7-3 dramatically improves the clarity and readability of the page.

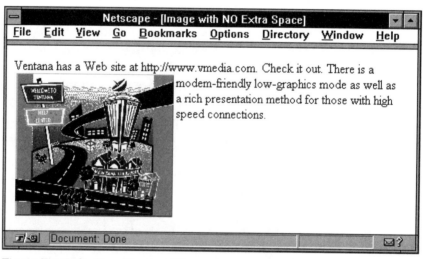

Figure 7-4: *Left-aligned image with no space.*

Two additional settings to the <IMG> tag that Netscape implements, WIDTH and HEIGHT, can help improve the performance of a client with a slow connection to the Internet. These settings allow you to specify, in pixels, the size of the image, and they let browsers like Netscape, which display pages as they arrive at the browser, render the text next to an image without having to wait to download the image. Without these settings, the rendering is delayed because the client must retrieve the image in order to calculate its size on the page. These settings also allow you to rescale images on the fly; you can simply specify different HEIGHT and WIDTH settings for an image's actual size, and Netscape scales the image to those dimensions.

To use these settings, you need to know the dimensions of your image. If you don't know the dimensions, you can use Paint Shop Pro to find these values. (See "Getting the Best From Inline Images," later in this chapter, for more about Paint Shop Pro.) You add the dimensions to the <IMG> tag as follows:

```
<IMG SRC="/pics/girl.gif" ALT="" HEIGHT=125 WIDTH=125>
```

Another Netscape extension, BORDER, lets you create a black border around an inline image. The value you provide is the thickness of the frame (in pixels):

```
<IMG SRC="/pics/girl.gif" ALT="" BORDER=4>
```

Although few people use BORDER to put frames around regular inlines, this setting is often given a value of 0 to remove the border around a hyperlinked inline that serves as a button (see "Commonly Used Inlines," later in this chapter).

Netscape also allows you to specify a lower resolution version of your inline image with the LOWSRC setting for the <IMG> tag. You can use this setting as follows:

```
<IMG LOWSRC="lowres.jpg" SRC="hires.gif">
```

When Netscape reads the page on which this tag appears, it displays lowres.jpg on its first pass through the document as it renders the text. It makes a second pass through the document, retrieving hires.gif and displaying it in the place of lowres.jpg. If the two images take up different amounts of space on the page and you don't explicitly specify a size with the HEIGHT and WIDTH elements, the second image is scaled to the size of the first one.

You should be prudent in the use of Netscape extensions. One of the Web's strengths is its openness and the cross-compatibility of documents across different platforms and browsers. There is a risk that nonstandard HTML implementations will splinter the Web between incompatible pages and viewers. Despite this, more people are using these extensions in their pages, because the extensions address the needs of page designers. Although using them increases the risk that some people viewing your pages won't see what you originally intended them to see, the fact remains that the majority of Web users use the Netscape browser, and other browser makers such as Spyglass have stated their intentions to add Netscape extensions to their browsers. (Spyglass provides OEM browsers and browser source code to many different companies, including Microsoft.) Many Web authors feel that the increased effectiveness of their pages for that majority outweighs the possibility of alienating a minority of their audience. On the other hand, not all current users can read the Netscape extensions, and by adhering to the standards, you ensure the long-term viability of your pages.

GIFs & JPEGs

Although the flexibility of MIME typing allows you to send any file format across the Web, only two graphics formats, GIF and JPEG, are commonly found on the Web. One sees the occasional XBM or even an XPM, and on the rarest of occasions, an IFF, but most authors use these two formats.

GIF

GIF is an acronym for Graphics Interchange Format. GIF was developed by the CompuServe Information Service in 1987. There are two variations on the format: GIF87a, which was the original specification, and GIF89a, which added some interesting features. Most of these features aren't important on the Web (but see "Transparent GIFs," later in this chapter, for an exception). All Web browsers that support inline GIFs understand both varieties of GIF.

As a graphics format, GIF has many advantages. First, it's not difficult to write a program that decodes and displays GIFs, so this format enjoys a wide level of support; almost every image-processing and drawing program can read and write graphics in GIF format. Also, the graphics information in GIFs is compressed with the LZW algorithm, so images in GIF format take a fourth or a fifth of the space taken by images in equivalent, uncompressed formats. This saves space on your server and saves time in transferring images over the network. An added bonus is that the compression used for GIFs is relatively fast to decode; once they're downloaded, GIFs can be displayed quite quickly on most computers.

The greatest disadvantage to using GIFs is that you're limited to only 256 colors in a single image. On the other hand, icon and cartoon-like images often use only a few colors, and GIF especially excels at compressing these sorts of images. For complex images though, such as scanned photographs, this limitation can lead to unattractive dithering. Dithering uses contrasting colors for adjacent pixels in order to create the illusion of additional colors. This process almost always degrades the quality of the image.

The Future of GIF

A controversy has recently risen about the legal future of the GIF format, which uses a patented compression technology. In the future, developers who use the GIF format in their programs will have to license the technology from the Unisys Corporation, which owns the patent. When Unisys announced this possibility in January 1995, a great outcry was heard from client developers, and many have started to look for a new format that could replace GIF.

Several new formats have been prototyped; all of them share the lossless compression and other features of GIF, and many sport added features, such as 24-bit color. One of these, the Portable Network Graphics (PNG) format, seems to be enjoying fairly wide support and has recently been embraced by CompuServe as its next-generation GIF24 format. You can learn more about the specification on the author's home page at http://www.boutell.com/boutell/. Whether or not this specification becomes a new standard for the Net, the controversy at least seems to have accelerated the development of browsers that support JPEG inlines (see "JPEG," below).

JPEG

The other commonly used graphic standard is JPEG. JPEG stands for Joint Photographic Experts Group, which is the name of the organization that developed the standard for the storage and transmission of photograph-style images with subtle gradations of color. JPEG isn't really an image format; it's a compression standard. Usually though, JPEG refers to the JFIF format, which uses JPEG encoding. JPEG compression is "lossy"; this means that some of the information in the image is lost in the compression.

This loss takes advantage of the natural limitations of the human eye, which perceives gradual changes in color with less accuracy than changes in brightness.

JPEG is the format of choice for storing complex real-world images. It supports "true-color," which is 24 bits of color information per pixel; this gives you a maximum of 16,777,216 colors, compared to the 256 offered by GIF. Not only does JPEG allow images much richer in color than GIF, but its compression algorithm really excels at compressing images that have subtle gradations of color. It's common for JPEG compression to shrink this sort of image to a tenth or a twentieth of its original size.

This clever algorithm has its downside: many clients are relatively slow when decoding JPEGs because the process is rather complex. For people downloading images over a slow connection to the Internet, the smaller size may make up for the greater time needed to display it. Another consideration to keep in mind when using JPEGs is that most computer displays are currently only 8-bit; therefore, they can display only 256 colors at a time. Programs displaying 24-bit images on 8-bit screens must dither them, which requires additional time. This situation is quickly changing; many new computers have true-color monitors, and as hardware standards change, JPEG will become more popular.

The most important consideration when deciding whether to use JPEG for your image is that JPEG stores simple images poorly. If your image includes only a few colors (fewer than 16) or large areas of the same color, JPEG's lossy compression will distort it. Also, applying JPEG's lossy compression to this sort of image often results in a final product that is larger than the GIF version.

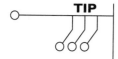

TIP

Until recently, graphical browsers allowed only GIFs as inlines. If you wanted to use JPEGs in your documents, you had to include them as hyperlinks. This situation has started to change. The current versions of the most popular graphical browsers (Netscape and Mosaic) support inline JPEG, and most other clients have plans to support them soon. Until all browsers support inline JPEGs, an excellent compromise is to link your high-quality JPEG images to icon-sized GIF inlines (see "Comparing Links & Inlines," earlier in this chapter). Those interested in seeing greater detail can click the link and download the JPEG. Not only does this allow anyone with a graphical client to get the full benefit of your page, but the small GIFs usually load faster than JPEGs.

Getting the Best From Inline Images

CD-ROM

Adding an inline image or two to your page is quite easy, and every page designer likes using them. Unfortunately, without care you could wind up producing awful images. By taking care in selecting and manipulating your images, you can dramatically improve the appearance and clarity of your pages. Paint Shop Pro, included on the Companion CD-ROM, is a shareware product with a wide variety of useful features for manipulating images. If what you need to do is import, edit, and export still images, it's likely that Paint Shop Pro is all you'll ever need. The Web site for Paint Shop Pro is at http://www.jasc.com/pspdl.html.

Table 7-2 shows all the formats of raster- (bitmap-) based images that can be imported into Paint Shop Pro. Many of these formats can also be written out, but as a Webmaster, you'll be much more interested in what images you can accept, since the output formats are likely to be either GIF or JPG. A great feature of Paint Shop Pro is that you can batch files up, and convert a bunch of files at the same time.

Format	Subformat	Source or Standard
BMP	RGB encoded	OS/2
BMP	RGB or RLE encoded	Microsoft Windows
CLP	Bitmap or Device Independent Bitmap	Windows Clipboard
CUT		Dr. Halo
DIB	RGB encoded	OS/2
DIB	RGB or RLE encoded	Microsoft Windows
GIF	Ver. 87a and 89, interlaced and noninterlaced	CompuServe
IFF	Compressed and uncompressed	Electronic Arts
IMG	Old and New Styles	GEM Paint
JIF	Huffman compressed	Joint Photo. Expert Group
JPG	Huffman compressed	Joint Photo. Expert Group
LBM	Compressed and uncompressed	Deluxe Paint
MAC	With and without header	MacPaint
MSP	Old and new versions	Microsoft Paint
PBM	Portable Bitmap	UNIX
PCD		Kodak Photo CD
PCX	Versions 0, 2, 3, and 5	ZSoft Paintbrush
PGM	Portable Graymap	UNIX
PIC		Pictor/PC Paint
PNG	Portable Network Graphics	
PPM	Portable Pixelmap	UNIX
PSD	RGB or indexed	Photoshop

Format	Subformat	Source or Standard
RAS	Type 1 (Modern Style)	Sun Microsystems
RAW	Unencoded pixel data	
RLE	CompuServe	CompuServe
RLE	Windows	Microsoft Windows
TGA	Compressed and uncompressed	Truevision
TIFF	Pack bits, LZW, Fax Groups 3 and 4, Huffman compressed and no compression	Aldus Corporation
WPG	Versions 5.0, 5.1, and 6.0	WordPerfect

Table 7-2: *Bitmap formats supported by Paint Shop Pro.*

Table 7-3 shows the meta and vector formats that can be read by Paint Shop Pro.

Format	Source/Standard
CDR	CorelDRAW!
CGM	Computer Graphics Metafile
DRW	Micrografx Draw
DXF	Autodesk
GEM	Ventura/GEM
HGL	Hewlett-Packard Graphics Language
PIC	Lotus Development Corp.
WMF	Microsoft Windows Metafile
WPG	WordPerfect

Table 7-3: *Vector and meta formats supported by Paint Shop Pro.*

Paint Shop Pro comes with an assortment of image filters with which you can enhance, deform, recolor, transform, redimension, and resize your images. There's also an assortment of drawing tools to touch up your images, as well as create new images.

GIFs & Interlacing

One of the features of the GIF file format is the option to use interlacing. Interlaced GIFs hold the same contents as regular GIFs, but the rows of pixels aren't encoded from top to bottom. Instead, the lines of the image are interlaced, like a television display, so that the complete image appears in stages. The encoding software breaks the image down into four groups, starting from different points.

It's easiest to understand interlacing with an example: Imagine an image with 20 rows, numbered from 0 to 19. The interlaced image begins with every eighth line of pixels and always starts with row 0; in the test image, this first group includes rows 0, 8, and 16. The second group begins at row 4 and includes every eighth row from there. This group is rows 4 and 12. After the second group of rows, the third starts with row 2 and includes every fourth row from there: 2, 6, 10, 14, and 18. The final group begins with row 1 and contains every odd row; a complete listing of the four groups is in Table 7-4.

Group	Rows
1	0, 8, 16
2	4, 12
3	2, 6, 10, 14, 18
4	1, 3, 5, 7, 9, 11, 13, 15, 17, 19

Table 7-4: *Interleaved encoding for a 20-row GIF.*

This permuted encoding allows users to see the image decode as it arrives, getting more detail as the process continues. This especially favors users with slow connections because it allows them to decide when they've seen enough of an image and to terminate the connection before the client downloads the entire thing.

When you save images with Paint Shop Pro in GIF format, you are given a choice of File Sub-Formats. If you select "Version 89a - Interlaced," the image will be saved in an interlaced GIF format. This is very handy for converting noninterlaced GIFs to an interlaced format. In addition, Paint Shop Pro has a "batch conversion" option which lets you convert images from any supported format to almost any other supported format, including from noninterlaced to interlaced GIFs.

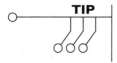

TIP

Recently, standards were set to allow for the creation of progressive JPEG images, which would offer a similar function to interlaced GIFs. At the time this was being written (March 1996) there were no converters available for Windows to convert standard JPEG images to progressive JPEG, but keep looking!

Scaling Images

As noted earlier, it's a common practice on the Web to have pages with icon-sized inline images (usually GIFs) linked to full-sized, high-quality images (usually JPEGs). Paint Shop Pro makes it simple to scale an image larger or smaller, while preserving the ratio between its X and Y dimensions (the aspect ratio). To do this, load an image into Paint Shop Pro, and select Image | Resize. The Resize dialog, shown in Figure 7-5, gives you several options for resizing the image. To scale the image equally in both X and Y directions, make sure that the Maintain Aspect Ratio box is checked. Then you can enter any X or Y dimension, and the other dimension will change to match, maintaining the original aspect ratio. With this technique, you can shrink or enlarge the image. If you're making thumbnail images, a typical width would be somewhere between 75 and 150 pixels.

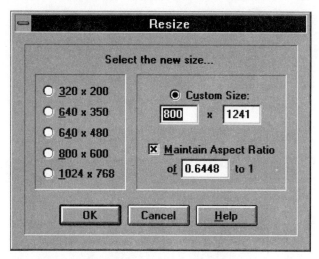

Figure 7-5: *Paint Shop Pro Resize dialog.*

Transparent GIFs

As you start dressing up your pages, you'll want to add special effects to them. A common desire is a logo that isn't rectangular, or words that appear over a background pattern. With standard GIF images, all images must be rectangular, and the background color of the image will cover the background of the browser—either the typical gray, a user-selected color, or perhaps a bitmap pattern. Fortunately, the GIF format provides a way around this annoying limitation—the transparency index.

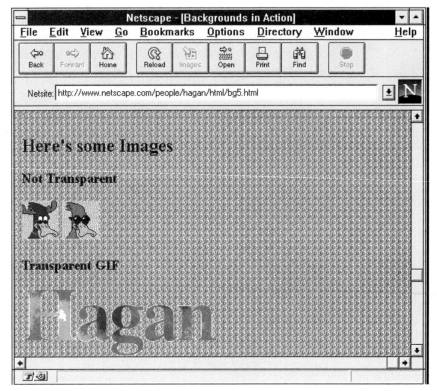

Figure 7-6: *Transparent and nontransparent images.*

The transparent color index is a field in the GIF header that indicates to the browser that one color in the image's colormap should be changed to a "color to be named later." The browser encounters this field when rendering the GIF and changes all occurrences of the transparent color to whatever color the background color of the page is. This feature is only available in the GIF89 version of the GIF standard.

Using Paint Shop Pro to enable transparency is easy, although perhaps not intuitive:

1. Open the image you want to make transparent into Paint Shop Pro.

2. With the Eyedropper tool, move to an area of the image that you want to become the background color.

3. Click the right mouse button to use that color as the background color.

4. Choose File | Save As, then click on the Options button, and select the File Type and Subtype as GIF - CompuServe and Version 89a - Interlaced.

5. Click on the Options button.

6. In the GIF Transparency Options dialog, choose "Set the Transparency Value to the Background Color" and click on OK.

7. Type the filename to save the file as, and save the file.

You probably noticed that there are other ways to set the color that will be the transparent color. You'll want to use the method that comes easiest to you as you gain familiarity with the program.

Transparent GIFs open all sorts of possibilities in your page design; you can use them for a variety of effects, including fancy headings, diagrams, and screen captures of tables and charts created in other programs. The appropriate use of transparent GIFs can give your page a professional appearance, while careless abuse of the feature might make people wonder about your eyesight.

Commonly Used Inlines

If you've done a fair amount of surfing on the Web, you've probably noticed that certain styles of inlines, as well as a few specific icons and images, pop up again and again. Although many people create these from scratch, several collections of images, icons, and clip art are archived on the Web. As we take a quick tour of these servers, we'll introduce you to the common uses of some of these simple, but useful, images.

Pretty Little Dots

Probably the most commonly used type of inline on the Web is
what we call PLDs—Pretty Little Dots. These small, 3D shaded
spheres are often used in combination with the <BR> tag in place
of HTML's bulleted lists, like this:

```
<h2>My Grocery List</h2>
<IMG SRC="pld.gif" ALT="*">Milk.<BR>
<IMG SRC="pld.gif" ALT="*">Honey.<BR>
<IMG SRC="pld.gif" ALT="*">Tofu.<BR>
<IMG SRC="pld.gif" ALT="*">Milkbones.<BR>
```

Figure 7-7: *A pseudo-list using dots and <BR> tags.*

As you can see in Figure 7-7, the previous markup gives you a
fairly satisfactory looking result, but it has a serious problem—it's
not a real unordered list. Although some clients may render it
identically to an unordered list, others use special indenting to set
lists off from the rest of the text. More importantly, this usage
violates HTML's purpose as a structural markup language. If you
don't use HTML's ability to indicate content and concentrate on
appearance instead, the client loses its ability to treat your text
intelligently.

Unfortunately, HTML v2.0 doesn't allow you to retain strict structural markup of your lists while using graphics for bullets. There is a compromise, though, that retains some structure and improves the appearance of your page on many clients. You can use HTML's defining lists (see Chapter 2, "The Basic Pieces") without definitions, to achieve the appearance of a bulleted list. The following is an example of how to do it:

```
<DL>
<DT><IMG SRC="pld.gif" ALT="*">Quail
<DT><IMG SRC="pld.gif" ALT="*">Pheasant
<DT><IMG SRC="pld.gif" ALT="*">Grouse
</DL>
```

This markup creates a three-item list with these attractive dots as bullets. Although the list is not really the proper type (<UL> would be the correct tag), at least this markup more closely represents the actual structure of the text.

URL Description	http://www.jsc.nasa.gov/~mccoy/Icons Lots of dots are in Daniel's Icon Archive.
URL Description	http://www.idb.hist.no/~geirme/gizmos/gizmo.html Mosaic Gizmos has color dots, lines, buttons, pointers, and illustrations.
URL Description	http://melmac.corp.harris.com/images.html This site prefers color squares to color dots.

Table 7-5: *Sources for pretty little dots.*

Color Bars

Another very common convention on the Web is the use of brightly colored horizontal bars, which take the place of the HTML <HR> tag that draws a horizontal rule across the page. Unfortunately, this usage also goes against the structural guidelines of HTML in the same way that using little dots for bullets does. Even worse, no semi-structural workaround is available for this usage; if you want to use color bars to divide your pages, you'll have to break the rules. Here's how to do it:

```
<IMG SRC="bar.gif"
ALT="------------------------------------------------">
```

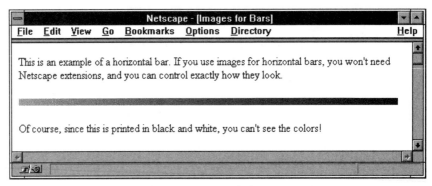

Figure 7-8: *Color bars on the sunsite.unc.edu home page.*

This ALT specification at least gives users of nongraphical browsers some sort of divider, although it's not identical to the horizontal rule that Lynx uses.

URL Description	http://www.jsc.nasa.gov/~mccoy/Icons/ Part of Daniel's Icon Archive (the root is at http://www.jsc.nasa.gov/~mccoy/Icons).
URL Description	http://pmwww.cs.vu.nl/home/dsbouma/rulers/ WEB Rulers offers an assortment of horizontal bars so that you don't need to use Netscape extensions.

Table 7-6: *Sources for color bars.*

Navigation Buttons & Icons

The Apple Macintosh and other GUIs have made the icon-laden desktop a familiar metaphor to most users. This paradigm has also become prevalent on the Web; thousands of icons are out there, used in many different ways. One of the most common uses for these icons is as buttons for navigational aids. Often, HTML pages are linked in series, like pages in a book. Thus, it's useful to add little buttons to the top and bottom of each page, so the user can simply click them to move to the previous or next page.

There are many different styles of navigation icons, but we especially like the look of 3D shaded buttons, with no borders (see "Netscape Extensions," earlier in this chapter), as shown in Figure 7-9. This is, of course, just our personal preference, and many variations are available, including pointing fingers and colored arrows. When using this type of navigation aid, don't forget to include text-only links as well, for users on nongraphical browsers, and for users who choose not to download images.

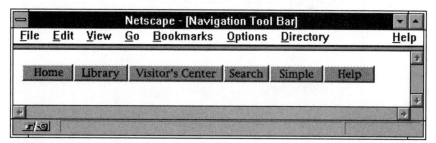

Figure 7-9: *A navigation button bar.*

If you position such a button bar at the top and the bottom of each page in your text, you give the user a quick and attractive way to navigate your pages.

You can also use icons to announce new features (as shown in Figure 7-10), work in progress (Figure 7-11), hyperlinks to sounds and movies (Figures 7-12 and 7-13), and whatever else you desire. (Remember, however, that many users have slow network links. They'll be annoyed if it takes a ridiculous amount of time to load your page because you've added too many spiffy icons. A picture is worth a thousand words, but that's only 5000 bytes; many icons are much larger.)

Figure 7-10: *Exclamation mark icon.*

Figure 7-11: *Under construction icon.*

Figure 7-12: *Audio hyperlink icon.*

Figure 7-13: *Film reel icon.*

In Table 7-7, you'll find a list of icon archives. Many of the icons accessed through the Yahoo reference are in an X format, which cannot be converted with the Windows editors. Steer clear of these—there are plenty of GIF images you can use!

URL	http://www.jsc.nasa.gov/~mccoy/Icons/
Description	Daniel's Icon Archive.
URL	http://www.yahoo.com/Computers/World_Wide_Web/Programming/Icons/
Description	The Yahoo Icon Page.
URL	http://www.di.unipi.it/iconbrowser/icons.html
Description	University of Pisa Searchable Icons.

Table 7-7: *Sources for buttons and other icons.*

The icons at these sites are excellent ways to spruce up your page, especially if you're not particularly gifted artistically. Before using them, be sure to carefully read their copyright statements. Even if free use is granted, it's always good manners to give credit to the people whose work has helped you.

Clickable Imagemaps

HTML provides a special type of inline image called an *imagemap*. You indicate that an inline is an imagemap with the ISMAP attribute. When a user activates the imagemap's hyperlink, the client sends the server the coordinates of the point on which the user clicked. These coordinates are processed by your web server, which then returns a URL to the client based on how you've mapped the image.

Using imagemaps on web pages gives the user the impression of real interactivity. A creative imagemap, in place of simple buttons embedded in a background, can be a very impressive addition to the page. However, do not rely exclusively on imagemaps to provide links to various parts of your site, because not all clients load images or are even able to. After you've constructed an imagemap, include links below the image to all of the pages that the imagemap is referencing or provide a link to a text page with those links on it. Doing so prevents your page from being nonfunctional when a text-based browser, or a user who chooses not to download images, accesses it.

An imagemap contains three components. One is the image itself, which must be in GIF format. This image can be anything you want. Outside of sensible design standards, there are no restrictions on how the image must look or on how large it must be.

Another component is the link that is put in whatever document contains the imagemap. Different web servers put this information in different places. For Alibaba, the web server available on the CD-ROM, a file called imagemap.cnf is located by default in the CONF subdirectory. This file contains the names of aliases that point to the location of the map file. Again, assuming that the map file is located in D:\ALIBABA\CLICK and is called persons.map, you would make the following entry into the imagemap.cnf file:

```
people :  D:\ALIBABA\CLICK\persons.map
```

The word *people* acts as an alias to the correct location of the map file. Then, in the reference that you make in the web page itself, you should enter the following link:

```
<A HREF="/IMAGE/people">
<IMG ALT="Our People" SRC="faces.gif" ISMAP></A>
```

This link passes the command people to Alibaba, which then turns to the imagemap.cnf file, which relies on the third component of the imagemap, the map file itself. The IMAGE portion of the HREF is an alias name that tells Alibaba to look in the imagemap configuration file. The alias name is configurable in the Alibaba setup. (See Chapter 3 for more about configuring Alibaba.)

The Map File

The map file is the file that contains the imagemap coordinates. While the map file typically goes in the CLICK subdirectory, you can put it anywhere. It's standard to give a map file the extension .MAP. The map file has the following format:

```
default http://www.domain.com/
# Send users to the House of Debuggin'
rect http://house.debuggin.com/info/index.html  101,234
152,300
circle gopher://gopher.doc.ic.ac.uk:7001/  53,42 53,96
poly index.html  25,10 39,1 52,29 45,40 28,40
```

The first line of the map file, beginning with "default," gives the location that the user goes to if he or she clicks outside any of the shapes that you identify in the imagemap. Subsequent lines consist of the shape of the range of coordinates to be linked, the location to which they are linked, and the coordinates that the program uses to construct the boundaries of the range. The imagemap program ignores comments, which begin with the pound sign.

The example gives the three shapes that the imagemap program can recognize: the rectangle, the circle, and the polygon. The coordinates for each shape are identified differently. For rectangles, use the coordinates of two diagonally opposite corners (left top corner and right bottom corner, in this case). For circles, give the coordinates of the center and any point on the circumference. For polygons, enter the coordinates of all of the corners. It is possible to overlap the coordinates for two images. Whichever set of coordinates comes first in the map file is the link that is followed. For example, if you want to create concentric circles that will have different links assigned to them, you could make a map file similar to the following:

```
default http://www.floofco.com/map-links-text.html
circle http://www.floofco.com/products/ 100,100 100,135
circle http://www.floofco.com/services/ 100,100 100,150
circle http://www.floofco.com/info/ 100,100 100,175
circle http://www.floofco.com/index.html 100,100 100,199
```

If the user clicked inside the innermost circle, with a radius of 35, he or she would be sent to the file index.html in the directory products; the second circle would take him or her to the services directory and so on. Clicking outside the circles would take the user to the file map-links-text.html, which could contain the text links to the various files or directories. It should be noted that the full URL, http://www.domain.com, is optional. If the file or files are on the same server as the imagemap, you can simply enter the path and filename, and the server assumes that it is opening a local file.

Creating Map Files With Web Hotspots

With the availability of programs that let you create map files graphically, you'll almost never need to manually create or edit map files. Some of the server programs available for NT come with these utility programs, but you can find imagemap editor programs on the Web. The Web Hotspots program, for example, can be found at 1automata's home page, at http://www.cris.com/~automata/.

Selecting File | New from the Web Hotspots menu allows you to specify the name of the graphics file you're using as the image. You can open files in a number of graphics formats, including JPEG, GIF, and TIFF. Once the image is open, you create the hotspot areas with rectangles, circles, polygons, or freeform modes. Each hotspot has an associated URL, which is the jump location for the hotspot area currently selected. Figure 7-14 shows a typical screen in the midst of editing. The URL that you enter can be either a full URL or a relative URL, just like any HTML link.

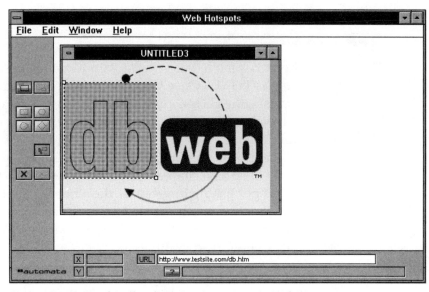

Figure 7-14: *Graphically editing an imagemap in Web Hotspots.*

Web Hotspots comes in two versions, a standard shareware version and a "professional" edition. In addition to the features in the standard edition, the professional edition includes verification of imagemap URLs with an integrated live test mode, scaling and rotation of hotspots, and realignment and resizing of hotspots relative to one another.

In addition to standard imagemaps, the professional version of Web Hotspots allows you to create a new version of imagemaps, called a client-side imagemap. With client-side imagemaps, the map itself is downloaded along with the document. This imagemap type provides several benefits: it allows the client, rather than the server, to make the jump determination, reducing the processing load on the server; the user can see the destination of a jump before taking it; the imagemap is not dependent on a server being there, so you can use imagemaps when accessing files local to your hard disk (or CD-ROM); and documents are more portable, since there is no dependence on a particular server.

Moving On

This chapter has moved us into the wonderful realm of image processing for HTML. Once you've learned the basic principles of image formats, the HTML <IMG> tag, and simple image processing, you'll pick up new skills and ideas as your pages become more complex.

Images have been an important part of traditional publishing for centuries. The next chapter introduces a capability that's really an electronic publishing innovation: the embedding of audio and animation directly onto the page. After you've grasped the essentials of electronic sound and movies, you'll have truly arrived in the world of networked multimedia.

8

True Multimedia: Adding Audio & Animation

The proliferation of graphical and intuitive user interfaces based on hypertext technologies has spawned an increasing interest in the use of computer networks for audio and video file distribution. While the basic technologies that permit such distribution have been around for quite a few years now, the Web has encouraged many individuals and companies that once shied away from multimedia to examine the ways in which the addition of sound and animation might enhance the content of their web pages. In turn, this increased interest has intensified the efforts of many software developers and media producers to customize their products for distributed-media environments.

The ability to embed audio and animation files into hypertext documents has astounding implications. Numerous high-quality media archives are already on the Net, and as the speed, storage capabilities, and available bandwidth of computer networks increase, we're sure to witness the continued migration of traditional media to the digital realm.

In order to understand the (r)evolution that media and communication are currently undergoing, it is imperative that you gain a basic working knowledge of the technologies involved. This chapter introduces the various audio and video file types currently in use on the Internet, the underlying concepts that have led to the proliferation of multimedia technologies online, and the software tools necessary for you to use these files. Finally, we discuss the ways in which you can incorporate audio and video files into your own pages so that you can get started right away.

Digital Audio on the Internet

The introduction of digital audio recording and playback techniques has revolutionized the ways in which music is made, stored, and transmitted. Since digital information can be copied and manipulated without degradation, digital audio recording technologies allow almost unlimited manipulation and processing of the audio signal. These same techniques can be used to prepare your own audio recordings for use on the Web.

Before discussing the various audio file formats in use on the Net, it's important that you gain an understanding of the basic underlying concepts of digital audio. We only scratch the surface in this section, but the information we provide should be enough to get you started and to help you decide which file formats are right for you.

Obviously, the first step in getting audio onto the Net is transferring it into your computer. In order to digitize an analog audio source, such as the output from a tape deck or microphone, the signal must be processed through an analog-to-digital (A/D) converter. Many workstations come equipped with sound cards that have A/D converters on them. If your computer has a sound input jack, it already has an A/D converter. If your computer provides only a sound output jack (usually a female 1/8-inch jack on the rear panel of the machine) or an internal speaker, you may only have digital-to-analog conversion capabilities.

Even if you're recording audio from a digital source, such as a digital audio tape (DAT) or compact disk (CD), some kind of A/D conversion is usually involved because most computers do not come equipped with digital audio inputs yet. In this case, the digital signal is converted to an analog signal within the hardware of the DAT or CD and sent through the analog output (usually a ⅛-inch jack). The analog signal travels along the line plugged into your computer and is redigitized by the workstation's sound board. The same is true of most CD-ROM players with regular audio-CD playback capabilities. Even though some CD-ROM players have digital outputs, most often the sound cards to which they connect do not.

The basic tenets of how audio is digitized are quite simple. An A/D converter utilizes a "sample and hold" circuit that records the voltage levels of the input signal at a fixed interval. This interval, or rate, at which the signal is sampled is determined by the A/D converter's *sampling rate*. The sampling rate determines the highest frequency that can be recorded or played back, which can be found by dividing the sampling rate in half. This is based on the Nyquist theorem, which basically states that a sampling rate must be twice that of the highest frequency to be sampled. For instance, if the highest frequency that will be recorded is 22,050 hertz (22.05kHz), then the rate at which the signal must be sampled is 44,100 times per second (44.1kHz).

Table 8-1 lists the most frequently used sampling rates.

Sampling Rate	Description
8kHz	A telephony standard that is emerging as a standard for 8-bit μ-law (.AU) mono files (you'll find more information on the μ-law forms in "Audio File Formats," later in this chapter).
11kHz	Refers to either 11.025kHz (one quarter of the CD sampling rate) or 11.1272727kHz (half the Mac sampling rate).
22kHz	Refers to either 22.05kHz (one half of the CD sampling rate) or 22254.545454545454kHz (the Mac sampling rate—the horizontal scan on the original 128K Mac). This is emerging as a standard for 8-bit unsigned mono and stereo file formats.
32kHz	The sampling rate of long-play (LP) digital audio tape decks, also of Japanese HDTV (high-resolution television) systems.
44.056kHz	Used by professional audio hardware to fit an integral number of samples into a video frame.
44.1kHz	The standard audio CD sampling rate. This is emerging as a standard for 16-bit linear signed mono and stereo file formats.
48kHz	The primary DAT sampling rate.

Table 8-1: *Popular audio sampling rates.*

Windows-based recording packages allow sampling rates to be user-defined. This allows the user to decide on the quality of the recorded sound. For example, on a system with a Windows Sound System from Microsoft, you can select sampling rates from 5.5kHz to 44kHz, in stereo (2 channels) or in mono (1 channel).

Another term you frequently encounter is *bit rate*, or *resolution*, which indicates the number of bits allocated for each *sample*, or output value from the A/D converter. Most audio files on the Net have been recorded at a resolution of 8 or 16 bits. An 8-bit sample size allows the digital signal to represent 2^8 (256) different levels in each sample, while a 16-bit sample size allows for 2^{16} (65,536) different levels.

With the basic Pulse Code Modulation (PCM) recording technique, the resolution bit rate determines the overall dynamic range of the output from an audio source. The dynamic range is a measure of the span between the quietest and loudest sounds an audio device is capable of recording or reproducing. Each bit of resolution contributes approximately 6 *decibels* (a decibel, or dB, is a measure of the ear's response to sound pressure levels) of dynamic range to the recording. Eight-bit audio files are therefore able to reproduce a dynamic range of 48dB, roughly that of an analog cassette deck, while 16-bit audio files are capable of yielding the 96dB of dynamic range found in CDs. Compression techniques can be applied to either bit rate to yield an even lower final bit rate.

The sampled audio file formats currently in use on the Net usually have either one or two channels. Naturally, single-channel files are often labeled mono, and dual-channel files are labeled stereo. This is important to consider when making your audio files available. Stereo files are twice as large as equivalent mono files, and often it is not necessary to distribute the stereo version of a recording. Combined with the varying sample rates, the Windows Sound System can record audio signals at rates from 62 kilobytes per minute, for a voice-quality, highly compressed recording, to over 10 megabytes per minute, for CD-quality stereo audio.

Before placing your audio files on the Net, you should consider all of these parameters. Since higher sampling rates and resolutions require more storage and throughput, you need to decide if you can sacrifice disk space and bandwidth for high-quality audio files. While one minute of an 8-bit mono file sampled at 8kHz is approximately 150K in size, a 16-bit stereo file of the same duration sampled at 44.1kHz can take up 10MB. Sometimes the low-fidelity version of an audio clip may well serve the purposes for which the clip is intended. Also keep in mind that many web browsers do not yet have their computer audio outputs plugged into stereo amplifiers, and lower resolution mono files are ideal for playback via internal computer speakers. Fortunately (or perhaps unfortunately), there are only a few recording rates and audio file formats that are commonly used on the Web.

Audio File Formats

Numerous digital audio file formats, many of which you'll probably never encounter, have been introduced over the years. As computer platforms have come and gone, so have their proprietary file formats. Even though MIME typing allows for any file format to be transmitted between a client and server, only a handful of prominent multimedia file types are commonly used on the Web. Since every new file type requires an appropriate helper application on the client end, simplicity and practicality have necessitated a decrease in commonly used file types. This section provides you with a brief introduction to the file types that are commonly used on the WWW today, as well as the ways in which you can convert files to these various formats. The name of each format is followed by its appropriate MIME type.

µ-law

```
audio/basic    au snd
```

The µ-law (pronounced mu-law) file format is the most frequently used audio file type on the Internet. Even though it's not the highest quality audio file format available, its relatively small file size and the availability of players for just about every operating system have made it a favorite for Net users. At a sampling rate of 8kHz, its sound quality is roughly equivalent to that of standard telephone receivers. Some systems, such as NeXT, use a sampling rate of 8.013kHz for the µ-law format. Since both Sun and NeXT machines commonly use this format, it is often referred to as the NeXT/Sun format.

Many people have found that the level of audio quality provided by μ-law files is sufficient for their particular applications, especially since most WWW users are still listening to audio they retrieve from the Internet through a monophonic computer speaker. For this reason, many sound archives now provide audio samples in both μ-law and higher quality formats like MPEG.

Windows systems can play μ-law sounds (.AU suffix) with web browsers as well as edit them with many sound editors, including GoldWave (see "Audio Software," later in this chapter).

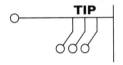

TIP

For a great archive of μ-law audio files, check out the WWW TV Theme Songs home page at http://www.parkhere.com/tvbytes/ tvthemes.html.

For hundreds of μ-law samples, see http://sunsite.unc.edu/pub/ multimedia/sun-sounds/.

AIFF & AIFC

`audio/x-aiff    aif aiff aifc`

The Audio Interchange File Format (AIFF) allows for the storage of monaural and multichannel sampled sounds at a variety of sampling rates. Since it is an interchange format, it's easily converted to other file formats. For these reasons, it is often used in high-end audio recording applications when storage space is not a concern. Originally developed by Apple, this format is used predominantly by Silicon Graphics and Macintosh applications.

AIFF files can be quite large. One minute of 16-bit stereo audio sampled at 44.1kHz usually takes up about 10 megabytes. Since AIFF does not allow for compressed audio data, Apple introduced the AIFF-C, or AIFC, format, which allows for the storage of compressed and uncompressed audio data. AIFC supports compression ratios as high as 6:1, but at the cost of the file's signal quality. Most of the applications that support AIFF playback also support AIFC.

Since AIFF supports multiple sample rates, some sites offer AIFF files roughly equivalent to standard μ-law files. These files are usually labeled as 1-channel, 8-bit, 8kHz AIFF files. Notice that when downsampled, AIFF files usually give a sample rate of 8kHz, not the 8.013kHz sampling rate of some μ-law files.

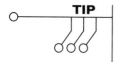

TIP *It's a very good idea to keep multimedia files as small as possible if you intend to distribute them over the Net. For this reason, many net.music archives are primarily using MPEG layer II (.MP2) and μ-law (.AU) audio files. MPEG layer II files are generally one-tenth the size of equivalent AIFF or WAVE files, and since MPEG audio compression schemes are based on psycho-acoustic models of how we perceive sound, there's minimal loss in sound quality during the compression process (see "MPEG," later in this chapter).*

RIFF WAVE

`audio/x-wav    wav`

A proprietary format sponsored by Microsoft and IBM, the Resource Interchange File Format Waveform Audio Format (.WAV) was introduced in MS Windows v3.1 and is supported by the tools supplied with every Windows-based PC. WAVE files support multiple encoding methods, most often ADPCM (Adaptive Differential Pulse Code Modulation) and all WAVE files follow the Rich Information File Format (RIFF) specification. Don't worry if these encoding techniques sound alien to you—you won't need to know these things for day-to-day use of the format.

This format is very similar to the AIFF format in that it supports monaural and multichannel samples and a variety of sample rates. Like AIFF, WAVE files require approximately 10 megabytes per minute for 16-bit samples with a sampling rate of 44.1kHz, but 8-bit, 8kHz, single-channel versions are often offered by sites.

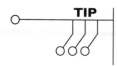

TIP *A large archive of WAVE sounds can be found at http:// sunsite.unc.edu/pub/multimedia/pc-sounds.*

MPEG

`audio/mpeg    mp2`

The International Standard Organization's Motion Picture Experts Group is responsible for one of the most popular compression standards in use on the Internet today. Designed for both audio and video file compression, the MPEG codecs (coder/decoders) have become a favorite of Net users working with audio/video files over the past couple of years due to the scheme's ability to compress large files without sacrificing much quality.

MPEG-1 audio compression specifies three layers, and each layer specifies its own format. The more complex layers take longer to encode but produce higher compression ratios while keeping much of an audio file's original fidelity. Layer I takes the least amount of time to compress, but layer III yields higher compression ratios for comparable quality files.

Numerous sites that offer high-quality music distribute it in the form of MPEG-compressed audio samples. The use of this compression technique is quite desirable because players have now been developed for just about every platform and operating system, and since MPEG audio compression is based on psychoacoustic models, it's an ideal format for distributing high-quality sound files online. Most sites with MPEG audio files offer layer II encoded files, which can compress files to anywhere from ⅓ to 1/24 their original file size (with higher compression ratios resulting in more data loss). The quality of an MPEG-1 layer II–compressed audio file remains very similar to the original uncompressed file at ratios from 5:1 to 12:1. These files are usually identified with the .MP2 extension, which does *not* mean that they're compressed with the MPEG-2 standard. MPEG-2 is still predominantly used for video compression, since the MPEG-2 audio compression standard is still being worked out. This is often confusing to many new Net users.

In addition to the numerous WWW sites that are using MPEG-1 to encode audio files, Phillips uses it for their new digital video CDs, and it has also been adopted by some digital radio standards bodies for use with digital radio broadcasts.

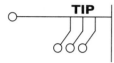

TIP

For more information on the MPEG compression standard, see the following Web sites:

- *http://www.crs4.it/~luigi/MPEG/ (the MPEG FAQ)*
- *http://www.crs4.it/~luigi/MPEG/mpeg1-a.html (information about MPEG-1 audio encoding)*
- *http://www.crs4.it/~luigi/MPEG/mpeg2.html#What is MPEG-2 AUDIO (information about MPEG-2 audio encoding)*

Creative Voice

`audio/x-voc`   `voc`

Creative Voice (.VOC) is the proprietary sound file format that is recorded with Creative Lab's Sound Blaster and Sound Blaster Pro audio cards. This format supports only 8-bit mono audio files up to sampling rates of 44.1kHz, and stereo files up to 22kHz.

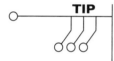

TIP

Creative Labs has a home page at http://creaf.com.
There is a Sound Blaster 16 programming information guide at http://www.xraylith.wisc.edu:80/~ebrodsky/sb16doc/sb16doc.html.

IFF/8SVX

`audio/x-iff`   `iff`

IFF/8SVX is the standard Amiga sound file format. Like AIFF, it is an interchange file format, meaning that it was designed for easy conversion to other formats. However, the IFF/8SVX format supports only 8-bit samples. The header section of an IFF/8SVX file differentiates it from other IFF format types. This format is rarely used for audio file distribution on the Net.

SND

The .SND extension is a bit ambiguous. Sun/NeXT sound files are sometimes identified with the .SND extension when they're actually µ-law files. Macintosh system sounds also have the .SND extension, as do some PC sounds. They vary in sample rate from 5.5kHz to 22kHz, with 11kHz being the most popular.

Macintosh .SND files are assigned as SFIL (sound file) in the "type" field of the Mac resource fork. These files can consist of AIFF/AIFC samples and/or synthesized sounds that can take advantage of the System 7 sound hardware and software.

Raw PCM data

Raw Pulse Code Modulated data is sometimes identified with the .PCM extension, but it sometimes has no extension at all. Since no header information is provided in the file, you must often specify the waveform's sample rate, resolution, and number of channels.

Streaming Audio

Internet Wave, RealAudio, and Streamworks are compressed audio types used to transmit streaming audio from a special server to a web browser helper application. Streaming audio differs from all the other encoding methods in that the sounds start to play before the entire sound is transmitted. This is very useful for sounds that are very long—such as a radio broadcast. Of course, this means that the audio must be compressed below the maximum rate that the user can receive data, which is typically 14.4 kbps or 28.2 kbps. Each of these three compression formats allows audio signals to be fed from a server to the client at rates that are suitable for modem communications. Windows clients (viewers) are available for all three formats, and Windows NT server products are currently available for the first two. Streaming audio technology is changing so rapidly that some of the information presented here may be obsolete by the time you read it. Be sure to check the home pages mentioned below for the latest information.

Internet Wave

```
application/vocaltec-media-desc    vmd
application/vocaltec-media-file    vmf
```

Vocaltec has been around for a while now with the Internet Phone, a very popular way of creating voice connections over the Internet. With the announcement of Internet Wave in September 1995, Vocaltec has joined the race to create a streaming audio server and clients for the Web. With the initial release of Vocaltec's server, Webmasters can create audio files in four different formats: VSC224, a 16 kbps rate; VSC154, an 11 kbps rate; VSC112, an 8 kbps rate; and VSC77, a 5.5 kbps rate. Naturally, the slower the bit rate, the lower the quality of the sound, but slower rates can be used by a larger group of people who may not have the fastest modems. The client program can dynamically select a position (fast forward or rewind) if the audio stream is already converted. If the audio stream is being converted in real-time, of course, it would be impossible to fast-forward. (If anyone figures out how to fast-forward real-time audio feeds, let us know, and we can all retire early!)

Vocaltec's transmission scheme uses a TCP connection, which places the burden of error correction on the network components and protocol stacks. Although there's a significant overhead with TCP connections (typically, every packet is acknowledged), there's also a good flow control mechanism, which will help reduce uncontrolled network overloads. For non-live applications, you can use your standard HTTP server to send the Internet Wave audio files; for live applications you'll need a separate server process.

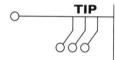

TIP *Vocaltec has a home page at http://www.vocaltec.com.*

Internet Wave Encoder

The Internet Wave encoder, available through the Vocaltec Web site listed above, is a simple program designed specifically to convert Microsoft .WAV files into the file type required by the Internet Wave client. The files created by the encoder are highly compressed using proprietary techniques. As an example, a .WAV file that started at a size of 24K at a 5.5 kbps rate was compressed down to 12K by the encoder at the highest quality rate, and to 4.1K at the lowest quality rate.

RealAudio

`audio/x-pn-realaudio    ra ram`

Progressive Networks's RealAudio was the first widely used streaming audio available on the Internet. Currently, over one million RealAudio players have been downloaded. At the end of 1995, RealAudio went into beta with version 2.0. With release 2.0, you can encode the audio stream at two different bit rates: one suitable for 14.4 modems, and one suitable for 28.8 modems and faster.

RealAudio uses User Datagram Protocol (UDP) packets to send information from the servers to the subscribed clients. The advantage of UDP is that it is a very lightweight protocol: when things are working, there's very little overhead to sending the packets. Since there's no error correction or flow control, the server and client programs must take care of this. When a UDP packet is dropped by the network (due to congestion, for instance), the server will never know unless the client was programmed to inform the server, and the client must recover the processing stream without the help of the network.

Version 2.0 of the client and server also opens up a number of Application Programmer Interfaces, which allow programmers to develop specialized audio-on-demand and live audio applications, integrate other or new codecs into the client and server, and provide OCX and OLE for better integration with other Windows programs. Since RealAudio is UDP-based, your listeners must make special provisions to allow the packets to pass through any firewalls that may exist between them and the server of the RealAudio stream. Progressive Networks provides a good amount of information about how to do this.

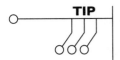
TIP

RealAudio has a home page at http://www.realaudio.com.

RealAudio Encoder

The RealAudio personal server allows you to offer a limited connection (two listeners at a time) RealAudio service from your own web server. Audio files must be converted into the RealAudio format before being used by the personal server, and the encoder program does this. With version 1.0 of RealAudio, a 24K .WAV file was compressed down to 4.3K. You can download a copy of the server from the Real Audio home page.

Streamworks

```
application/x-xdma     xdm
```

Xing's Streamworks is yet another streaming audio product, but with a significant difference—the addition of video. Of course at 28.8 kbps you hardly get television quality, but you *do* get an occasional moving picture along with the audio. At faster speeds, such as ISDN, you can receive a high-quality video channel. Xing has based the product on international standards, using MPEG video and audio compression, and TCP/IP connections, and can use Multicast packets as defined in RFC 1112 for data delivery. Because it can offer video as well as audio, the architecture can get more complicated than with the other two streaming audio products.

The application set for Streamworks is also broader than the other products, since it supports standalone and networked servers, is network-manageable with SNMP, and can also be simply integrated with a UNIX-based HTTP server. Note that at the time this was written, server products were only available for SGI, Sun, HP, and Linux variations of UNIX. By the time you read this, however, a Windows NT version of the server should be available. Clients are available for Microsoft Windows and X Window System.

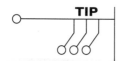
TIP

Xing has a home page at http://brain.xingtech.com.

MIDI & MOD

Not all audio file formats on the Net perform the sole function of storing digitized audio. In the following section, we discuss two unique file formats that you might consider using if you're interested in electronic music composition.

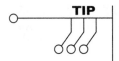

TIP *Links to electronic music software on the Net can be found at the Arachnaut's Internet E-Music Software List at http:// www.webcom.com/~hurleyj/music/emusic-sw.html.*

MIDI

`audio/x-midi    mid midi`

Unlike the formats discussed earlier, the Musical Instrument Digital Interface is not a specification for sampled digital audio. Instead, it is a serial communications protocol designed to allow the transmission of control data between electronic music instruments. It has been likened to a PostScript language for music. Since MIDI contains only instructions for controlling how and when devices, most frequently electronic synthesizers or samplers, produce sounds, the files are *much* smaller than digitized audio files. The MIDI Manufacturer Association (MMA), a group of electronic music instrument manufacturers, has been responsible for the evolution of the MIDI protocol since its inception in 1983.

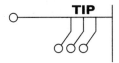

TIP *For information on MIDI, see the MIDI home page at http:// www.eeb.ele.tue.nl/midi/index.html.*

Modules

`audio/x-mod     mod`

Modules, usually identified by the .MOD extension, are somewhat like a cross between MIDI files and digitized audio files. Instead of consisting solely of sampled audio or control information, this format contains a bank of digitized sounds as well as information for controlling the ways in which the sounds are sequenced upon playback. The samples are raw, 8-bit audio data. The format also has simple digital signal processing (DSP) capabilities for adding effects.

Modules originated on the Amiga, but their relatively small file size and impressive breadth of usage has made them a favorite of many composers on the Net. Thanks to the readily available playback tools and gigantic collections of these files on the Net, module composition has in itself become an art form. Even though we've listed a MIME type with this entry, modules are usually compressed, and you must download them and decompress them before playing, so it may not be necessary for you to add the entry to your mime.types file.

Information about a MOD player called Mod4Win, version 2.3, is available at http://www.teleport.com/~smithtl/modpage/modpage.htm.

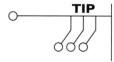

TIP

For detailed information on the MOD file format, see the MOD FAQ at http://www.cis.ohio-state.edu/hypertext/faq/usenet/mod-faq/top.html.

Also check out the MOD Page at http://www.teleport.com/~smithtl/modpage.htm for more information about MOD files.

Recommended Reading

Consult the following newsgroups and Web sites to find out more about the various aspects of audio on the Internet:

- *alt.binaries.multimedia* (encoded audio and video files)

- *alt.binaries.sounds.midi* (encoded MIDI files)

- *alt.binaries.sounds.mods* (encoded MOD files)

- *alt.emusic* (general discussions about electronic music)

- *comp.music* (discussions about computer music)

- *rec.music.makers.synth* (discussions about music synthesizers)

- *http://sunsite.unc.edu/emusic-l/* (the home page for the EMUSIC-L list, including the MIDI specification, a section about building MIDI triggers, tons of reviews of electronic music equipment, and tips on buying your first keyboard)

- *http://mitpress.mit.edu:/Computer-Music-Journal/ CMJ.html* (the Computer Music Journal archives at MIT, an *excellent* resource for technical articles about electronic music as well as a long list of links to other emusic sites)

- *http://ftp.ircam.fr/index-e.html* (the Institut de Recherche et Coordination Acoustique/Musique (IRCAM) WWW server)

- *http://akebono.stanford.edu/yahoo/Computers/Music/ MIDI/* (MIDI links at Yahoo)

Audio Software

The Companion CD-ROM contains two sound editors that should help you with creating sounds for your web site. (In the application descriptions that follow, we've also included the URLs of sites where you can find updates for these programs.) You can create the original material and get it just the way you want it with the sound editors. If the audio files are fairly short, you can publish them directly onto the web in one of the formats described earlier, probably μ-law (.AU) format. If you have lengthy files, you'll probably want to convert them to a highly compressed form with one of the two compression products, depending on what server you want to use and which helper application you want your listeners to use. The disadvantage of the compressed formats is, of course, that the client programs are not at this time integrated into the web browsers. Because of this, you'll want to include pointers from your web pages to places on the Web where the users can get the appropriate client programs.

GoldWave

http://web.cs.mun.ca/~chris3/goldwave/

 GoldWave is a great audio processing tool, accepting a wide variety of input formats, including Microsoft .WAV, Sound Blaster .VOC, Sun/NeXT .AU, Amiga .IFF, Raw/NeXT .SND, and Matlab .MAT. When saving in any format, you're presented with a range of save options that can be supported by the selected format. GoldWave offers a number of transformations, including echo, highpass and lowpass filtering, volume control with fade in and fade out, and reversing the sample. An interesting feature, called the expression evaluator, offers you the ability to enter a mathematical formula as the definition of the audio signal.

Cool Edit

http://www.netzone.com/syntrillium/

 Cool Edit is one of the finest sound editors available for Windows. It handles recording at all the popular rates, from 6kHz to 48kHz, in mono or stereo, with 8-bit or 16-bit samples. Files can be saved in any format you're likely to want: Apple .AIF, Sun .AU, MPEG, Sample Vision .SMP, Sound Blaster .VOC, Dialogic ADPCM .VOX, Windows (various formats) .WAV, A-law and μ-law Wave, and PCM raw data (.PCM). Cool Edit allows you to convert from any supported audio format to any other, and in the process change the sample rate if you need to.

Cool Edit has all the basic recording and playback capabilities plus transformations, such as echo, reverb, equalization filter, FFT filter, intensity control, noise reduction, flanging, and modulation with a tone or various noise types. You can also create tones, music, DTMF and MF signals, pink, white, and brown noise. Cool Edit is also an extendable program, offering programmers the opportunity to add their own filters or signal processing. (The MPEG import and export filter is an add-on program.) Cool Edit also offers a frequency spectrum view of the recorded signal so that you can visually inspect the spectral distribution of a recorded signal.

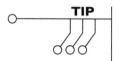

TIP

If you want to export to MPEG, you must *record at 32kHz or greater to use the add-on MPEG encoder. If you record at rates slower than this, the playback will sound as if you sped up the recording.*

Digital Video on the Internet

Most video signals (including videotapes and cable and off-air transmissions) in North America are *broadcast quality* as defined by the National Television Standards Committee. The NTSC standard dictates that the signal be displayed at 30 frames per second in an interlaced fashion, with the odd and even horizontal lines alternating during each pass. This process divides each frame into two fields, thus producing 60 fields per second. The vertical resolution of the video image is determined by the number of scanlines (defined as 525 by the NTSC standard).

Needless to say, digitizing and reproducing broadcast-quality video signals requires processing speed, hard disk storage space, and RAM at capacities typically unavailable on computer workstations. Even though some high-end digitizing systems are capable of meeting these requirements, the sheer volume of data would overwhelm most machines. One second of NTSC-equivalent digitized video consists of 30 full-screen (640 X 480 pixels), 24-bit images, which take up approximately 26MB of disk space. That's over 1.5 gigabytes a minute *without* audio!

These prohibitive requirements have generated the acceptance of lower-quality video clips on the Net. These files differ from analog and high-end digital video sources in that they are not displayed as interlaced fields but instead as a series of images. For this reason, digitized video files on the Net are often referred to as *animations*, because the method with which they are displayed resembles that of cartoons more than traditional video. Since animation playback software provides the illusion of movement by rapidly (or not-so-rapidly) displaying a series of individual images, the terms *video, animation,* and *movie* are often used interchangeably.

Making Movies With Windows

Unlike its audio counterpart, video hardware is rarely found preconfigured on Windows systems, and can be much more expensive than audio hardware. Thankfully, Microsoft has created a standard interface API for video hardware that allows almost any video card to work with the software of your choice. Microsoft has also created a video file format called AVI (Audio Video Interleaved) for Windows.

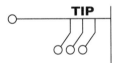

TIP *You don't necessarily have to have a video digitizing board in order to make a movie. Since animations are nothing more than a sequence of images, it's possible to string together a series of still images and convert them to a movie. Of course, doing this is much more time consuming than capturing video from an input board, but it's fun to experiment with if you don't have access to any video digitizing equipment. If you're interested in doing this, check out http://www.eit.com/techinfo/mpeg/mpeg.html.*

Animation File Formats

This section reviews most of the animation file formats in use on the Internet today. These don't represent every available animation or video file format out there, but they're the ones that you're most likely to encounter in day-to-day use. Actually, many of the formats covered are fading into obscurity and are discussed as points of reference so that you can get a better idea about the differences among the various formats. We've listed the appropriate MIME type following each file format.

QuickTime

```
video/quicktime      mov moov qt
```

QuickTime is Apple's proprietary dynamic data format originally implemented on the Macintosh. This format has become an increasingly popular animation file format on the Net since Apple released QuickTime enablers for the Microsoft Windows 3.1 environment. These movies can be played on almost any newer Windows 3.1–based PC system.

The most important thing to remember about QuickTime movies is that they're often created under the Macintosh operating system, which divides files into two separate "forks": *data forks* and *resource forks*. The resource fork contains small chunks of program code that describe various attributes of the file necessary for the Macintosh interface, while the data fork contains the actual numerical and textual data of the file. Since HTTP does not provide support for transferring multiforked files, QuickTime movies made on a Macintosh must be converted before they can be distributed over the WWW to be played on multiple platforms. This conversion process combines the resource and data forks into a single-forked file, commonly referred to as a "flattened" file. The resultant file can be stored on non-Mac file systems without the loss of important data.

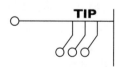

TIP

If you have access to a Mac, this conversion can be accomplished with the Movie Converter utility that comes with the Macintosh QuickTime Starter Kit, or the publicly available Flattmoov, at http://www.astro.nwu.edu/lentz/mac/qt/.

The latest version of QuickTime supports both digitized audio samples and MIDI (see "Audio File Formats," earlier in this chapter), so it's possible to include soundtracks that take up very small amounts of space. Most video files on the Net that include a soundtrack are in the QuickTime format.

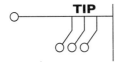

TIP *Apple has a Web site devoted to QuickTime at http:// quicktime.apple.com.*

MPEG

`video/mpeg    mpeg mpg mpe`

MPEG compression, discussed in "Audio File Formats," earlier in this chapter, can be used for both audio and video files. With the appropriate combination of hardware and software, real-time compression and decompression is possible on numerous platforms. The use of MPEG compression reduces the bandwidth necessary for high-quality audio/video file transfer without excessively sacrificing the original signal quality, making it an ideal way to efficiently distribute multimedia files online.

One viewer for MPEG video clips is the NET TOOB player, available at http://www.duplexx.com/. In addition to playing MPEG-1 video, it can also play .AVI and .MOV files.

AVI

`video/x-msvideo    avi`

AVI is Microsoft's proprietary video format, also known as Video for Windows. Its performance features are similar to QuickTime's, and numerous freely available AVI-to-QuickTime and QuickTime-to-AVI converters are available. Like QuickTime files, AVI files are capable of having an audio track. The Media Player that comes with all Windows systems can play AVI movie files, so you shouldn't need to search for a special player.

FLI & FLC

`video/x-fli    fli flc`

FLI and FLC are Autodesk's "Flick" formats. FLI, the original format of Autodesk's Animator, is limited to a maximum resolution of 320 X 200 pixels, a 64-color palette, and 4000 frames per file. FLC, the second generation of Autodesk's animation formats, introduced with Animator Pro, supports larger images (up to 65,536 pixels in width and height) but is limited to a 256-color palette for each frame. Neither of these formats supports audio.

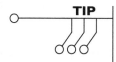

TIP

You can find a player for FLI and FLC files at http://www.ice.net/ ftphelp/viewers.html.

More detailed information about FLI (and many other graphics file formats) is available from http://www.dcs.ed.ac.uk/%7Emxr/ gfx/.

Video Software

Video editing and creation software is almost always bundled with video hardware that you can add to your PC, so if you get a video card for your Windows NT system, you'll start by using the software that comes with the card. There are some really good commercial programs available for manipulating video images, including Adobe Premiere, and the options are discussed at some length in *HTML Publishing on the Internet for Windows*, also from Ventana.

If you intend to publish video clips on your Web site, you'll probably want to offer them in a number of different formats, since not all formats are supported on every browser platform. The best three formats to publish in would be QuickTime MOV, Microsoft AVI, and the standard MPEG format. If you support all three on your site, there's a good chance that anybody accessing your site can find a compatible viewer program.

Serving Multimedia

Before the World Wide Web, audio and animation files were usually distributed on the Internet by either posting them to Usenet newsgroups or making them available at FTP sites. Both of these methods are still widely used today, but the Web is quickly becoming the preferred method for distributing multimedia files.

Don't be intimidated by the idea of incorporating multimedia files into your pages. The process of linking these files into your documents is *exactly* like the one described for linked images in Chapter 7, "Images on the Web." You simply need to call the file with the <A HREF> tag, as illustrated in the following examples:

```
<A HREF="/audio/bob.mov">"Bob"'s Loop of Endless Slack.</A>
(QuickTime movie - 3300 Kb)

Say, why don't you check out the 3.3Meg QuickTime movie <A
HREF="/audio/bob.mov">"Bob"'s Loop of Endless Slack</A>?
```

Notice that the file type and size of bob.mov is indicated somewhere near the link, either next to it or in the sentence before it. It's important to supply this information because some users may access the WWW through slow connections or they may not have the software necessary to play back the file. Including the file type and size helps them decide whether they have the time and capabilities to initiate the download. Also be sure to indicate the file format, sampling rate, and resolution of any audio files you have available for download. It's not written in stone anywhere that you have to do this, but this courteous gesture will save you the headache of dealing with irate users and tons of hate e-mail.

Other than the ones just mentioned, there aren't many "guidelines" for distributing audio/video files over the Net. If you plan to make multimedia files available on your server, the guiding force of your plan should be *common sense*. Obviously, larger files take up more disk space and increase the demand on the throughput of your system. If you observe that your server is incredibly loaded down and that your connection to the Net is perpetually maxed out, make sure that your entire system is not being choked by the transfer of large files that you could reduce in size or remove.

You can decrease the sizes of the files you offer by using the compression techniques discussed earlier in this chapter and/or reducing the resolutions of the files. For example, if you've got numerous 16-bit AIFF audio files that you need to make available, consider converting them to the 8-bit μ-law format with Cool Edit, or better yet, compress them to MPEG Audio so that they lose very little of their original quality. Likewise, you can limit the size of the animations on your server by reducing the pixel resolution (frame size) of the files. You can also reduce the number of bits allocated for each frame's color display, such as reducing a 24-bit movie to 8-bit. If you keep color images filled with solid colors instead of gradients, you can reduce the size of the compressed GIF files, because GIF compression works best on large areas of solid color.

Again, exercise common sense. This can't be stressed enough. Even though the Internet was designed to withstand a nuclear assault, it's having a hard time standing up to the barrage of multimedia files flowing through its wires. This problem will be partly remedied by the introduction of increasingly faster computers and the dissemination of high-bandwidth lines, but for now we need to take all the precautions we can to make sure that file sizes are kept to a minimum.

Moving On

This chapter has reviewed the most popular file formats currently in use on the Web for audio/video file transfer, as well as the ways in which you can include audio and video in your web documents. Multimedia on the Net is still in its infancy, and we hope this overview has provided you with enough information, tools, and jumping-off points to explore audio/video technologies and the ways in which they can be integrated into your web documents. As the available bandwidth on the Internet increases, so will your ability to utilize new communication technologies to transmit high-quality multimedia files. Chapter 13, "Future Directions," discusses many exciting developments in the field of distributed media currently in use on the Net, including advancements in real-time audio/video conferencing, improved protocols that support distributed computer-generated graphical environments, and general directions in which the Net is headed.

So far in this book, you've been reading about the delivery of documents and information in one direction: from you to the browser. One of the more exciting aspects of the Web, however, is the fact that information can also pass from the browser back to you, creating a highly interactive and reactive media form. In the next chapter, you'll read about gathering user input with the creation of simple forms and some of the programs that can process users' inputs.

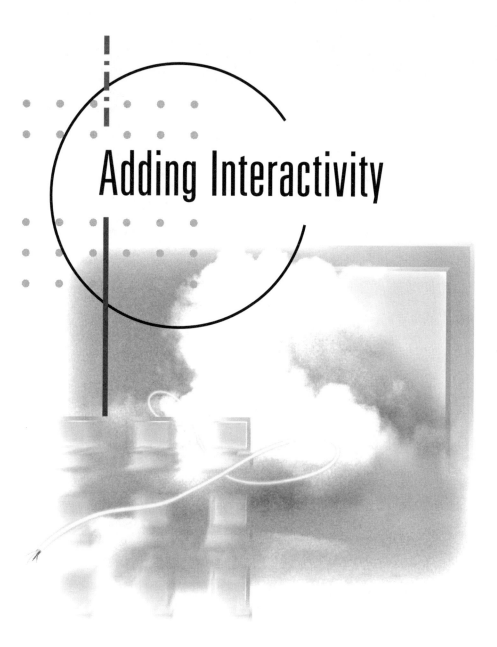

Adding Interactivity

9

Simple Forms

Most of the traditional publishing media communicate in only one direction. People read newspapers and watch television; they don't interact with them because these media are designed to carry information or entertainment from the provider to consumers. The distributed design of the Internet has the potential to break that mold and allow people to develop new patterns of communication. The recent emergence of embedded forms in HTML has realized some of this potential.

Forms allow the page designer to mix the traditional elements of the printed page with the user interface of a modern windowing system. They let you place pull-down menus and pushbuttons in the midst of formatted text and pictures. These user interface devices, or widgets, give those viewing your pages the opportunity to communicate upstream, allowing users to respond to what they're seeing, rather than being passive viewers. In this chapter we'll look at some of the ways in which forms can be useful on your web pages, and we'll look at the basics of how forms are created using several special HTML tags. Finally, we'll briefly describe a few of the many support programs available to help you process the data collected by your forms with a minimum of programming effort.

Forms on the Web

Web pages are often merely static catalogs of information and pretty pictures, but the proper use of forms can make your pages dynamic. For an excellent example of dynamic web pages, check out the Internet Underground Music Archive (IUMA) at http://www.iuma.com. Figure 9-1 is a form from IUMA that allows the user to look at the archive's music databases in several different ways: by artist, location, and genre. In other words, a form like the one in Figure 9-1 lets users get the information they want, organized the way that they want it.

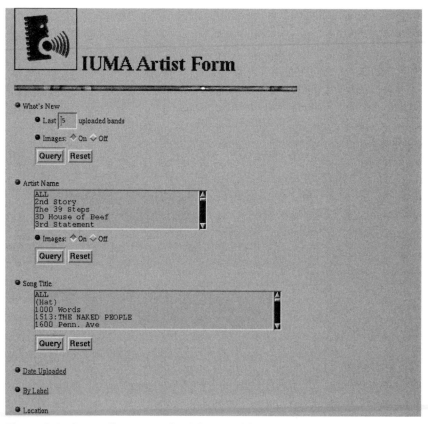

Figure 9-1: *An excellent example of the use of forms, from IUMA.*

Forms can also provide feedback on the job you're doing. Although you can attach your e-mail address to every page and ask for comments, users are more likely to give you useful information about your efforts if you give them an immediate, in-context opportunity to express their views.

Another important benefit of forms is psychological; forms can remove some of the feeling of faceless anonymity on the Net. This opportunity for feedback and interactivity reminds the user of the people on the "other side" who are responsible for the content that the user is enjoying. This somewhat intangible benefit is important, especially if you want your Internet presence to provide the basis of a dialogue or continuing relationship with a client, customer, or fellow-traveler.

Although they're extremely useful, forms have a few basic limitations. The major limitation is a result of the stateless design of the HTTP protocol. Web clients make a new connection to the server each time they download a page or upload the contents of a form, and the HTTP server keeps no record of the clients' previous transactions. Although certain programming tricks can get around some of the stateless limitations of HTTP (see Chapter 10, "CGI & DLLs: Programming Your Server"), the interactivity of forms cannot be used for tasks that require real-time control, such as arcade-style games. Additionally, since clients typically have to wait until they receive all of the expected data before displaying any of it, they can't use an HTTP connection for displaying video in real time, for example.

You should also keep in mind that the interactive tags that are the basis of forms are like the rest of HTML; they define functionality, rather than actual appearance. As you can see in Figures 9-2, 9-3, and 9-4, the exact implementation of these tags varies from client to client, depending on what makes sense for the platform. Although you can be assured that the user will be able to enter the appropriate data in each device, you should be careful not to depend on a particular implementation.

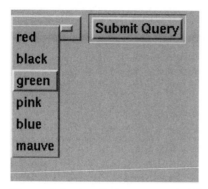

Figure 9-2: *A pull-down menu in Netscape for X.*

Figure 9-3: *A pull-down menu in Mac Mosaic.*

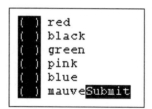

Figure 9-4: *A pull-down menu in Lynx.*

The Basic Structure of a Form

Unfortunately, HTML forms have gained a reputation for complexity, and many people believe that it takes great expertise to write and understand them. In reality though, you need to learn only a few simple elements to master the art of putting forms together effectively. Every form has the same basic structure, which follows:

```
<FORM ACTION="/cgi-bin/post-query" METHOD="POST">
Hi! Welcome to palace of Glinda the Good.<P>
Where are you trying to go? <INPUT NAME="home"> <BR>
<P>
<STRONG>Thank you</STRONG> for taking the time to complete
this form. </FORM>
```

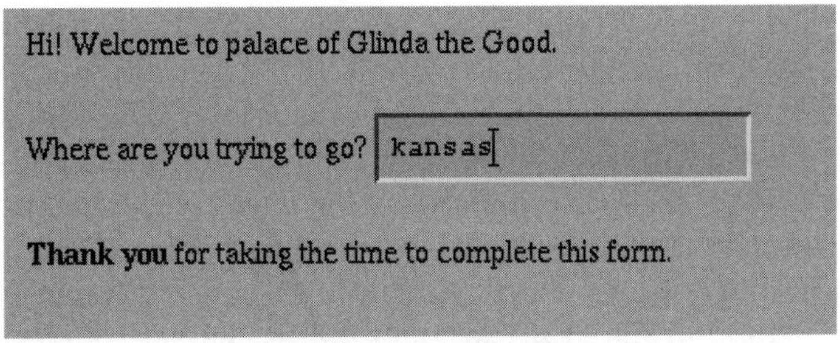

Figure 9-5: *A simple text-entry form with a response.*

As you can see in the example, it all begins with the <FORM> tag. This tag tells the client that an interactive area has begun and will continue until the client reaches the </FORM> end tag. Since the <FORM> tag has no effect on what the page looks like to the user, it's a good idea to use <HR> (horizontal rule) tags before and after the form to visually separate it from the rest of the page.

Every <FORM> tag must have an ACTION element, which specifies the CGI program that the server should send the form's data to. The program used in the previous example, post-query, is a utility for testing forms; it prints all the data that it receives from the client. For security reasons, programs that process submitted data are usually kept in special directories. The server is then set up to alias special URLs to these directories, such as the URL /cgi-bin.

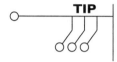

TIP

CGI stands for Common Gateway Interface, a programming standard for accessing data from HTML forms. Although programs that use this standard are commonly called CGI scripts, CGI is not a scripting language, but an interface that any programming language can use. We'll talk about CGI in detail in Chapter 10, "CGI & DLLs: Programming Your Server."

The other element in the <FORM> tag in the example, METHOD, tells the client how to send the entered data to the server. This element is optional; if you leave it out, browsers assume the default value GET. GET tells the client to embed the data from the form inside the URL; in fact, you can create hyperlinks that run CGI programs using METHOD=GET directly. When a form uses the POST method, the server sends the submitted data as if it were typed by the user. (The distinctions between these two methods is an advanced topic; it's covered in Chapter 10. For now, it's enough to know that we'll be using the POST method in all of the examples in this chapter.)

You can put any text or markup between the beginning and ending elements of a form, except for another <FORM> tag; you can't nest forms. In addition to regular markup, several special HTML tags are legal only inside a form; adding them elsewhere may even crash some (very poorly written) clients. Browsers render these special tags as areas for user interaction and input.

In our simple text-entry example, the form contains a question to answer, followed by two tags, <INPUT> and <BR>. As you can see in Figure 9-5, the client's rendering includes the text, followed by an embedded text-entry box into which the user has already typed a response. To finish the form, the user presses Enter, which tells the browser that the form has been completed. The browser assigns the entered text to the tag's NAME element (which is "home," in the example) and sends the NAME element along with the entered text to the server.

Every interactive tag should have a unique NAME that distinguishes it from the rest of the fields in the form. If you give two interactive elements the same NAME, the client sends both values, but the CGI program won't be able to distinguish which one came from which element. This is a result of the way that forms work in HTML; all the intelligence for understanding the entered data resides in the program that processes it. Neither the browser nor the web server has any way of knowing if all the elements have been filled out properly, or even if they've been filled out at all—the CGI standard leaves this task to the CGI program to figure out.

Although this example is simple, it demonstrates all of the basic elements of a form; it asks for information from the user and provides a widget in which to enter it. Of course, you can choose from many more interface elements; adding any of them is as easy as inserting the appropriate HTML tag.

The <INPUT> Tag

The most versatile of the tags that allows user input is, appropriately, the <INPUT> tag. Not only does it provide text-entry fields like the one you saw in the simple form at the beginning of the chapter, but it is also the source of toggle buttons, password fields, and hidden state information. You differentiate among all these options by adding the TYPE element to the <INPUT> tag.

Submit & Reset

We discuss the submit and reset settings first because they serve an important purpose in almost every form. The first of these settings creates a button that allows the user to signal that he or she has finished the form:

```
<INPUT TYPE=submit VALUE="Submit this form">
```

All forms require a submit setting; without it, the user has no way to send his or her responses to the server. For historical reasons, most browsers make an exception for forms that contain only a single text input (like the form shown in Figure 9-5). Pressing Enter in the entry field completes the form if no Submit button is available. This behavior is not required by the HTML v2.0 standard, and future browsers may not support it.

Although the second of these settings, reset, is not required, it's usually a good idea to add it, because it allows the user to change every element back to its default value (we'll learn how to set defaults for each interface element later in this chapter). Adding the reset setting is simple:

```
<INPUT TYPE="reset" VALUE="Reset to Defaults">
```

The default labels on the reset and submit buttons vary from browser to browser; for the submit button, for example, Lynx uses the simple "Submit," while Mosaic and Netscape both use the more technical-sounding "Submit Query." You can easily change the text on both submit and reset with the VALUE element.

Text-Entry

Text-entry widgets are the workhorses of the forms world. They're used for any fairly short, free-form response. In the following example, they're used for the fields of an address in a subscription form:

```
<FORM ACTION="/cgi-bin/post-query" METHOD="POST">
<EM>Enter your address below:</EM>
<P>
First Name: <INPUT TYPE="text" NAME="first" SIZE=15>
Last Name: <INPUT TYPE="text" NAME="last" SIZE=15><BR>
Street Address: <INPUT TYPE="text" NAME="address"
SIZE=40><BR>
City: <INPUT TYPE="text" NAME="city" SIZE=15>
State or Province: <INPUT TYPE="text" NAME="state" SIZE=2
MAXLENGTH=2>
Country: <INPUT TYPE="text" NAME="country" VALUE="USA">
Area Code: <INPUT TYPE="text" NAME="zip" SIZE=5><BR>
<P>
<STRONG>OR</STRONG>
<P>
<EM>Enter your secret subscriber's code:</EM>
<INPUT TYPE="password"><BR>
<P>
<INPUT TYPE="submit">
</FORM>
```

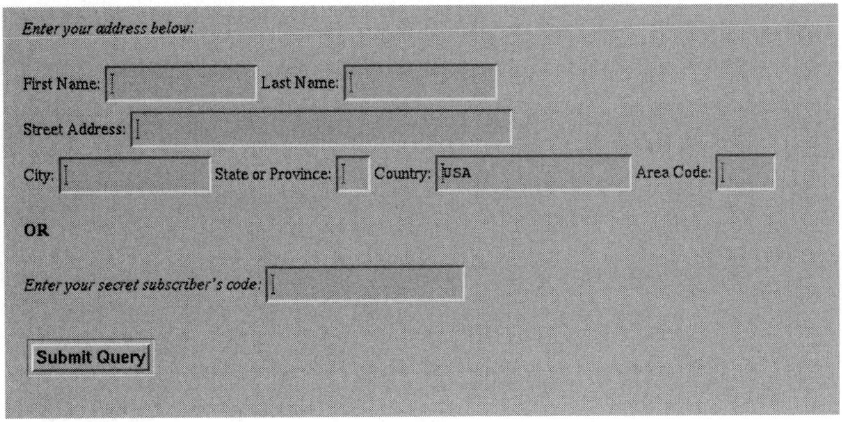

Figure 9-6: *An address form.*

This form allows the user to enter an address in a series of text-entry fields or to enter a special code, which must be kept secret for security reasons. For the address fields, we use regular text-entry <INPUT> tags. Even though text-entry is the default (as illustrated in the simple form shown in Figure 9-5), we explicitly specify text-entry with TYPE="text", which is a good idea because it clarifies the intentions of the author of the page and makes it obvious when he or she has forgotten the TYPE element in other INPUT tags.

For the subscriber's code, we use a special type of text-entry field, the password-entry field. This input type is identical to the regular text-entry type, except that characters typed into this box aren't echoed; instead, the client displays asterisks.

As you can see in the example, a number of elements modify the behavior of a text-entry widget. The first of these is SIZE, which changes the length of the field from the default of 20. If the user types more than this number of characters, the field scrolls left to provide more space; the SIZE value isn't a maximum limit on input.

The MAXLENGTH element, on the other hand, is such a limit. The user can't type more than two characters into the state field, for example. Although it stops the user from adding further input, MAXLENGTH doesn't automatically limit the length of the entry box; you must explicitly set that with SIZE.

The last of the optional elements that are valid with text-entry widgets is VALUE, which allows you to provide a default response for a field. You can see an example of this element in the Country field in the example. When the client renders this form, it places the text "USA" inside the area, as shown in Figure 9-6; if the user wants a different response, he or she must delete this default text first. The VALUE element is useful for providing examples of the type of input you desire, as well as for saving the user the trouble of typing the typical response.

Pushbuttons

The <INPUT> tag can also be used to create toggle buttons. These buttons allow the user to select one or more options from a series of choices. There are two varieties of pushbuttons: the check box and the radio button. The first of these creates a simple button that can be toggled on and off by the user. You can create a check box in your form using markup similar to the following:

```
Choose as many of the following toppings as you desire:
<P>
<INPUT TYPE="checkbox" NAME="sausage" CHECKED>
Italian Sausage? (our favorite!)<BR>
<INPUT TYPE="checkbox" NAME="mush">Mushrooms?<BR>
<INPUT TYPE="checkbox" NAME="olive">Olives?<BR>
<INPUT TYPE="checkbox" NAME="garlic">Garlic?<BR>
<INPUT TYPE="checkbox" NAME="fish">Anchovies?<BR>
```

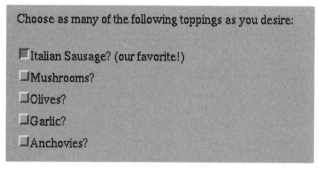

Figure 9-7: *A check box pizza menu with a preselected check box.*

As you can see in Figure 9-7, this HTML markup creates four options, each preceded by a button that the user can select to add that topping to a (virtual) pizza. Each button has its separate NAME element and can be independently chosen, and you can preselect a button with the CHECKED element. By default, browsers assign selected check boxes the value "on"; you can elect to give the buttons a different value with the VALUE element, as in the following example:

```
What commercial browser(s) do you use? (choose any that
apply)
<P>
<INPUT TYPE="checkbox" NAME="client1" VALUE="spyglass">
Spyglass Mosaic.<BR>
<INPUT TYPE="checkbox" NAME="client2" VALUE="netscape">
Netscape Mozilla.<BR>
<INPUT TYPE="checkbox" NAME="client3" VALUE="sesame">
Ublique's Sesame.<BR>
```

What commercial browser(s) do you use? (choose any that apply)

☐ Spyglass Mosaic.

☐ Netscape Mozilla.

☐ Ublique's Sesame.

Figure 9-8: *A form with specified VALUE settings.*

Each check box in this example has its own specified value; when the user submits the form, the browser sends the NAME and the assigned VALUE for each button that the user invokes instead of the string "on." Browsers send no data at all about nonactivated check boxes.

Unlike check boxes, radio buttons aren't independent entities. Multiple radio buttons are usually grouped together, all sharing the same name. Only one radio button of a group can be selected at any one time, because radio buttons behave like the presets on an old-fashioned car radio. When the user pushes a button, the last selection pops up. Radio buttons are used to select one from several exclusive options. This example creates two exclusive choices, each with its own radio button:

```
What is your sex?
<P>
<INPUT TYPE="radio" VALUE="male" NAME="sex">Male<BR>
<INPUT TYPE="radio" VALUE="female" NAME="sex">Female<BR>
```

Although this sort of either-or option excludes those who may be feeling confused about which option to select, it's often the easiest way to give the user concrete choices. If you want to suggest a choice, you can specify a preselected option for a single radio button with the CHECKED element.

As with all the interactive tags, you must give each button a NAME, but radio buttons are somewhat special; since the tags have the same NAME, radio buttons within the same form are linked together, no matter how far apart they appear on the page. And since radio buttons share NAME elements and the VALUE element is what distinguishes one button from the rest of its group, you always have to specify a VALUE element.

Hidden Fields

Besides text-entry and pushbuttons, the <INPUT> tag has one other important role, the hidden field. Although a hidden field is rarely important for simple forms, it allows the advanced forms author to get around one of the major obstacles to writing interactive applications for the Web: its statelessness.

Since the web server keeps no information about a client's previous connections, any information that the application needs to remember between transactions must be kept by the client. You can keep such information either by embedding the data itself, or a key to it, in the hidden fields of a form where it is invisible to the user unless he or she views the page's HTML source. These fields aren't really interactive. (The user can't even see them, let alone interact with them!) Rather, they are more like variable assignments in a programming language; they let you equate a NAME with a VALUE.

This example might be from some imaginary WWW tic-tac-toe game. It declares a variable named "gamestate" and assigns it a value that represents the status for each of the nine squares:

```
<INPUT TYPE="hidden" NAME="gamestate" VALUE="o--x-----">
```

In this hypothetical application, the user would initially pull down a form that contained three rows of three single-character text-entry fields (although using the <SELECT> tags might be a better choice—see the next section, "The <SELECT> Tag"). The user would enter an X in the center square, and click the Submit button. The forms-processing program on the server's end would find the user's move and make its own move, perhaps in the upper left-hand corner. It would then write out a new form, like the one in Figure 9-9, using the information in the hidden field. By keeping track of the game's progress inside the hidden field, the program can remember whose turn it is. It can also ensure that a user doesn't change his or her moves later in the game or try to make two moves in a single turn.

Figure 9-9: *A tic-tac-toe form.*

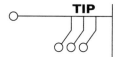

Hidden fields have an additional use in forms that serve applications: they can hold information that might change between sessions but that you don't want the user to have to supply. For example, if a user has to enter a password to read a set of pages, he or she should have to enter it only on the entry page. On each subsequent page, the password can be embedded in a hidden field, and the user can press the Submit button to request the next page of the series. Be careful, however, because even though a field is hidden, a user can still look at it with the View Source option available on most web browsers.

The <SELECT> Tag

Another special interactive tag is the <SELECT> tag, which allows the user to choose one or more options from a menu. Although you can use radio buttons and check boxes to provide similar functionality, the <SELECT> tag is often a better choice if you want to present lots of options. Too many pushbuttons can make your interface appear cluttered and can confuse the user. Like the <INPUT> tag, every <SELECT> tag requires a NAME to hold the selected option or options. The following is a brief, and absurd, example:

```
Which of the following performers do you like? <P>
<SELECT NAME="favbands" MULTIPLE SIZE=2> <OPTION> Culture
Club
<OPTION> Beastie Boys
<OPTION> Negativland
<OPTION SELECTED> Tito Jackson
</SELECT>
```

Figure 9-10: *A SELECT widget as a scrollable list with two options visible.*

As you can see, the <SELECT> tag requires both a beginning and an ending tag. Between these, you list each possible choice with the <OPTION> tag, indicating default choices with the <OPTION SELECTED> tag. All other HTML tags are illegal inside of an area enclosed by <SELECT> tags; most browsers ignore them, but some are so impolite as to crash when encountering an illegal tag.

In addition to NAME, there are also two optional elements that control the behavior and appearance of the <SELECT> tag. SIZE determines the number of menu options visible to the user at a time. In many clients, the default value of 1 (a single option visible) causes the SELECT widget to be rendered as a pull-down menu, as in Figure 9-11, while values greater than 1 make it a scrollable list, as in Figure 9-10. Although you can use SIZE to control the amount of vertical space that the widget occupies, browsers like Lynx, which render the <SELECT> tag in an odd way, won't honor it.

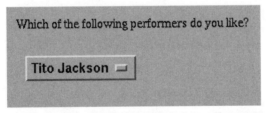

Figure 9-11: *A SELECT widget as a pull-down menu.*

The other optional element, MULTIPLE, allows the user to choose more than a single option from the menu. Usually, this element forces the browser to give the user access to more than one option at a time, and most graphical clients display such a menu as a browsable list. If the user selects more than one option, the client sends multiple copies of the same variable NAME, each with a different VALUE.

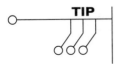

TIP *When you include the MULTIPLE element, you can specify more than one default choice with the <OPTION SELECTED> tag. Without the MULTIPLE element, the client usually uses the first SELECTED option as the default.*

The <TEXTAREA> Tag

The last of these special form tags is <TEXTAREA>, which gives you a multiple line version of the text-entry field. This area is suitable for any sort of free-form writing, and it's often used to give users a chance to send comments or e-mail to the author of the page. Although there's no official limit on the amount of text you can enter into this widget, individual clients will have their own limits, so we don't advise pasting in Shakespeare's complete works.

The <TEXTAREA> tag has three mandatory elements that control its use and size. Like the rest of the interactive tags, every <TEXTAREA> tag requires a NAME that tells the client where to store the results. The other two elements, ROWS and COLS, give the dimensions of the writing area in characters. The following is a brief example of the use of the <TEXTAREA> tag:

```
<TEXTAREA NAME="poem" ROWS=12 COLS=80> I've never seen a
purple cow.
I never hope to see one.
But I can tell you anyhow,
I'd rather see one, than be one.
-Gelett Burgess 1866-1951
</TEXTAREA>
```

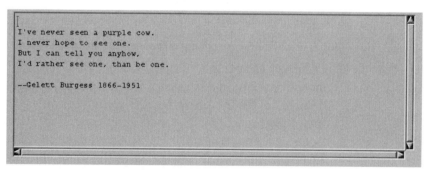

Figure 9-12: *A TEXTAREA widget with sample default text.*

Like the <SELECT> tag, the <TEXTAREA> tag requires both a beginning and an ending tag; any text that you place between them becomes the default response, as shown in Figure 9-12. If the user wants to fill the area with his or her own musings, he or she must delete the default text. In many clients, deleting the default text is a pain, and since there's rarely a need for default text, most page designers leave this space empty.

As you can see, the <TEXTAREA> tag pays attention to line breaks, both in the default text and in text entered by the user. Another important point is that ROWS and COLS specify the amount of space that the area occupies on the page, not the maximum amount the user can write. For example, if the user wrote a poem with 23 lines of 90 characters, the client would scroll the TEXTAREA widget both horizontally and vertically to make space for the additional characters.

Using Commercial Tools to Process Forms

Although designing an interface with HTML forms is fairly simple, writing a program to process the entered data can be quite complex. In the past, this problem has limited the use of forms to programmers, and most Web authors aren't programmers. Luckily, the problem of accepting data from forms has already been solved by a number of commercial and shareware programs.

Forms-processing is one of the areas of the Web in which the availability of support tools is simply exploding. There are a number of form types that are fairly popular on the Web, such as guest books, front ends to databases, comment forms, etc., and software companies have filled a need of nonprogrammers by writing "back-end" programs to process the data from these form interfaces. Although you can write your own CGI programs to process forms, as discussed in Chapter 10, if there's already a program written that does what you want, why bother?

Support programs that use perl can usually be used on Windows NT, since perl has been ported to NT (perl for NT is included on the Companion CD-ROM). Other programs are compiled executables, and usually don't include the source code. The executable programs will usually operate faster than the interpreted perl code, but in many cases the server processor is not heavily loaded, and response time is not a problem. In the next few sections we'll look at a number of shareware and commercial demonstration programs, most of which are included on the Companion CD-ROM.

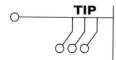
Just like the web server market, the support program market is growing daily, so be sure to check out the Web locations given below, and do your own surfing as well.

CGI PerForm

CGI PerForm is a CGI form support program that uses a few control files to customize its operation. It is a general-purpose CGI executable program (for Intel and DEC Alpha) that can be used for a variety of tasks that depend on storing data into files, retrieving that data and presenting it to users, and mailing input data. CGI PerForm uses specially coded form, template, and command files to instruct the main CGI processing program on what actions to take. The input forms and output template use a selection of command verbs defined by RealCom and encode them in HTML comments. CGI PerForm is shareware, and the basic version costs $149. The "pro" version, which allows you finer control over the way queries are made to the database, among other improvements, is available for $299. CGI PerForm is located in the cgiper directory on the Companion CD-ROM. The documentation is in the form of HTML files, and you can use your Web browser to read them.

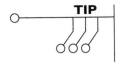

TIP

CGI PerForm's Web location is http://www.rtis.com/nat/software/ perform/default.htm.

dbWeb

dbWeb is designed to provide an interface between a web server and any ODBC database available to the Windows NT server system. Its strength is in creating query-by-example forms with which a user creates a database query, and then returning a result that uses a template you can modify. You can create an entire database interface web with no HTML coding. You can also modify the results pages to meet your own design guidelines by creating templates in HTML with special tags to indicate where the returned data should go. dbWeb is an executable (for Intel). The main program runs as a service, and it requires ODBC (which is supplied with the system). dbWeb is a commercial program, listing for $495, but a time-out version is available for free online.

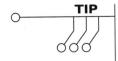

TIP

dbWeb's location on the Web is http://www.aspectse.com/.

Cold Fusion

Cold Fusion merges ODBC database functionality and web inter-faces. It allows fast creation of basic database interfaces, and with more time can offer very sophisticated query front ends. It also enables the creation of completely database-based web sites, as evidenced by the Allaire web at the location shown below. While Cold Fusion does require some HTML coding, it's a very powerful tool, and the additional syntax for HTML is quite straightforward. Cold Fusion is an executable (for Intel). It's a commercial product, with a cost of $495, but a time-out version is available for free, and is included in the cfusion directory on the Companion CD-ROM. The documentation is HTML-based.

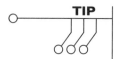

TIP

Cold Fusion's Web location is http://www.allaire.com/, which will bounce you to a database URL such as http://www.allaire.com/ cgi-shl/dbml.exe?template=/allaire/index.dbm.

Moving On

Now that you've read this chapter, you should have a basic knowledge of HTML forms, which you can use to write pages that are both attractive and interactive. By now you should be familiar with the basic structure of a form, understand the various HTML interactive elements, and know a little bit about the kinds of programs that are available, including Cold Fusion, dbWeb, and CGI PerForm, to help you process the data collected by your forms with little or no programming effort.

If you're not a programmer, the information in this chapter may be all you need to know about forms, but if you have a little programming experience (or programming aspirations), Chapter 10, "CGI & DLLs: Programming Your Server," shows you how to write CGI programs that process forms results, provide gateways to other Internet services, and generate pages dynamically. It is these skills that separate the everyday Webmaster from the true Web wizard.

10

CGI & DLLs: Programming Your Server

You can make your pages somewhat interactive by using form handlers like dbWeb or Cold Fusion, as discussed in the previous chapter, but if you want to create complex effects, you'll have to write the program yourself. Fortunately, server developers have crafted some simple ways to write programs that process forms and generate documents on the fly.

As explained in Chapter 9, "Simple Forms," CGI stands for Common Gateway Interface; it defines a method for the HTTP server and an outside program to share information. When the server receives a request from a client to run a gateway program (often called a CGI script), it summarizes the pertinent information about the request in a standard set of environment variables. The script then examines these environment variables in order to find the information it needs to respond to the request. In addition, CGI standardizes responses for the CGI script to give the server information that it needs, such as the MIME type of the script's output. CGI scripts are used for any task that requires a dynamic response from the server. The main purpose of CGI is to let you write programs that talk to web browsers. Using CGI, you can write programs that do the following:

- Dynamically create new web pages on the fly.
- Access databases.
- Process HTML forms input.
- Bridge the gap between the Web and other Internet services.

Most of the major server vendors are now also defining DLL-based APIs to speed up the process of responding to CGI-style requests, and to allow you to extend the functionality of web servers as you see fit. (Note that the general term "CGI program" is often used to refer to CGI-style programs created using these server APIs as well.) As flexible and powerful as CGI is, APIs allow even greater power and control over the operation of a web site, and while there's no universal API as there is a universal CGI interface, API-based programming will likely become the dominant way to provide extended services at many high-volume web sites.

In this chapter, we'll take a look at programming using standard CGI as well as DLL-based server APIs. We'll work through several examples of standard CGI scripts that accomplish typical tasks, including implementing a Web Finger gateway, processing the data from a simple form, and dynamically generating HTML pages. We'll also look at three popular server APIs (including the Alibaba API), and examine how a simple example application would be implemented with each.

Programming With CGI

The CGI standard is very simple. Any programming language that can access command-prompt environment variables can use it. CGI programs are most commonly written in C, C++, perl, and command-shell scripts.

Interpreted languages, like perl, have several advantages for writing CGI programs. Many CGI programming tasks require a lot of string handling, and most interpreted languages have powerful built-in functions for manipulating text. In addition, most interpreted languages let you write code without compiling, which saves time.

Of course, there are also disadvantages to writing CGI programs in interpreted languages. Although it's convenient to use the dynamic interpretation features of these languages, they can also be a security hazard if you aren't careful. In addition, programs written in scripting languages can run slower than those written in a compiled language like C if the scripts are large, which can be a significant problem if the CGI program is called frequently.

WinCGI

WinCGI is a variation of the standard CGI that allows servers that run as applications to utilize the services of Windows application programs—including Visual Basic programs. With this interface, a WinCGI-based program reads the information from a disk file instead of environment variables and the standard input, and writes the resulting data back to a file instead of standard output. The advantage of WinCGI is that you can use the advanced services of Visual Basic, such as ODBC support and MAPI functions.

Although there are many things you can do with perl and other interpreted-language scripts, you may be more familiar with a compiled language. Don't let that stop you from writing CGI programs. With standard CGI, the only requirement on the programming language is that it be able to use environment variables, read standard in, and write standard out. For Windows NT, this means a console application: Windows apps, services, and DLLs will not work as standard CGI programs. (For certain database applications, you may want to have a program that is running all the time to keep database connections open and speed database queries. You could program a service application under NT, and open shared memory areas or pipes that a console application—the program called by CGI—could read from and write to.)

In any case, since you can write CGI programs in almost any language for which you have a compiler or interpreter, you should use the language you're comfortable with. We like perl and C/C++; both are fairly common and very powerful. The examples in the first part of this chapter are written in perl. We've tried to avoid the more esoteric features of the language, so anyone with programming experience can understand the examples.

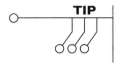

TIP

If you don't know perl but would like to learn it, we recommend Programming perl, *by Larry Wall and Randal L. Schwartz.*

Following are two important points to remember when writing CGI programs:

- You write any data or text for the client to the standard output.

- Any output must be preceded with a Content-type line, defining its MIME type, followed by a blank line.

Both of these rules are very important. They are the reason that generating new pages with CGI scripts is so easy. You simply write any data you want the client to receive to the standard output, preceded by its MIME type, and the server does the rest! Don't forget the Content-type and the blank line though: the server returns an error when it can't find them.

The <ISINDEX> Tag

Some of the most common applications for CGI programs are to bridge the gap between the web and databases, mail systems, search engines, and a myriad of legacy systems. Using CGI as the interface allows the web servers to provide access to information and services without reinventing the service programs. HTML and the CGI standard have come together to make basic searching as simple as possible with the <ISINDEX> tag. When a browser notes the <ISINDEX> tag within an HTML document, it marks the document as a searchable index and allows the user to enter terms for which to search. When the user's reply is submitted, the client retrieves the same URL as the document that included the <ISINDEX> tag, adding the user's search terms as follows:

```
http://www.vpizza.com/cgi-bin/isindex.bat?arg1+arg2+arg3
```

The words that the user entered in the search box follow the question mark; the browser replaces spaces with the plus sign. Furthermore, nonalphanumeric characters are specially encoded.

Although this encoding is relatively easy to undo in perl, it's very difficult to do with the NT command shell. To make <ISINDEX> scripts easier to develop, the server converts the information received from a client's <ISINDEX> query into command-line arguments for the CGI script; each word of the input is a different argument. For example, this silly little command-prompt script simply echoes the terms that the user enters:

```
echo off
echo Content-type: text/plain
echo.
echo %1 %2 %3 %4 %5 %6 %7 %8
```

The variables %1, %2, %3, and so on, represent the information passed to the script as command line parameters.

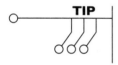

TIP

If a CGI script generates any output at all, other than a CGI header, the Content-type header must be the very first line it sends.

As you can see, this feature makes <ISINDEX> scripts fairly simple and to the point; to create more complex applications, most people use HTML forms. Because they're simple, <ISINDEX> scripts are often written quickly and somewhat carelessly. You should remember that all CGI scripts have the potential to be a security hazard and always follow these guidelines when writing your <ISINDEX> scripts:

- Check whether the script is being run with command-line arguments. If it is, it should print out searching instructions, including the <ISINDEX> tag.

- Check the validity of the arguments before executing the action (this is important if you're using an interpreted language like perl or a shell script, in which some characters have a special meaning to the interpreter).

🖎 Perform the proper action, and return the results, properly preceded by a Content-type header.

Listing 10-1 shows a CGI script that uses <ISINDEX> to provide a gateway to the Finger service, which lets you obtain information about a user on any host that supports it. You should probably check that the Finger command runs properly from the command prompt before trying out this script. Also, since we're working with NT, you must create a command or batch file that invokes the perl script, as follows:

```
perl finger.pl %1 %2 %3
```

Call this file something useful, like finger.bat. Now here's the perl script itself:

Listing 10-1: finger.pl, a WWW finger gateway using the <ISINDEX> tag.

```
#
# finger.pl An <ISINDEX> gateway to the finger service
#

$finger='finger';

if ( $#ARGV < 0 ) {
   &print_header("Finger2Web Gateway");
   &print_form;
   &print_footer;
   exit;
}
elsif ( $#ARGV > 0 ) {
   &print_header("Finger2Web Error");
   &print_form;
   print "The Finger Gateway takes only a single argument.";
   print "Please try again.\n";
   &print_footer;
   exit;
}
else {
   $user = $ARGV[0];
   if (! &safety_check($user)) {
```

```perl
    &print_header("Finger2Web Error");
    &print_form;
    print "You've submitted a request with an illegal
character.";
    print "Please try again.\n";
    &print_footer;
    exit;
  }
  unless(open(FINGDATA,"$finger $user|")) {
    &print_header("Finger2Web Error");
    &print_form;
    print "Fatal Error executing the finger command.\n";
    &print_footer;
    exit;
  }
  &print_header("Finger2Web Results for $user");
  &print_form;
  print "<PRE>\n";
  while (<FINGDATA>) {
    print $_;
  }
  print "</PRE>\n";
  close(FINGDATA);
  &printfooter;
}


####################
####################
##
## SUB-ROUTINES
##

# make sure that argument is made up of only "safe" characters.
sub safety_check {
  local($tocheck) = @_;
  ($tocheck =~ /^[a-zA-Z0-9_+\-%@\t ]+$/)
}
```

```
# print HTML header data. Takes 1 argument, which is printed
# as both the title and a level-1 header.
sub print_header {
   local($title) = @_;
   print "Content-type: text/html\n\n";
   print "<HTML>\n";
   print "<HEAD>\n";
   print "<TITLE>$title</TITLE>\n";
   print "</HEAD>\n";
   print "<BODY>\n";
   print "<H1>$title</H1>\n";
}

# finish off the HTML page.
sub print_footer {
   print "</BODY>\n";
   print "</HTML>\n";
}

# print ISINDEX and search instructions
sub print_form {
   print "<ISINDEX>\n";
   print "<P>This is a finger to Web gateway. Enter the name
of a user\n";
   print "for whom you need information, in the form: ";
   print "<VAR>user@hostname</VAR>";
   print "<HR>\n";
}
```

The finger.pl script performs all the essential actions of an
<ISINDEX> CGI script. The main code of the program is a block of
"if" statements, which check the number of arguments that the
program has received. If no argument is found, the gateway prints
the <ISINDEX> tag and the search instructions, as shown in
Figure 10-1, while more than one argument causes the gateway to
print an error message.

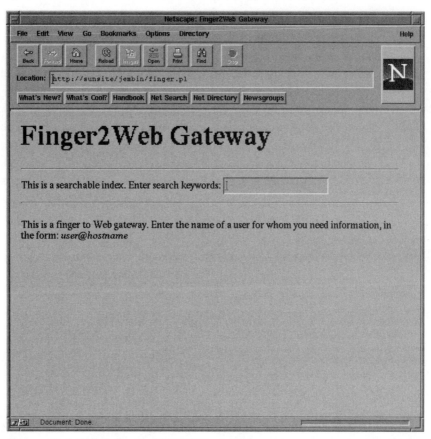

Figure 10-1: *The finger.pl <ISINDEX> input page.*

If the program receives only a single argument, the gateway makes sure that the argument is safe to interpret. In this case, "safe" means that it contains no characters that have a special significance to the perl interpreter, which is an important security safeguard. Without it, a malicious user might be able to fool the CGI script into violating system security. You should get in the habit of always checking user-supplied input for dangerous characters.

After the script has checked the supplied input, it opens a pipe to the Finger command and prints the output between the <PRE> tags. A more advanced program might try to parse the output and add more interesting HTML markup, but since different Finger servers have extremely varying output, this would be difficult to implement. After the script has finished with its output, it closes the pipe and sends the closing <BODY> and <HTML> tags.

This Finger gateway shows what's required to write a simple <ISINDEX> script. Like all such scripts, this one checks its arguments in order to find how it's being called. The argument can be supplied in two ways. You can link the URL of the gateway to the document and allow the user to use the search input box, as follows:

```
We offer a <A HREF="/cgi-bin/finger.bat">finger gateway</A>
```

You can also directly add the argument to the URL in a hyperlink:

```
Want to see if I'm online?
<a HREF="/cgi-bin/finger.bat?jem@sunsite.unc.edu">
Finger me</a>
```

Each time it returns a result or an error message, the gateway reprints the <ISINDEX> tag and the search instructions, separated from the rest of the text with a horizontal rule. This makes it easy for a user to check multiple addresses without needing to use the Back button on the browser to return to the search page.

Handling HTML Forms

In Chapter 9, "Simple Forms," you learned how to use the <FORM> tag to create interactive areas in your HTML pages. Although you can use prewritten CGI programs to process the results, they are limited by their designers to the functions originally intended. You gain a lot of flexibility by "rolling your own" CGI scripts to process the forms that you create.

GET vs. POST

A browser can pass data from an HTML form to the server in two ways, GET and POST, which you specify with the METHOD attribute of the <FORM> tag, as follows:

```
<HTML>
<HEAD>
<TITLE>Sample Guestbook</TITLE>
</HEAD>
<BODY>
<H1>Sample Guestbook</H1>
<FORM ACTION="/cgi-bin/guest.bat" METHOD=POST>
Full name:
<INPUT TYPE=text SIZE=30 NAME="fullname"><BR>
E-mail address:
<INPUT TYPE=text SIZE=20 NAME="e-mail"><BR>
<P>
Comments:<BR>
<TEXTAREA COLS=60 ROWS=15 NAME="comments">
</TEXTAREA>
<BR>
<INPUT TYPE=submit VALUE="Sign Guestbook">
</FORM>
<HR>
You can see <A HREF="/guests/guestbook.txt">
what other people have written</A>
</BODY>
</HTML>
```

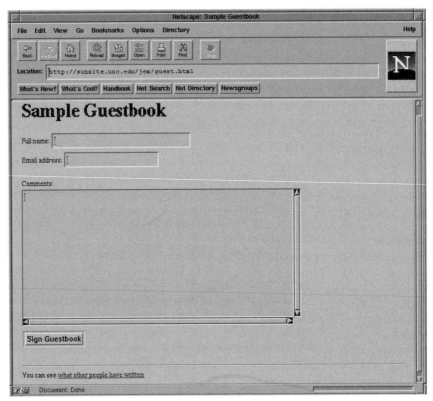

Figure 10-2: *A sample guestbook form.*

This sample guestbook form provides three different areas for user input; each of these areas contains a variable (given by the NAME attribute) to which the browser assigns whatever the user enters. If the user leaves a widget blank and the widget has no associated default, the browser doesn't bother to transmit that widget's NAME. CGI programs that process forms are responsible for making sure that the user has completed all the required parts of the form; there's no way to tell the client which bits must be filled out.

Browsers would invoke this guestbook with the POST method. When a browser submits form data with this method, it transmits the data in a way that's similar to that which the server uses to send HTML and other objects to clients. You could change this form to use the GET method by modifying the METHOD element of the <FORM> tag. When form data is submitted with the GET method, the client attaches it to the end of the URL that is named by the ACTION element; the encoded information (see the next section, "URL Encoding") is separated from the name of the CGI script by a question mark. This is identical to the browser's method for sending data from an <ISINDEX> query; in fact, both of these types of scripts use the HTTP GET method (see Chapter 2, "The Basic Pieces").

Deciding which method to use with your form and program can seem somewhat arbitrary. Some web developers consider any use of the GET method a bad idea. They say that attaching dynamic information to the end of the URL is a distortion of the URL's purpose because the writers of the standard had intended the URL to be a unique *locator* for network resources. In addition, this feature is a liability when dealing with forms that hold information that the user might not want other people to see. Most browsers boldly display the current URL at the top of the window, and few people like having private information broadcast across the office.

Although these objections may be valid, we believe that the GET method does have its place. By using this method, you allow users to store their responses to commonly used forms on the hotlist, or bookmark file. The GET method is particularly useful for queries in databases that change regularly, for example.

The POST method, on the other hand, is preferred when creating forms that users rarely complete or always send with different data. The POST method is more efficient and more reliable than the GET method because different operating systems have different limits on the maximum amount of data that can be passed that way. For example, forms that contain <TEXTAREA> boxes, which allow users to enter large amounts of text, should always use the POST method.

Whether you use the GET method or the POST method makes little difference in the amount of work that you need to do to write your script. That's one of the appealing features of the CGI standard—simplicity. The interface between the script and the server that runs it is unobtrusive; usually only a few lines of code are required in order to access the submitted data or to gather information about the server that is running the script (see "CGI Environment Variables," later in this chapter, for details).

Since it's so easy to provide support for both methods, many scripts support both by changing their behavior depending on the value of the REQUEST_METHOD variable (see "Processing the Form Data," later in this chapter). Although supporting both methods is an excellent way to increase the flexibility of your program (especially if you're going to make the program publicly available), you should keep in mind the preceding guidelines about when each method is most appropriate.

URL Encoding

Although browsers transmit the data to the server differently depending on the method the form specifies, they encode that data in the same way, regardless of whether they're using GET or POST. The client gathers the user's input from all the widgets and packages it with its corresponding NAME; variables are separated by ampersands. Data from the form in Figure 10-2 might be encoded as follows:

```
fullname=Fred+Mbogo&e-mail=mbogof@zappa.shoop.com&
comments=hi+y%27all
```

In this example, you see the three HTML variable names in the form. An equals sign separates each one from its proper value.

Since the GET method adds form data to the end of the URL, the form information must be specially coded so as not to conflict with the URL standard. In the URL standard, several characters (such as the ampersand) are reserved; they have a special meaning to clients and servers. Other characters are simply illegal. The following list describes the characters that can't be used:

- = ; / # ? : (reserved characters that have special meanings in a URL)

- Any nonprintable ASCII control character

- The space character

Browsers replace the space character with a plus sign and replace reserved and control characters with a percent sign followed by their ASCII code in hexadecimal. Browsers also often encode characters that have special meanings, either in the URL or to most interpreted languages, in this hexadecimal format. For this reason, the apostrophe in the previous example, "hi y'all," is replaced by the ASCII hexadecimal code of %27.

Although most browsers properly encode these special characters, your program shouldn't count on it. Not only may a buggy browser fail to change them to their hexadecimal equivalents, malevolent crackers may directly send improperly encoded data to your script hoping to trick it into performing a security-breaking action. To ensure the robustness of your program and the integrity of your system, always make sure that any user-provided data that will be interpreted by a shell is free of any characters with special meaning to the shell.

Processing the Form Data

When an HTML form uses the POST method, the server sends the data that it receives from the client to the handling CGI script on its standard input. It also sets the REQUEST_METHOD environment variable to POST. Your script should check this variable to ensure that it's receiving POST data; it can then read this data almost as if it were being piped to the script from the command line:

```
type form-data | cgi-script
```

A major difference between writing a normal command-line utility that reads data from the standard input and a CGI script for use with the POST method is that the HTTP server sends no signal that it has finished transmitting data. Usually, when a utility has finished reading all the available data from the standard input, it receives a special end-of-file value; CGI programs never receive this notification. Instead, the HTTP server sets the CONTENT_LENGTH environmental variable, which gives the amount of input the script should read in bytes. When your script has read that amount of data, it should stop; the results of further reads are not defined by the CGI specification and therefore may vary from server to server.

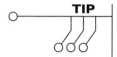

TIP

A CGI script that's written to be used with the GET method works essentially in the same way as a POST-based script except for the way that the server passes the data. Instead of sending browser-submitted data to the standard input of the script, the server encodes this data in the environment variable QUERY_STRING, using the conventions described in the "URL Encoding," earlier in this chapter. An additional difference is that the CGI variable REQUEST_METHOD is defined as GET rather than POST.

Like the data that the server sends to the client, this information that the client transmits with the POST method has a MIME type. Currently, only one possible MIME type is defined for client-transmitted data: application/x-www-form-urlencoded, which defines data from an HTML form. The server records the MIME type of the client-sent data in the CONTENT_TYPE environment variable. Although there's currently only a single type for data from an HTTP POST, this may change in the future, so you should check the value of this variable in order to make sure that your scripts will work in the future.

After you've finished checking that the REQUEST_METHOD and CONTENT_TYPE variables have the expected values and you've read the number of bytes indicated by CONTENT_LENGTH from the standard input, you're ready to process the actual data from the form. Processing the data requires that you undo the URL encoding previously described, which includes four steps:

1. Break up the pairs of HTML form variables and their values, which are separated by ampersands.

2. Separate each HTML form variable from its value; the variables and their values are linked by equal signs.

3. Convert all hex sequences (escaped by a percent sign) in each of the variables and the values to their ASCII equivalents.

4. Replace all plus signs in each of the variables and values with spaces.

After you've gone through these steps in order and extracted the HTML variables and values in their original form, you can do whatever you like with them. The output of a CGI script always follows the same guidelines; you must precede data with a Content-type header, specifying the MIME type, and a blank line.

Debugging Perl Scripts

One of the most common questions CGI novices ask is, "How do I debug my perl script?" The answer, at least part of it, is simple—fake it. You need to define (with the SET command) all the CGI environment variables that your script is looking for; you must also provide data on the standard input for scripts that use the POST method. An easy way to do this is to write a simple shell script that defines the proper environment variables and echoes your script's input; you can run this script before using your debugger. A more complex issue is how to trace program functions during the execution of the program. Unfortunately, there are no tools available to debug perl scripts in the same way you can visually debug C or C++ code. This is because perl was designed for fast and convenient text processing and string parsing, but not for large-scale programming. If you find your perl program is getting just too big to debug with debugging print statements, you might consider switching to a compiled language.

Listing 10-2 is a simple CGI script that processes the POSTed data from the sample guestbook form in Figure 10-2. It appends the user-supplied name, e-mail address, and comments to a text file. When it's finished, it prints a simple but friendly message expressing its thanks. Again, you must create a command or batch file that invokes the perl script, as follows:

```
perl guest.pl
```

Name this file guest.bat. This will be the script first called by the form in Figure 10-2. This short script will in turn call the longer perl script, below.

Listing 10-2: guest.pl, a CGI script to process the results of the simple guestbook form.

```perl
#
# guest.pl: A cgi script to handle user input from
# guestbook.html
#

# The server's document root
$root = 'D:/alibaba/docs';

# path, relative to $root, to the guestbook file
$guestbook = '/guests/guestbook.txt';

# email address of the server's administrator
$webmaster = 'webmaster@www.shoop.org';

# copy the values of these environment variables
$method = $ENV{"REQUEST_METHOD"};
$type = $ENV{"CONTENT_TYPE"};

# make sure the script was called with the POST
# method and the HTML form's MIME-type
if ($method ne "POST" ||  →
    $type ne "application/x-www-form-urlencoded") {
  &print_header("Guestbook Method Error");
  print "Guestbook data must come from a form and ";

  print " be invoked with\n";
  print "the POST method.\n";
  &print_footer;
  exit;
}

# read form data from standard input
%input_values = &break_input;

# convert from the strange URL syntax to normal ascii
# and translate non-NT ) line
# endings to NT convention
$fullname = &normalize_query($input_values{"fullname"});
$email = &normalize_query($input_values{"email"});
$comments = &ntify_eols(&normalize_query  →
  ($input_values {"comments"}));
```

```perl
# you must log at least your name or your email address
if ($name eq '' && $email eq '') {
  &print_header("Guestbook Input Error");
  print "You must give either your full name or ";an
  print "an email address\nto sign the guestbook.\n";
  &print_footer;
  exit;
}

&log_entry("$root/$guestbook", $fullname, →
   $email, $comments);

&print_header("Thanks!");
print "Thanks for your comments...\n";
&print_footer;

####################
####################
##
## SUB-ROUTINES
##

# read CONTENT_LENGTH bytes from standard input and
# decode the URL format input, breaking it into an
# associative array of HTML variable names and their
# values.
sub break_input {
  local ($i);
  read(STDIN, $input, $ENV{'CONTENT_LENGTH'});
  @form_names = split('&', $input);
  foreach $i (@form_names) {
    ($html_name, $html_value) = split('=', $i);
    $input_values{$html_name} = $html_value;
  }
  return %input_values;
}

# given a title, print the return header
sub print_header {
 local($title) = @_;
 print "Content-type: text/html\n\n";
  print "<HTML>\n";
  print "<HEAD>\n";
```

```perl
  print "<TITLE>$title</TITLE>\n";
  print "</HEAD>\n";
  print "<BODY>\n";
  print "<H1>$title</H1>\n";
}

# finish off the HTML page.
sub print_footer {
  print "</BODY>\n";
  print "</HTML>\n";
}

# URL syntax converts most non-alphanumeric characters
# into a percentage sign, followed by
# the character's value in hexadecimal.
# This function undoes this weirdness.
sub normalize_query {
  local($value) = @_;
  $value =~ tr/+/ /;
  $value =~ s/%([a-fA-F0-9] →
    [a-fA-F0-9])/pack("C",hex($1))/eg;
  return $value;
}

# clients don't translate the end-of-line from TEXTAREA
# widgets to the server's convention. this function
#  does it for this program.
sub ntify_eols {
  local($string) = @_;
  $string =~ tr/\n/\n\r/;
  $string =~ tr/\r/\n\r/;
  return $string;
}

# given a filename and user data,
# this function logs it.
sub log_entry {
  local($log, $fullname, $email, $comments) = @_;
  unless (open(BOOK, ">>$log")) {
    &print_header("Guestbook Open Error");
    print "Failed to open $guestbook. →
        Please inform $webmaster\n";
    &print_footer;
  }
```

```
    print BOOK "Entry by: $fullname\n";
    print BOOK "E-mail address: $email\n\n";
    print BOOK "$comments\n\n";
    print BOOK "---------------------------- →
    -----------------------------\n";
    close BOOK;
}
```

Although we've made the program and its comments mostly self-explanatory, you should note the following:

- Look at the subroutines break_input and normalize_query. See how little code it requires to do this sort of complex text processing in perl? That's why we like to write as many ad hoc CGI scripts as possible in perl. Writing this sort of script can be more difficult in languages that are not designed to do this kind of string parsing.

- The subroutine ntify_eols translates the end-of-line characters inside the input from the <TEXTAREA> box to the NT convention (a newline followed by a carriage return). Since browsers send text using the characters appropriate to their operating systems (UNIX-compatible systems use only a newline, and the Mac operating system uses only a carriage return, for example), you should always translate before you write the input to a file.

- The script checks to make sure that essential HTML variables (such as *fullname* or *email*) are present. It's always the responsibility of the CGI script to verify that the user has correctly filled in the form.

- Unlike Listing 10-1, the <ISINDEX> Finger gateway example earlier in this chapter, this form-processing script doesn't bother to check for illegal characters in the input. Since the script never employs the user input in a way that could possibly interpret the input as a command, it's not necessary to check for illegal characters.

Except for the previous few points, this is a simple script for a simple form; it merely processes the data that the browser sends and acknowledges it. More complex scripts write the form itself, without relying on a prewritten page.

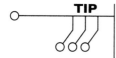

TIP

The concept of combining control logic and HTML code into a single piece of perl code, while convenient for fast prototyping and ad hoc work, can be problematic when working with large-scale CGI and server extensions, particularly when code must be maintained by someone other than the original programmer. This is why many large-scale server extensions, particularly those at sites that have a high hit rate, are written in a real programming language like C or C++, and make every effort to separate control logic and HTML code into different spaces.

Generating Pages Dynamically

CGI can be used for much more than writing forms and handlers. You can also use CGI programs to generate new HTML pages on the fly, which is an incredibly useful and powerful capability. With dynamic documents, you can alter the appearance, interface, and features of your web pages as you desire. You can also use them to extend the functionality of the web, adding features that are difficult or impossible to get from traditional media. The main reasons to create a document dynamically instead of by hand are as follows:

* To present the current state of some changing resource.

* To save you the trouble of writing pages that would be difficult, annoying, or impossible to write by hand.

* To present information that has been customized in some way for a particular user or group of users.

The task might be as simple as appending the current date and time to a page, or it could be as complex as constructing a personal newspaper from the hundreds of megabytes in a day's Usenet news.

Of course, the price you pay for this flexibility is the overhead of running the CGI program every time someone retrieves the page. (If you elect to use a server API interface, however, as described later in this chapter, you can avoid some of the overhead involved in the standard CGI interface.) Dynamically created documents have a further disadvantage in that they can't be cached (the server automatically marks them as uncacheable). This problem will become more important as more organizations direct all their web requests through a locally caching server to reduce outside traffic.

Despite these disadvantages, using CGI programs (or API-based server extensions) in this way is the best—or only—solution to many of the problems you encounter in maintaining a large, complex web site. One such problem is the major differences from user to user in client software, available bandwidth, and preferred data formats. Although the HTTP protocol contains some support for negotiating such things, and HTTP-NG (see Chapter 13, "Future Directions") has even more, few WWW clients and servers take real advantage of it.

From WWW to SQL

More and more companies and organizations wish to gateway their traditional MIS departments and databases to the Web. For this reason, CGI interfaces to SQL-based relational databases have become increasingly important. Fortunately for the NT-based server programmer, the task is not at all difficult. In Chapter 9, we discussed two commercial programs, dbWeb and Cold Fusion, that remove almost all the effort in creating database interfaces to your NT-based web server. With the functions available in Microsoft MFC and the ODBC SDK, you can also write your own programs that access databases with ODBC. Once you're using ODBC, you can access almost every major database available on all major operating systems.

The example CGI perl script included in this section, condit.pl, helps solve the problems associated with matching returned HTML with the capabilities of the user's browser and the user's preferences by allowing you to do the following:

* Embed one or more Boolean flags in a URL.

* Test for these flags in a simple conditional macro language.

You can use condit.pl to maintain a single set of HTML pages that have different sets of features. You could use this ability to implement a pre-home page (discussed in Chapter 12, "Fitting In: Joining the Virtual Community"), which allows users to choose the type of access—for example, graphics only, graphics with text, or text only—that is most appropriate for the abilities of their clients and the speeds of their Internet connections. In this pre-home page, you could create a list of links offering the same home page in many different ways, as illustrated in the following markup:

```
Choose which homepage:
<UL>
<LI>Graphical Interface Only (imagemap)
   <OL>
   <LI><A HREF="/cgi-bin/condit.bat/NOTEXT/home.html"> →
   GIF graphics</A>
   <LI><A HREF="/cgi-bin/condit.bat/USEJPEG:::NOTEXT/ →
home.html">
   JPEG graphics</A>
   </OL>
<LI>Graphical Interface with text
   <OL>
   <LI><A HREF="/cgi-bin/condit.bat/home.html">GIF graphics
</A>
   <LI><A HREF="/cgi-bin/condit.bat/USEJPEG/home.html"> →
   JPEG graphics</A>
   </OL>
<LI><A HREF="/cgi-bin/condit.bat/NOGRAPHICS/home.html"> →
Text-only Interface</A>
</UL>
```

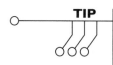

TIP

If a slash follows the name of a CGI script in a requested URL, the HTTP server puts everything between this slash and the beginning of the query string into the PATH_INFO CGI environment variable.

When a user activates one of the hyperlinks in this markup, the server runs condit.bat, which in turn starts condit.pl, stuffing all the URL information after /cgi-bin/condit.bat into the PATH_INFO environment variable. condit.pl interprets the PATH_INFO variable as a list of option flags, followed by a relative URL. This relative URL points to an HTML document to which the options should be applied (home.html, in the example). The condit.pl script opens this document and scans it for commands within the HTML comment tag, <!-- >. Each condit.pl command tests for the presence of one or more flags and includes a section of text if the command and its flags evaluate as true. The condit.pl commands and their functions are shown in Table 10-1.

Command	Description
INCLUDE-IF	Include this section if all flags match.
INCLUDE-IF-ANY	Include this section if any flags match.
INCLUDE-IF-NOT	Include this section if no flags match.
INCLUDE-IF-NOT-ALL	Include this section if not all flags match.

Table 10-1: *Commands understood by condit.pl.*

Each command to condit.pl, followed by a comma-separated list of flags to test, must be on a line by itself in the HTML document. The markup for the example home.html home page might look similar to the following:

```
<HEAD>
<TITLE>The SHOOP Home Page</TITLE>
</HEAD>
<BODY>
<!-- INCLUDE-IF-NOT NOGRAPHICS
 <!-- INCLUDE-IF USEJPEG
 <A HREF="/cgi-bin/imagemap/homemap"><IMG     SRC="graphics/
home-map.jpg ISMAP>
 </A>
 -->
<!-- INCLUDE-IF-NOT USEJPEG
```

```
      <A HREF="/cgi-bin/imagemap/homemap"><IMG   SRC="graphics/
      home-map.gif ISMAP>
      </A>
      -->
   -->
<!-- INCLUDE-IF-NOT NOTEXT
   <OL>
   <LI>We have lots of <A HREF="goodstuff/first.html">good
stuff</a>.
   <LI>Most people find this <A HREF="boringstuff/first.html→
   "> boring</a>.
   <LI>This is all very <A HREF="importantstuff/first.html→
   ">important</a>.
   </OL>
-->
</BODY>
```

Following is what the condit.bat file should look like:

```
perl condit.pl
```

And here's the condit.pl script itself:

Listing 10-3: condit.pl, a CGI script that allows conditional inclusion of markup code.

```
#
# condit.pl: A cgi script to handle
# conditional includes
# Written for The Web Server Book by:
# Simon E Spero (ses@eit.com)
#

# root of document space
$root="D:/alibaba/docs";


# regular expression identifying html files
$html = '\.html$|\.htm$|/$';

# the default page to load, if the URL
# represents a directory
$default = "index.html";

# Get the path info and split off the flags
$path_info = $ENV{"PATH_INFO"};
```

```perl
($slash,$flags_given,$rest) = split('/',$path_info,3);

# set $key{$flag} to true for each flag
for (split(/:::/,$flags_given)) { #
  $key{$_} = 1;
}


# Check to see if the request is for an html file
unless($rest =~ /$html/) {
  # If it isn't, let the system handle
  # the request directly
  print "Location: /$rest\n\n";
}


# Otherwise, we need to try and open it.
# Let's find the filename
else {
  $filename = "$root/$rest\n";
  if($filename =~ /\/$/) {
    $filename .= $default;
  }

  # and try and open it
  unless(open(INPUT,"$filename")) {
    # couldn't open the file - let the system
    # have a go.
    print "Location: /$rest\n\n";
    exit;
  }


  &print_header;

  #
  # $print_it will be used to enable and disable
  # printing. At first,
  # we'll want to print anything until we
  # get told otherwise
  # we'll also be keeping a stack of
  # old print_it's so we can nest
  # conditional includes.
```

```perl
$print_it = 1;
@print_it_stack = ();

# now, for each line in the file
while(<INPUT>) {

  #is this a command for us?
  if( /^\s*<!--\s*INCLUDE-IF/) {
    #yes it is -
    # if we're printing at the moment, we
    #need to parse it - otherwise,
    # we'll just push the
    #current state onto the stack to make sure we
    #keep track of nesting
    if($print_it) {
      # ok, we do have to check it
      # -let's parse the
      # request into command and requirements
      ($command,$requirements) =
        /^\s*<!--\s*(INCLUDE-IF →
          [^\s]*)\s*(.*)$/;

      # We'll test the requirements
      # as requested.
      # &satisfy_all is true if
      # all requirements match
      # &satisfy_any is true if
      # any requirements match

      if($command eq "INCLUDE-IF") {
        $should_include=&satisfy_all ($requirements);
      }
      elsif ($command eq "INCLUDE-IF-ANY") {
        $should_include =&satisfy_any ($requirements);
      }
      elsif ($command eq "INCLUDE-IF-NOT") {
        $should_include =!&satisfy_any ($requirements);
      }
```

```
                    elsif ($command eq  →
                       "INCLUDE-IF-NOT-ALL"){
                       $should_include =!&satisfy_all ($requirements);
                    }
                 }
                 # let's save the current value of print_it
                 # and set print_it to its new value.
                 # If we're not printing now, this won't
                 # start us printing; we're just
                 # balancing brackets

                 push(@print_it_stack,$print_it);
                 $print_it = $print_it && $should_include;
              }
              elsif (/^\s*-->\s*$/) {
                 #this wasn't a command -
                 # but it was the end of a
                 #conditional. we'll restore print_it
                 # from the stack
                 $print_it = pop(@print_it_stack);
              }
              else {
                 # It's a real line -
                 # if print_it is set, let's, er, print it
                 print $_ if $print_it;
              }
           }
       }
   }



   ####################
   ####################
   ##
   ## SUB-ROUTINES
   ##

   # print the MIME type, and # add a comment saying how
   # this document was created
   sub print_header {
      print "Content-type: text/html\n\n";
      print "<!-- This file generated by condit.pl\n";
      print " original source was /$rest\n";
```

```
    print " keys used were ",join →
      (", ", keys(%key)),"  -->\n\n";
}

# given a comma-separated list of requirements, return
# true if all exists in %key
sub satisfy_all {
  local ($requirements) = @_;
  local ($all_match);
  $all_match = 1;
  for $i (split(/,\s*/,$requirements)) {
    unless($key{$i}) {
      $all_match = 0;
    }
  }
  return $all_match;
}


# given a comma-separated list of requirements, return
# true if any exists in %key
sub satisfy_any {
  local ($requirements) = @_;
  for $i (split(/,\s*/,$requirements)) {
    if($key{$i}) {
      return 1;
    }
  }
  return 0;
}
```

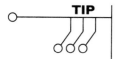

TIP

While condit.pl is a good example of a CGI script that dynamically writes HTML, it also demonstrates another feature of CGI that we haven't yet discussed: CGI redirection. As you can see from the comments in the script, if the relative URL passed to condit.pl doesn't seem to point to an HTML document, the script asks the client to retrieve the URL directly. It sends the client to that document with an HTTP redirect, which you can create in CGI scripts by printing the string "Location:" followed by a URL and a blank line.

You should note that clients place the URL for condit.bat before any relative links in the documents that it generates, which has both advantages and disadvantages. Although this automation allows you to easily use the condit.pl macros in the pages beneath the top directory of the hierarchy, it also means that condit.pl is run for every relative link the user follows. To avoid this, use a full URL (including the protocol and hostname) in the hyperlinks.

condit.pl gives you an idea of the power of CGI in generating and modifying documents on the fly. It also illustrates an approach to solving programming problems on the web. By implementing a general solution, you gain a lot of flexibility; not only is condit.pl a good way to maintain a set of pages with different interfaces, but you could use it to take advantage of the new HTML tags that only some browsers support (see Chapter 13, "Future Directions").

Programming With Server APIs

Standard CGI scripts and programs have a significant disadvantage: they always involve a process separate from the server process, and in the case of perl for NT, they are interpreted languages—which makes them slower and more resource-intensive. When you use the CGI interface with a compiled language, you achieve faster program execution, but the server must still spawn a new process to load your executable every time a browser calls the CGI script. Most major server vendors have solved this problem by introducing server APIs, which make it possible for you to create server extensions with DLLs under Windows NT, instead of using standard CGI executable programs or scripts. There are many advantages to this in terms of execution speed, program loading speed, and server scalability. The DLL is preloaded and will execute much faster than standard CGI programs and scripts.

There are several disadvantages to using DLLs, however. First and foremost, the DLL you write becomes part of the server address space. If your DLL crashes, the entire server crashes. You must test your server extensions thoroughly before turning them loose on a live service. Also, since the DLLs are loaded at the time the server starts, you must stop and restart the server in order to change the program, and since NT will lock open DLLs, you must stop the server in order to even replace the DLL file. Programs called as CGI programs do not have this restriction, since when no one is calling them, they're not in use.

Another significant disadvantage is that there is no "universal API" defined for DLLs yet as there is with CGI. Microsoft and Process Software have teamed up to produce a potential de facto standard called ISAPI, and many server manufacturers have stated their intention to support it, including the Alibaba server, Spyglass, and others. A notable exception to this is Netscape, which had already defined an API called NSAPI. The NSAPI will undoubtedly become popular if for no other reason than it is offered by Netscape.

Also, if your web server is running as a service, debugging your DLL can be tricky. Although there are ways around the issues surrounding the debugging of services, if your server can run as an application as well as a service, you should start your debugging of new DLLs with the server running as an application. This greatly simplifies the debugging process if you're using a visual debugging environment like Visual C++. (The DLL programs are trivial to debug with the advanced visual debugging environments available with Windows compilers.)

Finally, writing DLLs is not as easy as writing executables, since under NT, they must be written to be re-entrant: the same DLL code can be active in more than one server request at the same time. This places special constraints on things like global data and data queues.

Even with these disadvantages, DLLs are the best way by far to create server extension programs that can operate at high speeds for web sites that support high volumes of users.

In the next few sections, we'll take a closer look at three server APIs—the ISAPI and NSAPI mentioned above, as well as the Alibaba API. In each section, we'll review the API from a high level, then implement a sample application. The application that we'll implement with each of the three APIs is a very simple program that looks at the name of the browser making a standard GET request (from the HTTP_USER_AGENT variable) and returns a different page to different users based on that information. In the simple case presented here, all we do is change the last letter in the filename before the .HTM suffix from its original letter to a letter that corresponds to the offset of the browser's name in our internal look-up table. For example, the Netscape 2.x browser is the sixth entry in our internal table, so a request of the file testfile.htm would be changed to testfilF.htm. (There are obviously better solutions for a production system, but the point of this chapter is to compare how each API is used for a sample program.)

Using the Alibaba API

The Alibaba API is nothing more than a DLL-based replacement for the CGI interface. Instead of loading and executing your program every time a CGI call is invoked, the Alibaba server preloads the DLL, and then only spawns a thread for each DLL call. Because the API is so similar to the CGI interface, you'll find few new concepts in using the Alibaba API.

The Alibaba server comes with an example DLL that echoes back all the data sent to it by either a POST or a GET request. When you write this kind of extension, your program will do exactly what a CGI program would do, and you'd program the control flow in the same way you would a standard CGI interface program.

API Definition

Every DLL created to be an Alibaba extension must have two common entry points: DLLMain, which is called when the DLL is loaded, unloaded, attached to a thread, or detached from a thread; and AlibabaDLLEntry, which is called by the server whenever your DLL is run. The prototype of AlibabaDLLEntry is as follows:

```
int AlibabaDLLEntry(struct CGIDLLIN *DLLIn,struct CGIDLLOUT
*DLLOut)
```

The structures of information passed to the DLL are shown in Listing 10-4 below. All of the parameters normally found in environment variables are passed to the DLL in the structure called CGIPART.

Listing 10-4: Structures passed to DLLs with the Alibaba API.

```
struct CGIDLLIN {
 struct CGIPART  cgipart; /* CGI information */
 struct ACCEPT   accept;  /* AcceptFields   */
 SYSTEMTIME localtime;
      /* Local Time DLL was called by */
      /* the Server, only useful for */
      /* performance timing          */
 char *PostData;
      /* Filled only when POST is used*/
}; /* end of struct CGIDLLIN */

struct CGIPART {
  char ServerSoftware[DLL_SHORTSTR];
  char ServerName[DLL_SHORTSTR];
  char GatewayInterface[DLL_SHORTSTR];
  char ServerProtocol[DLL_SHORTSTR];
  int  ServerPort;
  char ServerAdmin[DLL_MIDDLESTR];
  char RequestMethod[DLL_MINISTR];
  char PathInfo[DLL_MIDDLESTR];
  char PathTranslated[DLL_LONGSTR];
  char ScriptName[DLL_MIDDLESTR];
  char QueryString[DLL_BIGSTR];
  char RemoteHost[DLL_SHORTSTR];
  char RemoteAddress[DLL_MINISTR];
  char AuthType[DLL_SHORTSTR];
  char RemoteUser[DLL_SHORTSTR];
  char RemoteIdent[DLL_SHORTSTR];
  char HTTP_REFERER[DLL_LONGSTR];
  char HTTP_USER_AGENT[DLL_LONGSTR];
  char ContentType[DLL_SHORTSTR];
  long ContentLength;
};
```

```
struct OneAcceptField {
  char      MimeType[DLL_MIDDLESTR];
  double    Quality;
};

struct ACCEPT {
 struct OneAcceptField  →
        OneAccField[DLL_MAXACCEPTFIELDS];
 char DefaultMimeType[DLL_MIDDLESTR];
 int  MaxAcceptUsed;
};

struct CGIDLLOUT {
  int    WithHeader;   /* TRUE .... Full HTTP Header  */
                       /* is written by DLL           */
                       /* FALSE ... Server sends 200  */
                       /* Message - Content-type by   */
                       /* DLL                         */
  int    DataLength;   /* Length of DataRecord        */
  int    DoFree;       /* If TRUE Server has to free  */
                       /* AnswerData                  */
  char   *AnswerData;  /* Data                        */
}; /* end of struct CGIDLLOUT */
```

Registration of New Extensions

To make a new DLL work with the Alibaba server, open the
Alibaba Administration Tool and flip to the Aliases tab. Select the
DLL alias option. Add a new alias for your DLL by entering the
URL alias you want to use in the Alias box, then entering the fully
specified path name to your DLL in the Value box, including the
name of the DLL itself. Click Add, and then click OK to save the
change. The next time the Alibaba server is started, it will go
through the list of DLL aliases and load all the DLLs in the list.

Creating the Sample Program

Of the three APIs discussed in this chapter, returning different
filenames based on browser ID is hardest to do with the Alibaba
API. This is because the API is a simple CGI replacement, so once
we determine the type of browser, and the name of the file to
return, we must actually return the file in the program, instead of

letting the server do the work for us. Also, since this program is called instead of a CGI script, we need to tell the Alibaba server that it should call the program in the first place. Fortunately, we can do this through the use of aliases. For example, you can tell the server that whenever a URL starts with /CUSTOM, the DLL should be called. So if a browser were to request http://hostname/custom/sample.htm, the server would call up our sample program, which would return the file /samplX.htm. Unfortunately, if there are things such as images embedded in the HTML file, they, too, will be processed through this program, and must be returned with the appropriate MIME type indictor. Listing 10-5 shows the code for the program. This program is fairly complicated, as it is pretty much replacing the functions of the server itself to the point of returning the file to the client. Since the server still views this as a CGI script, the results will still be uncacheable. (This source code, along with the header and makefile for Visual C++ 4.0, is also included on the Companion CD-ROM.)

Listing 10-5: Alibaba API sample.

```c
#include <sys\types.h>
#include <sys\stat.h>
#include <windows.h>
#include <io.h>
#include <stdlib.h>
#include <stdio.h>
#include <string.h>
#include <fcntl.h>
#include <malloc.h>

#include "alidll.h"
int newprocess(void);
int endnewprocess(void);
int AlibabaDLLEntry(struct CGIDLLIN *DLLIn, →
        struct CGIDLLOUT *DLLOut);
int DoCustomResponse(struct CGIDLLIN *DLLIn, →
        struct CGIDLLOUT *DLLOut);
int ReturnFile(struct CGIDLLIN *DLLIn,struct →
        CGIDLLOUT *DLLOut, char *PName);
```

```c
char *FNAME="ALITEST.LOG";
char hlpstr[DLL_LONGSTR];
char *errstr1="<TITLE>ERROR IN CALLING  →
   CGIDLL</TITLE><H1>Calling CGIDLL failed</H1>";
char *errstr2="<TITLE>Post Not →
   Supported</TITLE><H1>Post Not Supported</H1>";
char *errstr3="<TITLE>Document Not →
   Found</TITLE><H1>Document Not Found</H1>";


#define MALLOCSIZE      30000
#define VAR             1
#define VALUE           2
char DocRoot[254];

BOOL APIENTRY DllMain( HANDLE hModule, DWORD →
     ul_reason_for_call, LPVOID lpReserved )
{
 switch( ul_reason_for_call )
 {
  case DLL_PROCESS_ATTACH:
   newprocess();
   break;
  case DLL_THREAD_ATTACH:
   break;
  case DLL_THREAD_DETACH:
   break;
  case DLL_PROCESS_DETACH:
   endnewprocess();
   break;
 } /* endswitch */
 return TRUE;
} /* end of DllMain */

int newprocess()
{
 int fh;
     HKEY hKeyMe;
     DWORD dwBufSize = 254;
```

```
if ((fh = _open( FNAME, _O_RDWR | _O_CREAT |
 _O_BINARY |_O_APPEND, _S_IREAD | _S_IWRITE )) == -1)
{
 return 0;
} /* endif */
    // The next two lines get the server root from the
    // registry so that this program
    // knows where to go to fetch the real file
    // later on
    RegOpenKeyEx(HKEY_LOCAL_MACHINE,
       "SOFTWARE\\Alibaba\\CurrentVersion →
       \\BaseServer \\ServerRoot",
       0,KEY_ALL_ACCESS,&hKeyMe);
RegQueryValueEx(hKeyMe,"SERVERROOT",NULL,NULL,DocRoot,
       &dwBufSize);

 wsprintf(hlpstr,"New Process called\r\n");
_write (fh,hlpstr,strlen(hlpstr));

_close(fh);
}

int endnewprocess()
{
 int fh;

 if ((fh = _open( FNAME, _O_RDWR | _O_CREAT |
     _O_BINARY |_O_APPEND, _S_IREAD | _S_IWRITE ))
         == -1)
 {
  return 0;
 } /* endif */
wsprintf(hlpstr,"End New Process called\r\n");
write (fh,hlpstr,strlen(hlpstr));
_close(fh);
}


int AlibabaDLLEntry(struct CGIDLLIN *DLLIn, →
     struct CGIDLLOUT *DLLOut)
{
  SYSTEMTIME endtime;
  char hlpstr[DLL_LONGSTR];
  int fh;
```

```
DLLOut->DoFree = TRUE;
if (!strcmp(DLLIn->cgipart.RequestMethod,"GET")) {
  if ((fh = _open( FNAME, _O_RDWR | _O_CREAT
    | _O_BINARY |_O_APPEND, _S_IREAD
    | _S_IWRITE )) == -1)  {
    DLLOut->AnswerData = errstr1;
    DLLOut->WithHeader = FALSE;
      /* Server sends 200 OK Command */
    DLLOut->DataLength = strlen(errstr1);
    DLLOut->DoFree = FALSE;
    return 0;
  }
  GetLocalTime(&endtime);
  wsprintf(hlpstr,
    "DLL called at: %02d.%02d.%02d:%03d,  ",
    DLLIn->localtime.wHour,
    DLLIn->localtime.wMinute,
    DLLIn->localtime.wSecond,
    DLLIn->localtime.wMilliseconds);
  write (fh,hlpstr,strlen(hlpstr));
  if (DoCustomResponse(DLLIn,DLLOut) == -1) {
    /* DATA KO        */
    DLLOut->AnswerData = errstr1;
    DLLOut->WithHeader = FALSE;
   /* Server sends 200 OK Command */
    DLLOut->DataLength = strlen(errstr1);
    /* Be sure to set DoFree correctly, */
    DLLOut->DoFree = FALSE;
    _close(fh);
  }
  GetLocalTime(&endtime);
  wsprintf(hlpstr,
    "done at: %02d.%02d.%02d:%03d\n",
    DLLIn->localtime.wHour,
    DLLIn->localtime.wMinute,
    DLLIn->localtime.wSecond,
    DLLIn->localtime.wMilliseconds);
  _write (fh,hlpstr,strlen(hlpstr));
  _close(fh);
  return 0;
}
```

```c
    if (!strcmp(DLLIn->cgipart.RequestMethod,"POST")) {
        /* This is a "GET" only routine */
        DLLOut->AnswerData = errstr2;
        DLLOut->WithHeader = FALSE;
            /* Server sends 200 OK Command */
        DLLOut->DataLength = strlen(errstr2);
        DLLOut->DoFree = FALSE;
        return 0;
    } /* endif */
}


/**********************************/
/* DoCustomResponse               */
/*    This program responds       */
/*    with a different page based on */
/*    the client that called it   */
/*    This could also be accomplished */
/*    by using a redirect response in */
/*    the header                  */
/**********************************/
#define NUMAGENTS 10
char UserAgents[NUMAGENTS][50] =
    {"Mozilla/X","Mozilla/1",
        "Microsoft Internet Explorer/0",
        "NCSA Mosaic/2","Spyglass_Mosaic/2",
        "Mozilla/2","","","",""};
    // Specify as much of the User Agent line as you
    // need to identify the browser at
    // the level of granularity you want
    /* A sample of HTTP USER AGENT lines is as follows:
        Mozilla/2.0b5 (WinNT; I)
        Microsoft Internet Explorer/0.1 (Win32)
        NCSA Mosaic/2.0 (Windows x86)
        Spyglass_Mosaic/2.10 Win32 Spyglass/9
    */
int DoCustomResponse(struct CGIDLLIN *DLLIn, →
        struct CGIDLLOUT *DLLOut)
{
    int   i,iRtn;
    char PName[254];
    char *PSrch;
```

```c
BOOL bSlashFound,bFound;
strcpy(PName,DLLIn->cgipart.ScriptName);
PSrch = strchr(&PName[1],'/');
if(PSrch == NULL) {
  // We did not find a /
  PSrch = PName;
}
i = strlen(PName);
// Look to see if there is a . between the end and
// the first /
bSlashFound = FALSE;
while((i>0)&&(PName[i]!='.')) {
  if(PName[i]=='/') {
    bSlashFound = TRUE;
    break;
  }
  i--;
}
if(bSlashFound==FALSE) {
  // No slash at the end.
  if(i==0) {   //
    DLLOut->AnswerData = errstr3;
    DLLOut->WithHeader = FALSE;
    /* Server sends 200 OK Command */
    DLLOut->DataLength = strlen(errstr3);
    DLLOut->DoFree = FALSE;
    return 0;
  } else {
    // /CUSTOM/FILE.HTM
    // or /CUSTOM/PATH/FILE.HTM
    // or FILE.JPG, FILE.GIF, etc.
    // We want to substitute a different suffix,
    // depending on the client that called
    // Put the lookup table in the registry
    // in a real program!
    // Chop off the last letter, and substitute
    // A-Z depending on the index into the
    // user agent table.
    bFound = FALSE;
    for(i=0;i<NUMAGENTS;i++) {
      if(_strnicmp(DLLIn->cgipart.HTTP_USER_AGENT,
```

```
                    UserAgents[i],strlen(UserAgents[i])) == 0) {
                      PSrch[strlen(PSrch)-1] = 'A' + i;
                      bFound = TRUE;
                      break;
                    }
                  }
                //if(bFound == FALSE)
                // Just return the HTM file as is
              }

              if ((iRtn=ReturnFile(DLLIn,DLLOut,PSrch)) == -1) {
                DLLOut->AnswerData = errstr3;
                DLLOut->WithHeader = FALSE;
                  /* Server sends 200 OK Command */
                DLLOut->DataLength = strlen(errstr3);
                DLLOut->DoFree = FALSE;
              } else if (iRtn == -2) {
                DLLOut->AnswerData = errstr2;
                DLLOut->WithHeader = FALSE;
                  Server sends 200 OK Command */
                DLLOut->DataLength = strlen(errstr2);
                DLLOut->DoFree = FALSE;
              }
          } else {
            // Found a slash, so no file specified.
            // /CUSTOM/name  /CUSTOM/name/
            DLLOut->AnswerData = errstr3;
            DLLOut->WithHeader = FALSE;
              Server sends 200 OK Command */
            DLLOut->DataLength = strlen(errstr3);
            DLLOut->DoFree = FALSE;
            return 0;
          }
        } /* end of DoCustomResponse */

        int ReturnFile(struct CGIDLLIN *DLLIn, →
              struct CGIDLLOUT *DLLOut, char *PName)
        {
          // Return the file specified.
          char RealPath[254];
          char *lpContent;
          int len;
          DWORD dwFileSize,dwRS;
```

```
HANDLE hFile;
unsigned int i;
len = strlen(PName);
len--;
 // Get the name of the file from the URL
while(len > 0) {
   if(PName[len]!='/') {
      len--;
   } else {
      break;
   }
}
if(PName[len]=='/') {
   len++;
}
// Create a path to the disk file location
strcpy(RealPath,DocRoot);
strcat(RealPath,"\\");
len = strlen(RealPath);
PName++;
while(*PName != 0) {
    if(*PName == '/') {
    RealPath[len] = '\\';
   } else {
      RealPath[len] = *PName;
   }
   len++;
   PName++;
}
RealPath[len]=0;
// Open the file
_fmode = _O_BINARY;
hFile = CreateFile(RealPath,GENERIC_READ,
   FILE_SHARE_READ,NULL,
   OPEN_EXISTING,FILE_ATTRIBUTE_NORMAL,NULL);
if(hFile == INVALID_HANDLE_VALUE) return -2;
dwFileSize = GetFileSize(hFile,NULL);
 // Create a memory area to read in the file
lpContent=
   (char *)GlobalAlloc(GMEM_FIXED,dwFileSize);
ReadFile(hFile,lpContent,dwFileSize,&dwRS,NULL);
DLLOut->WithHeader = FALSE;
   /* Server sends 200 OK Command */
```

```c
// Create a buffer for the returned data
if((DLLOut->AnswerData =
   calloc(1,dwFileSize+10)) == NULL) {
   return -1;
}
// Select the return type based on MIME Mappings.
// For now, hard code it.
// Get the suffix from the file name
while(RealPath[len] != '.') {
   len--;
   if(len < 3) {
      break;
   }
}
if(len >= 3) {
   len++;
   if((_strnicmp(&RealPath[len],"ht",2))==0) {
    wsprintf(hlpstr,"Content-type: text/html\n\n\n");
    i = strlen(hlpstr);
    strcpy(DLLOut->AnswerData,hlpstr);
    memcpy(&(DLLOut->AnswerData[i]),
        lpContent,dwFileSize);
    DLLOut->DataLength = i+dwFileSize;
   } else if((_strnicmp(&RealPath[len],"gi",2))==0) {
    wsprintf(hlpstr,
      "Content-type: image/gif\nContent-Length: →
        %d\n\n",dwFileSize);
    i = strlen(hlpstr);
    strcpy(DLLOut->AnswerData,hlpstr);
    memcpy(&(DLLOut->AnswerData[i]), →
        lpContent,dwFileSize);
    DLLOut->DataLength = i+dwFileSize;
   } else if((_strnicmp(&RealPath[len],"jp",2))==0) {
    wsprintf(hlpstr,
      "Content-type: image/jpeg\n\n\n");
    i = strlen(hlpstr);
    strcpy(DLLOut->AnswerData,hlpstr);
    memcpy(&(DLLOut->AnswerData[i]), →
      lpContent,dwFileSize);
    DLLOut->DataLength = i+dwFileSize;
   } else {
```

```
        // If we don't know what it is, say it is text...
        wsprintf(hlpstr,"Content-type: text/html\n\n\n");
        i = strlen(hlpstr);
        strcpy(DLLOut->AnswerData,hlpstr);
        memcpy(&(DLLOut->AnswerData[i]), →
          lpContent,dwFileSize);
        DLLOut->DataLength = i+dwFileSize;
        }
      GlobalFree(lpContent);
      CloseHandle(hFile);
      }
    return 1;
}
```

Using the ISAPI

Microsoft and Process software got together to define an API that can emulate CGI, plus provide additional functions to extend server functionality. At the time this is being written, there were still some differences between the exact specification of the Microsoft version and the Process Software version. This section will use the Microsoft version as the reference standard.

The ISAPI is split into two parts: a CGI replacement part and a filter callback part. The CGI replacement part has some very convenient features, such as the ability to furnish a document that resides at a different spot in the local web without doing a redirect, and adding additional information to the standard log entry for the current request. The filter callback is a scheme that allows you to install special filter DLLs that request to be called on every event of a particular type. This filter callback mechanism is useful for developing programs that add compression, perform encryption, perform custom authentication, do special logging, or perform special traffic analysis. There are a number of good samples provided with the Microsoft Server, which will make programming filter extensions easy.

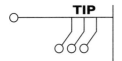

You can run the Microsoft server as a regular program as well as a service, which makes debugging DLLs a lot easier!

API Definition for ISAPI CGI

There are two required functions for the CGI functions: a version-checking function, called GetExtensionVersion, and the main entry point, called HttpExtensionProc. The prototype for HttpExtensionProc is as follows:

```
BOOL WINAPI HttpExtensionProc(_EXTENSION_CONTROL_BLOCK
*lpEcb);
```

The control block (ECB) is defined as shown in Listing 10-6.

Listing 10-6: ECB definition for the ISAPI.

```
//
// passed to extension procedure on a new request
//
typedef struct _EXTENSION_CONTROL_BLOCK {

    DWORD    cbSize;   // size of this struct.
    DWORD    dwVersion;       // version info of this spec
    HCONN    ConnID;   // Context number not to be modified!
    DWORD    dwHttpStatusCode;       // HTTP Status code
    CHAR     lpszLogData[HSE_LOG_BUFFER_LEN];
        // null terminated log info specific to this Extension
DLL
    LPSTR    lpszMethod;       // REQUEST_METHOD
    LPSTR    lpszQueryString; // QUERY_STRING
    LPSTR    lpszPathInfo;    // PATH_INFO
    LPSTR    lpszPathTranslated;      // PATH_TRANSLATED
    DWORD    cbTotalBytes;    // Total bytes indicated from
client
    DWORD    cbAvailable;     // Available number of bytes
    LPBYTE   lpbData;  // pointer to cbAvailable bytes
    LPSTR    lpszContentType; // Content type of client data

    BOOL (WINAPI * GetServerVariable)
    (HCONN hConn, LPSTR lpszVariableName, LPVOID lpvBuffer,
    LPDWORD lpdwSize );
```

```
    BOOL (WINAPI * WriteClient)
      ( HCONN ConnID,LPVOID Buffer,LPDWORD lpdwBytes,DWORD
  dwReserved );
    BOOL (WINAPI * ReadClient)
      ( HCONN ConnID,LPVOID lpvBuffer,LPDWORD lpdwSize );
    BOOL (WINAPI * ServerSupportFunction)
      ( HCONN hConn,DWORD dwHSERRequest,LPVOID lpvBuffer,
          LPDWORD lpdwSize,LPDWORD lpdwDataType );
  } EXTENSION_CONTROL_BLOCK, *LPEXTENSION_CONTROL_BLOCK;
```

You can see from the ECB definition that instead of passing every parameter to your function in the original call, only the most important data is passed, and you can retrieve the rest through the use of the GetServerVariable callback. The ReadClient and WriteClient functions are what you think they are: functions that read data from the client and write data to the client. These functions are used instead of standard in and standard out pipes. The last function, ServerSupportFunction, has some interesting properties. With it, you can start a standard response, when dwHESRRequest is set to HSE_REQ_SEND_RESPONSE_HEADER; you can send a redirect message, with dwHSERRequest set to HSE_REQ_SEND_URL_REDIRECT_RESP; and you can send the data of another URL on the current server *without doing a redirect* by specifying the URL and setting dwHSERRequest to HSE_REQ_SEND_URL.

API Definition for ISAPI Filters

The filter functions allow you to extend the server functionality beyond that normally possible with CGI replacement functions. There are two required entry points in the DLL: GetFilterVersion and the main entry point, HttpFilterProc. When your GetFilterVersion function is called, you return the notifications, described in the following table, you're interested in processing.

Notification	Description
SF_NOTIFY_SECURE_PORT	Notify application only for sessions over a secure port.
SF_NOTIFY_NONSECURE_PORT	Notify application only for sessions over a nonsecure port.
SF_NOTIFY_READ_RAW_DATA	Allow the application to see the raw data. The data returned will contain both headers and data.
SF_NOTIFY_PREPROC_HEADERS	The server has preprocessed the headers.
SF_NOTIFY_AUTHENTICATION	The server is authenticating the client.
SF_NOTIFY_URL_MAP	The server is mapping a logical URL to a physical path.
SF_NOTIFY_SEND_RAW_DATA	The server is sending raw data back to the client.
SF_NOTIFY_LOG	The server is writing information to the server log.
SF_NOTIFY_END_OF_NET_SESSION	The session with the client is ending.

Table 10-2: *Notifications.*

Table 10-2 illustrates the wide variety of notifications that can take place. Further, at the conclusion of your filter processing, you can tell the server if any more processing of any kind should take place. The return codes are shown in Table 10-3.

Return Code	Description
SF_STATUS_REQ_FINISHED	The filter has handled the HTTP request. The server should disconnect the session.
SF_STATUS_REQ_FINISHED_ KEEP_CONN	Same as SF_STATUS_REQ_ FINISHED except that the server should keep the TCP session open if the option was negotiated.
SF_STATUS_REQ_NEXT_ NOTIFICATION	The next filter in the notification chain should be called.
SF_STATUS_REQ_HANDLED_ NOTIFICATION	This filter handled the notification. No other handlers should be called for this particular notification type.
SF_STATUS_REQ_ERROR	An error occurred. The server should use GetLastError and indicate the error to the client.
SF_STATUS_REQ_READ_NEXT	The filter is an opaque stream filter and we're negotiating the session parameters. Only valid for raw read notification.

Table 10-3: *Return codes.*

The prototype for HttpFilterProc is as follows:

```
DWORD WINAPI HttpFilterProc(
    PHTTP_FILTER_CONTEXT pfc,
    DWORD NotificationType,
    LPVOID pvNotification
    );
```

The structure used in the *pvNotification* structure varies depending on the type of notification.

Registration of New Extensions

All the data needed to load filter extension programs are stored in the Windows NT Registry:

```
HKEY_LOCAL_MACHINE\
  SYSTEM\
    CurrentControlSet\
      Services\
W3SVC\
  Parameters
    Filter DLLs= fully specified path to the .DLL
```

CGI extension DLLs are called as needed, and can remain loaded or be removed from memory after a period of time, depending on the design of the server. To call a CGI extension DLL, you simply specify its name on a form, just as you would with a regular CGI program.

Creating the Sample Program

The sample program uses the filter capabilities of the ISAPI, and requests that the server notify it when the path is being translated from the URL to a physical path. By the time this program is called, the physical URL is already filled in, so we just need to call a support routine to find out the HTTP_USER_AGENT variable, compare it to our internal list, modify the name, and let the server do its work.

Listing 10-7: ISAPI implementation of the sample program.

```c
/*
    mstest.c
*/

#include <windows.h>
#include <winsock.h>
#include <stdio.h>
#include <stdlib.h>
#include <httpfilt.h>
#define NUMAGENTS 10
char UserAgents[NUMAGENTS][50] =
  {"Mozilla/X","Mozilla/1",
    "Microsoft Internet Explorer/0",
    "NCSA Mosaic/2","Spyglass_Mosaic/2",
```

```
    "Mozilla/2","","","",""};
BOOL WINAPI __stdcall
   GetFilterVersion(HTTP_FILTER_VERSION * pVer)
{
  pVer->dwFlags = (SF_NOTIFY_NONSECURE_PORT |
      SF_NOTIFY_URL_MAP | SF_NOTIFY_ORDER_HIGH);
  pVer->dwFilterVersion = HTTP_FILTER_REVISION;
  strcpy( pVer->lpszFilterDesc,
    "Browser specific file name translator, →
       Version 1.0");
  return TRUE;
}

DWORD WINAPI __stdcall
   HttpFilterProc(HTTP_FILTER_CONTEXT *pfc, →
   DWORD NotificationType,VOID *pvData ) {
  CHAR  *pPhysPath;
  PHTTP_FILTER_URL_MAP pURLMap;
  BOOL bFound;
  char ReturnBuf[250];
  int i,PathLen;
  DWORD BufSize;
  BufSize = 250;
  switch ( NotificationType ) {
    case SF_NOTIFY_URL_MAP:
      pURLMap = (PHTTP_FILTER_URL_MAP) pvData;
      pPhysPath = pURLMap->pszPhysicalPath;
      pfc->pFilterContext = 0;
      // Get the HTTP User Agent
      (pfc->GetServerVariable)(pfc,
        "HTTP_USER_AGENT",ReturnBuf,&BufSize);
      // This is the string sent by the browser that
      //identifies the brand and
      // version of the browser
      // Use a really dumb comparison,
      // and replace the "m" in .htm with A-Z
      // depending on what the offset into
      // the comparison array was
      PathLen = strlen(pURLMap->pszPhysicalPath);
      if((strcmp(&pURLMap->pszPhysicalPath[PathLen-4],→
        ".htm"))==0) {
      bFound = FALSE;
      for(i=0;i<NUMAGENTS;i++) {
```

```
        if(_strnicmp(ReturnBuf, UserAgents[i], →
          strlen(UserAgents[i]))  == 0) {
          pURLMap->pszPhysicalPath[strlen →
          (pURLMap->pszPhysicalPath)-1] = 'A' + i;
          bFound = TRUE;
          break;
        }
      }
    }
    break;

    default:
      break;
    }
    return SF_STATUS_REQ_NEXT_NOTIFICATION;
}
```

You can see that this is much less complicated than the Alibaba
API example, because the server itself is still doing the job of
parsing the URL and returning the file to the browser. Furthermore, since we're just tinkering with the filename, the document
looks like all the other documents on the web. The downside to
this is that this program will be called on each and every request
in the server, and it's up to the program to figure out if and when
it should play with the filename. In the case of the example, every
.HTM file has its filename changed.

Using the NSAPI

Netscape was one of the first server makers to realize that an API
into the functions of the server would allow third-party programmers to extend the functionality of the server. Strictly speaking,
the NSAPI is not a replacement for CGI: in fact, it's quite difficult
to write a function with NSAPI to replace a CGI script. Netscape
supports multiple platforms with their server, and NT was not
their first choice, so much of the API documentation favors UNIX
lingo over that of NT, and many of the questions you may have
about the NSAPI will need to be answered by people rather than
the skimpy documentation provided by Netscape. For this reason,

if you intend to develop server extensions with the NSAPI, you should almost certainly join the Netscape Developer Partner's program. This program gives you access to a secure newsgroup where you can post questions and scan for answers to problems you may be having. Netscape has a presence on the newsgroup, and will answer many of the questions themselves. For more information about this program, see http://developer.netscape.com/.

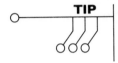

TIP

Netscape includes samples of every kind of extension program you may want to write with the server, and you should spend time with those examples before you try to create your own server extensions.

API Definition

Netscape has defined six points at which you can have a server extension DLL intercede in the processing (these are essentially the same steps taken internally by the server in the processing of every HTTP request):

- *Authorization Translation.* This phase of processing simply checks the validity of the user's authorization information against a user database. The Path Checks phase uses the results from this phase. You could add your own authorization scheme and database accesses instead of using the built-in capabilities.

- *Name Translation.* This phase translates the URL virtual path specified by the client browser into an internal physical path to the information requested. You could add your own alias processing at this point.

- *Path Checks.* The permission for a particular user to access a particular object is checked in this phase. Together with the Authorization Translation phase, you could implement your own security mechanisms.

❖ *Object Type.* This phase locates the appropriate information on the file system based on the preceding steps. For instance, if you wanted to do suffix replacement (.HTM to .HTT or .HTX), you could do it at this phase.

❖ *Respond to Request Service.* The "meat" of processing takes place in this phase. This is the code that actually returns information to the client browser through writes to the server's output stream. You could substitute your own functions for special file or information types.

❖ *Log the Transaction.* Standard logging takes place in this phase. If you had a special logging function, such as writing to a database or real-time stream, you could implement it in this phase.

You select the point in the processing at which you want your server extension to operate. In some cases, your extension will be called for almost every request, such as functions that verify permissions of users based on an authentication mechanism. In other cases, your function will be called only when the server is processing information that your extension supports—for instance, if you came up with a new MIME type that passed data back to the client in a way not already handled by the standard file-return mechanisms. You could probably add server extensions that return data for an extended period of time, such as audio streams, but be careful, because every active request being handled by an extension DLL ties up a thread in the server for the lifetime of the request.

There are no required entry points in the DLLs you write, since you tell the server the names of the entry points you want used from any particular DLL. There are, however, many different header files that need to be included in your extension DLLs. These header file are much too long to be reprinted here, but they're available at http://home.netscape.com/newsref/std/server_api.html.

Registration of New Extensions

The Netscape server keeps all its configuration information in the Registry, and you need to add entries in the Registry to activate new DLL extensions. A typical Netscape server initial installation might have a Registry tree that looks like Figure 10-3.

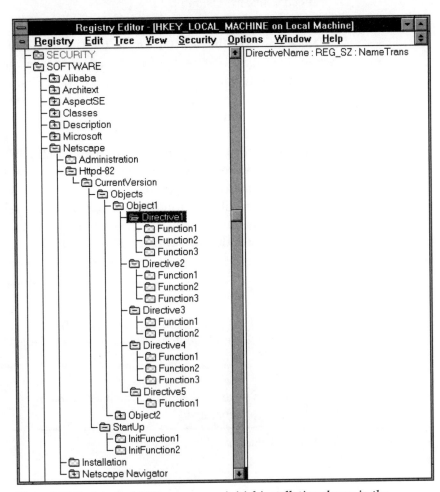

Figure 10-3: *A typical Netscape server initial installation shown in the NT Registry.*

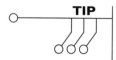

TIP

This section describes the basic principles behind how extensions are added to the Netscape server. The sample source files provided with the Netscape server include specific instructions for installing extension programs for each of the phases shown above. Please refer to the specific instructions in the sample code when you actually add a new extension DLL.

Netscape uses the StartUp key to tell the server what to do when starting up. To load your DLL when the server is starting, you'll add a key and value to the StartUp key. First, add a key called InitFunction01. You should leave the Class entry blank. If you're adding multiple DLLs, the next one would be InitFunction02, and so forth. Since the startup functions are performed in the order they're found in the Registry, by making the number 01, you're telling the server to load your DLLs before other startup actions are taken.

Next, under InitFunction01, add three values, as shown in Table 10-4. With this information, the server will know to load your DLL and will register the functions you've specified.

Value Name	String
fn	load-modules
shlib	The fully qualified path name to your DLL, such as c:\netscape\ns-home\nsapi\WinDebug\mydll.dll.
funcs	The name of the function you want called in this DLL. You can enter more than one function name, separated by commas, such as auth-function, path-translator.

Table 10-4: *Values added to the Registry.*

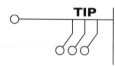

TIP

If you're using C++, be sure to declare the exported functions as "C" convention names with an extern "C"{ function-name } declaration. If you forget, the C++ compiler mungs the names into the C++ format for export, and the Netscape loader will never find them.

The next thing you need to tell the Netscape server is when to *call* your function. As mentioned in the previous section, Netscape has defined six points at which you can have a server extension DLL intercede in the processing. These are reflected in the Registry as directives, as shown in Table 10-5. (Note that the default Registry entries in Figure 10-3 show only five of the six possible directives.)

Processing Phase	Registry Directive
Authorization Translation	Not in default configuration
Name Translation	Directive1
Path Checking	Directive2
Object Type	Directive3
Respond to Request Service	Directive4
Log the Transaction	Directive5

Table 10-5: *Netscape processing phases and corresponding Registry directives.*

Typically, your DLL function will perform actions that are related to one of these six stages of processing, and you'll specify to the server under the appropriate key that it should call your function. For example, if you're adding a server extension to manage the retrieval of objects (files) based on the file extension, as in the example supplied by Netscape, you'd add below the Directive3 key a new function, called Function01. This new key would have at least the function name, with a Key Value of "fn." Other parameters could also be placed in this key if they were required by your function.

Creating the Sample Program

The sample program using the NSAPI is placed in the Registry as detailed in the source code, and is called every time a path is being translated from the URL to a physical path. By the time this program is called, the physical URL is already filled in, so we just need to call a support routine to find out the HTTP_USER_AGENT variable, compare it to our internal list, modify the name, and let the server do its work, just as with the ISAPI example. This code is even simpler than the ISAPI example, because there are no required functions. The only tricky part is that the Netscape server can only operate as a service, and there's no straightforward way to hook the visual debugger up to a DLL called by a service. Instead, the following code manually inserts a breakpoint at the top of the program:

```
if(iDebug == 1) {
  _asm{int 3};
  iDebug = 0;
}
```

The variable iDebug is set as a global variable to 1, so that only the first time the DLL is run, the breakpoint will be hit. When the breakpoint is hit, you'll have the option of either killing the program or opening the debugger—which is what you want to do. Once the program is open in the Visual C++, you can set your own dynamic breakpoints. Just don't forget to do a release build before you start using this on a live service!

Listing 10-8: NSAPI implementation of the sample program.

```
/*
The following three are standard headers for SAFs.
They're used to get the data structures and prototypes
needed to declare and use SAFs.
*/

#include "base/pblock.h"
#include "base/session.h"
#include "frame/req.h"

/* ------------- custom_page ----------------- */

/*
  Usage:Alter these registry parameters
  ( Run the registry editor as regedt32.exe)
  (1) Add a registry key number below
    HKEY_LOCAL_MACHINE\\Software\\Netscape\\
    Http[d/s-port]\\CurrentVersion\\StartUp
    as Key "InitFunction01"
```

(2) Add these parameters as values to the key
    just added.
fn:load-modules
shlib:c:\netscape\ns-home\nsapi\nstest\→
    WinDebug\nstest.dll
funcs:custom_page

(3) Go to
  HKEY_LOCAL_MACHINE\\Software\\Netscape
    \\Httpd\\CurrentVersion
  \\Configuration\\Objects\\Object1
  Check to see that you have a NameTrans Directive
  Key.If you do, go to (6)

(4) If you don't have a NameTrans Directive Key,
    add one in below the Object Key
    specified above, after the AuthTrans
    Directive as Key "Directive02"
    or whatever value is suitable to keep the
    NameTrans Directive Key after the AuthTrans
    Directive Key in the list of Directive Keys.

(5) Add this value to the Key just added
    "DirectiveName:NameTrans"

(6) Now Add a Function Key below the
    NameTrans Directive Key as "Function01"

(7) Add these values to the Function Key
    you just added.
    fn:custom_page
    separator:,

This NameTrans should appear before
  other Nametrans keys in the default object
  (default object is usually key "Object1")

Note that you can load more than one
  function using one load-modules command. If you
  want to try another function from this file, you
  can load it by separating the names to the funcs
  parameter with commas.

*/

```c
#include <string.h>    /* strchr */
#include "frame/log.h" /* log_error */
#define NUMAGENTS 10
char UserAgents[NUMAGENTS][50] = {"Mozilla/X","Mozilla/1",
    "Microsoft Internet Explorer/0",
    "NCSA Mosaic/2",
    "Spyglass_Mosaic/2",
    "Mozilla/2","","","",""};
int iDebug = 1;

__declspec(dllexport) int custom_page
        (pblock *pb, Session *sn, Request *rq)
{
  BOOL bFound;
  int i,iStrLen;
  char *ua;
  char *ppath = pblock_findval("ppath", rq->vars);

#ifdef _DEBUG
#pragma message ("Breakpoint enabled in NSTEST.C")
  if(iDebug == 1) {
    _asm{int 3};
    iDebug = 0;
  }
#else
#pragma message ("Breakpoint Disabled: Not a debug →
    build")
#endif

  if(request_header("user-agent", &ua, sn, rq)
      == REQ_ABORTED)
    return REQ_ABORTED;

  bFound = FALSE;
  iStrLen = strlen(ppath);
  if((_strnicmp(&ppath[iStrLen-4],".htm",4))==0) {
    for(i=0;i<NUMAGENTS;i++) {
      // If the user agent that is requesting this
      // file is found in the user agent table,
```

```
                // add a letter that corresponds to its
                // position in the table
                if(_strnicmp(ua,UserAgents[i],
                      strlen(UserAgents[i])) == 0) {
                   ppath[iStrLen-5] = 'A' + i;
                   bFound = TRUE;
                   break;
                }
             }
          }
       return REQ_NOACTION;
    }
```

CGI Reference

The examples in this chapter are an excellent introduction to the most important and commonly used features of CGI, but there is a lot that they don't cover. This section provides a brief overview of all the features that the Common Gateway Interface offers.

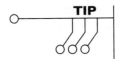

TIP *You can find a formal specification for the CGI v1.1 standard at http://hoohoo.ncsa.uiuc.edu/cgi/overview.html.*

CGI Environment Variables

As you've learned throughout the chapter, the CGI standard mandates that servers pass information to scripts through environment variables. Although the example scripts in this chapter demonstrate how to use most of the important CGI variables, many more aren't discussed. The following tables describe the environment variables that are a part of the CGI standard.

CGI Variable	Description
SERVER_SOFTWARE	The name and version of the HTTP server that accepted the request, separated by a slash.
SERVER_NAME	The advertised hostname of the server.
GATEWAY_INTERFACE	The version of the CGI standard that the server implements.
SERVER_PROTOCOL	The name and version of the protocol that sent the request. Currently, only HTTP supports the CGI standard.
SERVER_PORT	The number of the port on which the request was received.
REMOTE_HOST	The hostname of the machine from which the request originated. If reverse lookups are disabled, this variable isn't defined.
REMOTE_ADDR	The IP address of the machine where the request originated.
REMOTE_USER	The authenticated username of the user, if the script is protected by client authentication.
AUTH_TYPE	The type of client authentication (if any) that protects the script.

Table 10-6: *Simple CGI environment variables.*

The simple variables summarized in Table 10-6 give the gateway information about the server's configuration and the origin of the request. The environment variables summarized in Table 10-7, are, in general, more important, because they relate to the actual contents of the client's request.

CGI Variable	Description
REQUEST_METHOD	The HTTP method the client used to make the request (GET, POST, or HEAD). CGI gateways receive data from the client differently depending on the method (see "Processing the Form Data," in the "Handling HTML Forms" section, earlier in this chapter).
HTTP_ACCEPT	A comma-separated list of MIME types that are acceptable to the client. Asterisks are wildcards and signal that any type of data is acceptable. Most servers and clients make no use of this data; in the future, servers may do on-the-fly conversions to the client's preferred type.
HTTP_USER_AGENT	The name (brand name and version, typically) of the browser making the request.
PATH_INFO	The extra pathname information that follows the name of the CGI script. This is an easy way to send information to your gateway.
PATH_TRANSLATED	The pathname information from PATH_INFO preceded by server's root data connection. If PATH_INFO specifies the name of a file beneath the server's directory, a gateway can use this variable to get the full pathname to that file on the system.
QUERY_STRING	The data from the browser, if the client invokes the gateway with the GET method (see "URL Encoding" and "Processing the Form Data," in the "Handling HTML Forms" section, earlier in this chapter).

CGI Variable	Description
CONTENT_TYPE	The MIME type of the transmitted information. Currently, only one value, application/x-www-form-urlencoded, is valid for data from a submitted HTML form.
CONTENT_LENGTH	The number of bytes of data sent from the browser if the client invokes the gateway with the POST method (see "URL Encoding" and "Processing the Form Data," in the "Handling HTML Forms" section, earlier in this chapter).

Table 10-7: *Client data CGI variables.*

Most of the environment variables listed in Table 10-7 are explained and used in the examples throughout this chapter; the only two exceptions are PATH_TRANSLATED and HTTP_ACCEPT.

The PATH_TRANSLATED variable is closely related to the PATH_INFO variable. The latter consists of everything within the URL, from the end of the name of the script to the query string (which begins with a question mark). This variable is often used to pass a relative URL on which to operate to the CGI script. The server sets the PATH_TRANSLATED variable to be the same as the PATH_INFO variable, modified to represent a valid path on the system. The server makes all necessary translations—if your server supports tilde expansion for user document directories, the requested URLs are also converted to their proper paths. For this reason, it's a good idea to use the PATH_TRANSLATED variable when getting the name of a file from a CGI program.

The other important CGI variable we haven't really covered is HTTP_ACCEPT. This variable contains a comma-separated list of the MIME types that the browser is prepared to accept from the server. The list is ordered from most welcome to least welcome. Although this feature has great potential, no web client or server really takes advantage of it; most clients just give a long list of data types, followed by */*, signifying any and all MIME types, which obviously isn't very useful.

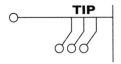

TIP

Although HTTP_ACCEPT is the only one specifically mentioned in the CGI v1.1 standard, the server creates environment variables for every line of HTTP header information that the client sends with the request. Each variable is the string "HTTP_" followed by the name of the HTTP header field. You can find a full list of possible HTTP headers at http://www.w3.org/hypertext/WWW/ Protocols/HTTP1.0/draft-ietf-http-spec.html.

CGI Headers

While the HTTP server communicates with the CGI program through environment variables, CGI programs write to the standard output to send information to the server. The CGI standard describes three header lines that a CGI script can use. Table 10-8 lists these headers.

Header	Description
Content-type	Specifies the MIME type of the following output. If the script generates any output at all, other than a CGI header, Content-type must be the very first line it sends.
Location	Specifies that the output is the location (a URL) of another document, rather than a document itself.
Status	The HTTP status code that the server should return with the response. You'll find a list of HTTP status codes at http://www.w3.org/hypertext/WWW/ Protocols/HTTP/HTRESP.html.

Table 10-8: *Standard CGI headers for script-to-server communication.*

Each of these headers must be sent on a line by itself, followed by another blank line. The server then interprets this output and generates a proper HTTP response from it, thus saving the programmer the trouble of learning the full HTTP v1.0 standard. This also provides a layer of data abstraction, preventing future upgrades to the HTTP standard (such as HTTP-NG—see Chapter 13, "Future Directions") from breaking pre-existing CGI scripts.

Cookies
Cookies, which have nothing to do with snacks, are not supported by all browsers, but they offer a very convenient way to store information at the client for those that do. A cookie is an extra bit of information that your CGI script attaches to the HTTP header that's returned to a client. This information is stored at the client, and is returned to your script whenever it is called. This allows you to maintain state in an environment that is essentially stateless, and can be used for keeping track of users who visit your site, or to create lists of goods that a user is purchasing from your online store, to give two examples. For a complete description of cookies, see http://home.netscape.com/newsref/std/cookie_spec.html.

Moving On

The CGI standard provides an easy way to extend the basic functionality of your web server. The standard gives your programs a simple way to access information about the server's configuration and the client's request from any programming language; this allows you an incredible amount of flexibility in expanding your pages from a static catalog of documents into a dynamic, interactive presence on the Web. Although the standard is simple in concept, it defines a lot of variables that can be difficult to keep track of. Fortunately, most scripts require only a few that are easy to remember.

Various server APIs are also being defined, to speed up the process of responding to CGI-style requests, and to allow you to extend the functionality of web servers as you see fit. Even though there is no universal API as there is a universal CGI interface, API-based programming will likely be the dominant way to provide extended services at many high-volume web sites. As flexible and powerful as CGI is, APIs allow even greater power and control over the operation of a web site.

One of the most common applications for CGI scripts on a server is implementing a search capability on your web site. The next chapter focuses on various search engines that are available to help create full text indexes of your web site, and provide readers of your site with an efficient means to locate information.

11

Searching & Indexing

The Net provides access to a great amount of information, but it can be difficult for users to find the exact bit they need. This was true when most data on the Net was in text files, and the problem has grown with the explosion of hypertext on the Web, because each link represents another possible path to the information you seek. Most of the world's best computer scientists have worked on the problem of searching; it's one of the most important topics in computing. When applied to the Internet, this field of study is often referred to as Networked Information Discovery and Retrieval (NIDR). Computer scientists in the area of NIDR are working to apply the ideas and algorithms of computer-based searching to tools that will allow users to easily and intuitively find information on the Net.

Like many of the best ideas in computer science, the approach to most of these tools is an extension of a familiar concept. When you're looking for a particular bit of information in this book, you probably check the index. This index has been prepared by a professional; while the indexer's expertise isn't specific to the Web, he or she understands how to organize the topics of a book so that they're easily searched. The indexer combines his or her understanding of the way people read computer books with the author's knowledge of the material. The result is a table of ideas and concepts that are important to the author and the reader.

Similarly, most of the Internet's searching tools are broken into separate modules: an indexer and a search engine. The indexer reads a collection of documents and builds several files containing tables of all the words within the collection. Of course, the software indexer can't duplicate the experience and knowledge of a human being. Instead, it substitutes thoroughness for understanding, by giving every word or phrase an entry in the index. The search engine is like a reader leafing through a book. It understands the tables created by the indexer and uses them to quickly locate documents that match a user's query. This full-text indexing allows users to search the database in English, without having to learn a complex query language.

Full-text indexing allows you to create searchable databases of all the web pages on your server. Doing so allows browsers of your web site to find information very quickly without knowing how you have arranged your information. Some sites have found this to be such a useful capability that they have included a Search button that jumps to the search interface on every page in their web. In this chapter we'll look at a couple of free programs, included on the Companion CD-ROM, that allow you to create searchable indexes on your NT web server. We'll also look briefly at a couple of commercial programs available for searching NT-based web sites, which add many additional features beyond those offered by the freeware and shareware products.

ICE

CD-ROM

ICE, written by Christian Neuss, is a set of perl scripts that implement a simple yet very useful search index and interface. ICE will work with any web server, and will index all disk-based files. ICE cannot index documents and records located in a database, although you could write a simple program to create an ICE-compatible index file based on database documents or records. ICE is useful for sites containing up to a few thousand documents.

The indexing part of ICE goes through a list of directories that you specify and creates a large text index file, listing all the indexable words and where they came from. The searching part of ICE performs two functions: the first is to return a search form for the user to enter data on. The second is to accept the data from the form and return search results. (You don't need to use the forms-generation capability of ICE—you can make your own search form if you prefer—but it is convenient.) The ICE searching and indexing programs, ice-idx.pl and ice-form.pl, are included in the ICE directory on the Companion CD-ROM. Since the programs are written in perl, to run them you'll need to have perl for NT installed. (Perl for NT is also included on the Companion CD-ROM.)

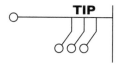

TIP

The home of ICE is at http://www.informatik.th-darmstadt.de/~neuss/ice/ice.html. ICE is officially listed as "beerware" (read the home page!); if you want to use ICE at a commercial site, please contact the author of the program to make appropriate arrangements. The U.S. site is http://ice.cornell-iowa.edu/.

Creating the Index

The ice-idx.pl script is the part of ICE that creates the index. Embedded in ice-idx.pl are several hard-coded names that you'll need to adapt to your system. The first thing you need to do is create a list of directories that will be searched by the indexer. The search directories specification starts around line 30. The script does not recursively search directories, so you'll need to specify each and every directory that you want indexed. For example, if you want to index the web of documentation for the Website web server, which is under the D:\WEBSITE\HTDOCS :\alibaba\docs directory, you'd enter the following:

```
@SEARCHDIRS=(
"D:/WEBSITE/HTDOCS",
"D:/WEBSITE/HTDOCS/CFDOCS",
"D:/WEBSITE/HTDOCS/CFDOCS/EXAMPLES",
"D:/WEBSITE/HTDOCS/CFDOCS/EXAMPLES/COMMENTS",
"D:/WEBSITE/HTDOCS/CFDOCS/EXAMPLES/COMMENTS",
"D:/WEBSITE/HTDOCS/CFDOCS/EXAMPLES",
"D:/WEBSITE/HTDOCS/CFDOCS/EXAMPLES/CONFER",
"D:/WEBSITE/HTDOCS/CFDOCS/EXAMPLES/COURSES",
"D:/WEBSITE/HTDOCS/CFDOCS/EXAMPLES/DIRECT",
"D:/WEBSITE/HTDOCS/CFDOCS/EXAMPLES/EVENTREG",
"D:/WEBSITE/HTDOCS/CFDOCS/EXAMPLES/ORDERS",
"D:/WEBSITE/HTDOCS/CFDOCS/EXAMPLES/TRAINING",
"D:/WEBSITE/HTDOCS/CFDOCS/TEST",
"D:/WEBSITE/HTDOCS/CFDOCS/TUTORIAL",
"D:/WEBSITE/HTDOCS/CFDOCS/USERGUID"
);
```

You can either use the / or \\ separator in the pathnames: the script will understand either form.

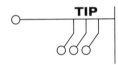

TIP

It's common to modify perl programs for specific configurations since perl is interpreted at the time it is run and it's so easy to modify.

Next, specify the name and location of the index file. This is located right after the directory specification. Enter a full path and filename for the file that will contain the index information. Pick a spot for the index, and enter it as follows:

```
$INDEXFILE="C:/tmp/index.idx";
```

You can choose any path and name for the index file, but remember what you chose, as you'll be using it when you edit the search script. It is common for index files to end with the suffix .IDX so that you'll know what the purpose of the file is later.

A few lines farther down is a system type indicator. To correctly specify your system type, change "UNIX" to "PC" in the following line:

```
$TYPE="UNIX
```

Toward the end of the perl script is a line that looks like this:

```
chop($cwd = 'pwd');
```

To modify the script to work under NT, change "pwd" to "cd" so that the system call will work properly.

That's it for the indexing script. Check to see if everything is working by running the script from a command prompt. Make sure the directory containing the perl program is in your path, then change directory to the location of the ICE scripts and type the following:

```
perl ice-idx.pl
```

You won't see anything while the program is running unless there are errors. Now, go to the location of the index file, and open it with any text editor. You should see the index of words, such as the following example:

```
@f /D:/WEBSITE/HTDOCS/INDEX.html
@t Your Home Page Goes Here
@m 821646357
1 README
1 WebSite
1 WebView
1 build
1 button
1 check
1 choose
1 click
1 client
1 default
1 demos
1 directory
```

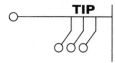

TIP

If you want to have your site indexed automatically on a regular basis, you can use the NT "at" service to run the ice-idx.pl program at regular intervals. A convenient front end for this service comes as part of the Windows NT Resource Kit.

Creating a Thesaurus

Although full text searching is a very powerful tool for users trying to find information on a web site, there are limits. For instance, you might want to find information on trains, but the information on the site is written using the word railroads. Without using a thesaurus function on the full text search engine (or thinking to try different words yourself), you might never find the information you want. The ICE search tool supplies a thesaurus capability, but you must create the thesaurus file yourself.

The thesaurus file is set up as a list of pairs. Each pair can define a word and a synonym (EQ), a word and a corresponding abbreviation (AF), or an abbreviation and a corresponding word (AB). For example, a simple thesaurus file might include the following entries:

```
Image EQ Picture
Picture EQ Image
Database AF DB
DB AB Database
```

Creating the Search Form

The second ICE script, ice-form.pl, serves two functions. The first thing it does is to return a search form to the browser, based on entries you make in the script. For example, a typical search form returned by ice-form.pl might look like Figure 11-1.

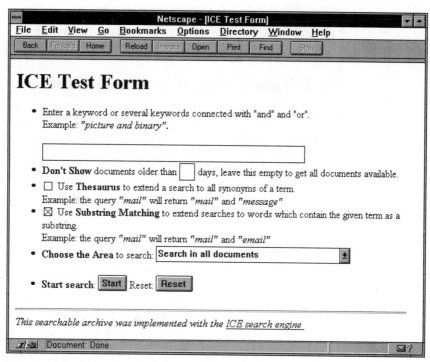

Figure 11-1: *A typical search form created by ice-form.pl.*

This form is returned when the script is called without any additional parameters. If you enter a search term or terms, this form will run the ice-form.pl script again, this time with the extra information of your search terms, and return the results of the search, as shown in Figure 11-2. The results programmed into the WAIS engine are the filename, the modification date on the HTML file, the physical path to the file, and the number of times the search term appeared in the file.

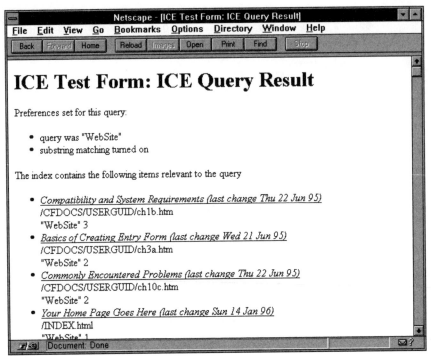

Figure 11-2: *The results page of a search.*

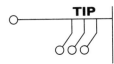

TIP

You're not required to use the ice-form.pl script to create the search form: you can create your own if you want. See Chapter 9, "Simple Forms," and Chapter 10, "CGI & DLLs: Programming Your Server," for information on creating your own forms.

There are a number of sections in ice-form.pl that you'll need to customize, and a number of sections that you may want to customize. First, create a title for the search form page. The variable $title determines the title at the top of the search form page. The default is "ICE Indexing Gateway"; and you should change this to your own title.

Next, create a list of what the index contains. In the example, there are a number of directories listed along with the physical path on the disk. Not only is it unnecessary to show the path names in this list, it is probably a bad idea. Just create a list of the identifiable web areas (if you have more than one major area) in the index.

Now, for the $indexfile variable, enter the full path and filename for the index file you created with ice-idx.pl. For the $thesfile variable, enter the path and filename for the thesaurus (synonym and abbreviation) file, if you've created one.

Finally, establish mappings from real directory paths to the URL path used by your web server. Since the perl scripts are run on your file system directly, they need to know how to change the physical path they find on the disk to the URL path needed by your server. For example, if you have a document root for your server specified as D:\website\htdocs, you'd need a single entry in the mapping section of the ice-form.pl file that looks like this:

```
%urltopath = (

    '/',  'D:/website/htdocs')
```

Now you can check basic functions by running the ice-form.pl file from the command line. Enter the following:

```
perl ice-form.pl
```

You should see a result similar to the following:

```
You have called the ice forms interface manually.
Optionally, provide search word as an argument.
Test mode: search for "the"
____
```

If this works, you can now create a page on your web that calls the ice-form.pl script. First create a simple batch file that in turn calls the perl script. The batch file should contain a single line, as follows:

```
perl ice-form.pl
```

Call this file anything you want, such as search.bat.

Now, in a page on your web, put in a link to the batch file. For example:

```
<P>You can<A HREF=/cgi-bin/search> search this web site by
keyword!</A></P>
```

Clicking on this link should bring up the search form, and typing in search terms and entering the search form should bring up a list of results. Be sure to check the links given to the document; it's easy to make a mistake in the %urltopath variable, which would in turn create bad document links on the search results form.

If you want to change the look of the search form, or the results formatting, find the appropriate spot in the ice-form.pl script and modify the HTML code. The section of the script with the following comment contains the HTML code for the query form:

```
# display the Forms interface
```

The subroutine identified as "sub main" is the part of the script containing the code that creates the search results return page.

WAIS for NT

WAIS stands for Wide Area Information Servers and refers to a protocol standard for search and retrieval over a network. The WAIS protocol is based on Z39.50, the 1988 version of the ANSI standard for communicating with electronic library catalogs. WAIS was first designed and implemented by Thinking Machines, Inc., for the enormous text databases needed by customers like Dow Jones. Thinking Machines generously donated an implementation of the protocol and its full-text search and index system to the public domain. Eventually, the programmers who designed WAIS left Thinking Machines to found WAIS, Inc., a company devoted to further developing the WAIS technology. Support for the public domain version of WAIS passed to the Clearinghouse for Networked Information Discovery and Retrieval (CNIDR), who changed the package's name to freeWAIS. The NT version of WAIS is based on freeWAIS version 0.3, which is one of the most powerful and widely used full-text indexing packages on the Net.

On the Companion CD-ROM there are versions of the NT WAIS toolkit for the Intel, MIPS, and DEC Alpha architectures, along with complete documentation. If you have an Intel-architecture system, use the programs from the Intel toolkit directory. You should see the files in the following table:

File	Description
waisindx.exe	The indexing program
waislook.exe	The searching program
waisserv.exe	The Z39.50 searching program
waistool.doc	The manual in Word for Windows format
waistool.wri	The manual in Windows Write format
waistool.ps	The manual in PostScript, ready for printing
read.me	Summary of new features, etc.

Table 11-1: *Files included in the WAIS toolkit.*

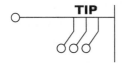

TIP

The WAIS toolkit can also be found at http://clyde.emwac.ed.ac.uk/. It's part of the Internet Toolchest for Windows NT.

Copy waislook.exe into your Windows system32 directory so that a server can find it when running as a service. This is the program that searches your index and returns the results. You can copy waisindx.exe either to the same directory, or to a working directory of your choice. You'll manually invoke waisindx.exe when creating the index, so it must be in your path. Check that the programs are installed properly by checking the version number at the command prompt. Following are the commands you should use along with the results you should see:

```
C:\>waisindx -v
waisindx: freeWAIS Release 0.3 beta 2/16/93
Version 0.73 for Windows NT

C:\>waislook -v
Version 0.73 for Windows NT
```

Creating the Index

The waisindx.exe program is the part of the WAIS toolkit that creates the index database. To create an index, first change directory to the root of the directory tree on your web that you want to index—for example, \website\htdocs. To create a database called "myindex" that indexes files in the \website\htdocs directory, start the WAIS indexer by entering the following:

```
waisindx -t html -d myindex *
```

The -t html option tells the indexer how to find titles in the files being indexed, and the -d myindex option specifies the name of the index database to be created. This command will create a number of files that all start with the name myindex.

Sometimes a straight full-text search isn't good enough, because not everyone thinks up the same word for the same idea. To help with this problem, WAIS allows you to create a synonym file that lets you provide a list of synonyms for your index. To create a synonym list, you can create a synonym file in the same directory with the same name as the database you've created plus the file extension .SYN. This file is very simple, with the first word on each line interpreted as the base word, and all other words on the line as synonyms for the first word. Following is a sample synonym file from the WAIS toolkit documentation:

```
# First word is base term, rest are synonyms
boat ship yacht launch galleon destroyer dinghy
shoe slipper boot sneaker trainer
```

Creating the Search Form

You can test the database you just created by using the waislook program, as in this example:

```
waislook -d myindex -http -h www.myhost.com -p 80 search
string
```

Search string is a word or combination of words that specifies your search. If there's more than one word, the default interpretation is to combine them in an OR specification. Other Boolean operators that can be used are AND and NOT. The -d myindex option specifies that the myindex database should be used in the query; the -http option tells waislook to return an HTML page as the result; the -h localhost option specifies that the system name to be listed in the returned document URLs is *www.myhost.com*; and the -p 80 option is the port number to be used in the URL. Each of these fields must be specified to make the references work properly.

The result of this test will be a display on your screen of the HTML file that would normally be returned to the browser of your web site. You can quickly determine if the waislook program is working by using words you know are in the index, then seeing if waislook finds them.

Now that you've created an index and tested it, you're ready to incorporate the search capability on your web. The waislook program was not designed specifically to be a CGI program, so there might be some special measures you'll need to take, depending on the server you're using. If you're using the EMWAC server or Purveyor from Process Software, it's easy to invoke the waislook program. Just create an HTML form with the same name as the database (for example, myindex.htm, if the database name is myindex, as in the example above), and include an <ISINDEX> tag somewhere on the page. The <ISINDEX> tag creates a text input field that prompts a user to enter search terms. When the server gets the request for the page with a search term specified, it automatically invokes waislook.exe with the database myindex. The results of the search will be returned to the browser.

For servers that do not take this special action, such as the Alibaba server, the process is more involved. First, you need to create a short batch or command file that invokes the waislook program when called, as follows:

```
echo Content-type:text/html
echo.
echo.
if "%1" == "abc123" waislook -d myindex -http -h 127.0.0.1 →
    -p 80 %2 %3 %4 %5 %6 %7 %8 %9 & goto CONT1

waislook -d myindex -http -h 127.0.0.1 -p 80 %1 %2 %3 %4 %5 →
%6 %7 %8 %9
:CONT1
```

For our example we'll name this file waislook.cmd. You must also move the WAIS database files that waisindx.exe created into the same directory as this command file. For Alibaba, that would be the cgi-bin directory.

You can see that there are two branches in the command file: the first branch invokes the waislook program for the initial search of the database, and the second invokes waislook for subsequent searches. To allow the user to submit the initial search of the database, create a form-submission page with the following HTML:

```
<HTML><HEAD>
<TITLE>Example Search Form</TITLE></HEAD>
<BODY>
<FORM ACTION="/cgi-bin/waislook.cmd" METHOD="GET">
<P>Enter search terms here:</P>
<INPUT TYPE="text" NAME="abc123" SIZE=40>
<INPUT TYPE="submit" VALUE="Search Web">
</FORM> </BODY></HTML>
```

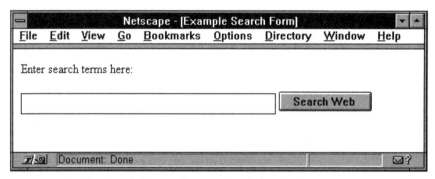

Figure 11-3: *The sample form-submission page for the initial search of the WAIS database.*

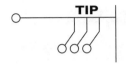

TIP

For more information about the <INPUT> and <ISINDEX> tags, and about the creation and use of interactive forms in general, see Chapter 9, "Simple Forms," and Chapter 10, "CGI & DLLs: Programming Your Server."

The form has a single text box, defined by the first <INPUT> tag, with the name "abc123." The second <INPUT> tag is the button the user selects to submit the form to your web server. When the user types a search term into the text box and clicks the Search Web button, the browser program sends the content of the form to your web server. The browser doesn't send everything you see in the HTML form, only the names of the controls along with their values. The web server, seeing that the destination is a CGI program (through the ACTION parameter of /cgi-bin/waislook.cmd), starts up the waislook.cmd script, and passes the contents of the form to the script via the command line. The fourth line in the waislook.cmd file checks to see if the first command-line parameter that has been passed to it is our special flag word, "abc123," and if so, it invokes the waislook.exe program *without* using the first parameter. The remaining parameters (%2 to %9) are passed to waislook as command-line parameters, which are the words that the user is searching for. Figure 11-4 shows a typical return from a database search.

The WAIS search engine evaluates the potential that the returned search result is what you are really looking for by counting the number of times a search term occurs in a document, and whether the search term appears in the title of the document. The highest score is 1000. The size is the number of bytes in the document.

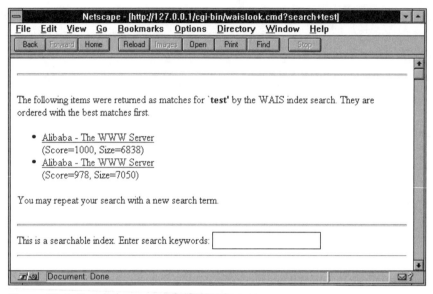

Figure 11-4: *Result from a waislook search.*

The waislook program allows the user to enter another search term at the bottom of the returned results page. This is accomplished with an <ISINDEX> tag. When the user enters a search term in this field and presses Enter, the waislook.cmd command file will be called again, only this time, since the first string passed to the command file is *not* "abc123" (the NAME of the text box on the initial search form), waislook.exe is invoked by the second branch of the command file, and the first search term *is* used as the first command-line parameter. (The odd name "abc123" was given to the text box on the initial search form because it's unlikely that a user will ever really specify "abc123" as a search term.)

If you forgot to move the WAIS database files into the same directory as the waislook.cmd file, when you submit the initial search page you'd get the error message shown in Figure 11-5, instead of the search results page shown in Figure 11-4.

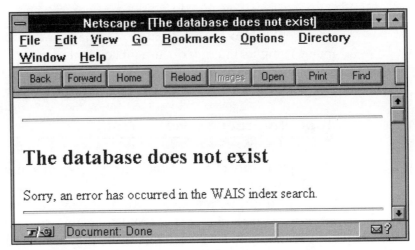

Figure 11-5: *Error return from waislook.exe.*

Commercial Search Engines

The Topic Internet Server and the Excite search engines are commercial products in use at major corporate sites around the world. Both add many additional features beyond those offered by the ICE and WAIS programs we've discussed. If you have the money to spend, these products offer great solutions to your Windows NT web-indexing and -searching needs.

Excite

Excite, from Architext, takes full-text searching to a new level that is not available from freeware or shareware tools. In addition to simple Boolean searches, Excite adds the ability to search based on concepts, instead of words. The Excite indexer creates its own concept comparisons, so you don't need to keep up your own database of synonyms. Of course, this means that you're stuck with the way Excite does things, and you may get back documents you didn't expect with the concept search. Upon the return of a document list, Excite can create a summary of the document found using its internal document concept identifier. Excite is available not only for Windows NT, but also for a variety of UNIX systems. The home page for Excite is at http://www.excite.com.

Topic Internet Server

The Topic Internet Server from Verity is part of a broad line of searching and document-serving products, and you can check them out at http://www.verity.com. The Internet Server product offers word-matching and concept-searching, and integrated support not only for HTML but for 50 different word processing formats, TIFF, and Adobe Acrobat. Verity also advertises a scaleable architecture that allows them to support millions of documents.

Moving On

By now, you should be able to use ICE and WAIS for NT to create full-text-searchable indexes of your web site, and to create basic forms to access the indexes. You should also understand that there are more sophisticated commercial programs available if straight text-searching does not meet all your needs. The searching and indexing of web sites is an evolving field, and you should always check for the latest developments by searching the Web for yourself.

Local searching and indexing, however, is by no means the only issue involved in making your web site highly accessible to users. As in all human endeavors, design and promotion are key. In the next chapter, you'll learn how to use these skills to create an effective site. You'll also learn about the various channels and forums that are available for advertising and promoting your site.

Final Considerations

12

Fitting In: Joining the Virtual Community

Y ou can approach putting a new site on the World Wide Web in two ways. One is to have a relatively isolated site, with little publicity and few external links. For some sites, there's little reason to encourage users from all over the Web to connect. For example, if your site is providing technical support for specific products, it would probably be enough to include the URL for the site in your product documentation, along with instructions on how to connect and access information. However, the majority of sites will want to use their presence on the Web both for publicity and for information distribution. This chapter will focus primarily on this second approach, providing information on how to create a site that is easy to locate and use and that encourages users to come back often.

Location & First Impressions

The location of your site—that is, both the machine name and the filename—determines, in part, how easy it is for a user to find you without using any search tools or Web indices (which are discussed later in this chapter). It has become standard for the machine that is hosting a Web site to be named "www." Ventana Communications Group's site, for example, is running on the machine www.vmedia.com. This does not mean that the host machine has to be renamed. To create an alias that sends a user to the correct machine, simply add an alias name to your nameserver. Alias www.*domain*.com to the machine that you'll be using to serve your information, and from that point on, using either the machine's real name or its new alias will enable a user to access your site. If you're working with a service provider who handles your name service, contact them and ask them to do this for you.

The site name itself is all users need to find information on your site. Since all servers should be configured to return a default page when no page name is given, the user does not need to enter a starting page name. The directory or machine name alone will take her or him to this default page.

This first page, index.htm, provides a sort of conceptual center for your site. It is commonly referred to as the *home page* of the site. The home page provides users with their first impressions both of the site itself and of the company, department, or individual that is being represented there. Assuming that you're not operating entirely on name recognition to draw users, you'll want to make sure that the presentation of your home page encourages exploration of the content presented throughout the rest of the pages. There are, obviously, an infinite number of potential layouts for home pages. Several different types are seen consistently throughout the Web:

- the graphical interface
- the graphics/text hybrid
- the pre-home page

Each of these types is discussed in more detail below.

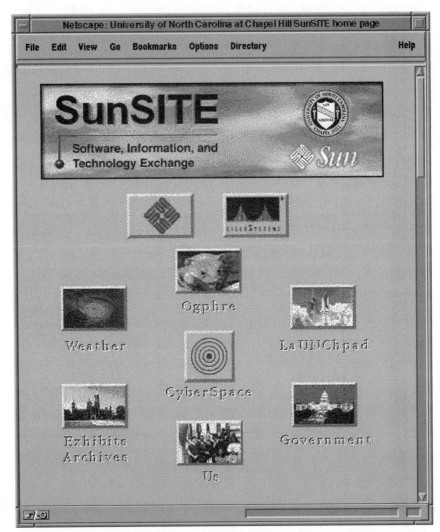

Figure 12-1: *A graphical interface—the SunSITE.unc.edu home page (http:// sunsite.unc.edu/).*

Graphical Interface

The graphical interface, shown in Figure 12-1, attempts to present, in one image or set of images, all of the categories into which information is organized, using the graphics themselves as the links to different areas of the site (see "Clickable Imagemaps," in Chapter 7, "Images on the Web"). This sort of layout should be used by designers who are expecting high-speed output on the server end and users with high-speed connections who are looking specifically for impressive graphics layouts.

One way to determine whether a large-scale graphical interface on your home page is practical is to analyze in advance the type of information that the site will be serving. If you're primarily focused on distributing text information or have limited multimedia content (a few audio clips or photographs of a small number of products, for example), having a complex front end limits the number of people who go beyond your first page. Users who could benefit from text files, such as catalogs or news briefs, or from small images alongside product descriptions, could very well be frustrated by a detailed home page. Since many people use the Web through modem connections or text-based browsers like Lynx, it's a good idea to remember that for every large graphic you include on a page, you're substantially increasing the time the page takes to load.

If, on the other hand, your focus is on multimedia products, graphic design, or other, more technically oriented materials, you will, and will want to, draw users who are looking for impressive page design and layout. The graphical interface, in this context, can convince users at first glance of your ability. Even in cases where it's appropriate to use the graphical interface, however, you should provide a text menu at the bottom of the page as an alternative. Also, each image should always carry an alternate text name, so that a browser not using images will receive some indication of what the image is.

Figure 12-2: *A graphics/text combination—the NCSA home page (http://www.ncsa.uiuc.edu).*

Graphics/Text Hybrid

The graphics/text hybrid, as shown in Figure 12-2, is used by the majority of sites on the Web. This layout integrates hyperlinked text and graphics, primarily for visual effect. This layout can have two advantages over a straight graphical interface. One advantage is the amount of time required for the page to load, because, by and large, the graphics are relatively smaller at a site with the graphics/text combination layout. However, a number of small graphics can take as long to load as a larger graphic, because each has to load in turn. Since most browsers cache images after loading them, it's advisable to use a bulleted list with a single icon (as described in "The Basics of HTML," in Chapter 2, "The Basic Pieces") or to include a small number of pictures repeated throughout the page. This allows images to be loaded out of the client's memory instead of off the server itself.

The second advantage to the graphics/text combination format is that it can establish a sense of consistency beyond the home page. A banner on the top of the home page can be repeated on all of the pages in the site or can be modified slightly to indicate one's location relative to the home page. Also, icons can be reused to link to pages with similar content, furthering design continuity.

Finally, the inclusion of text obviously allows for greater elaboration about the site and the products than does the use of a completely graphical interface. In both layouts, however, it's a good idea to include an "About this site" link, which provides the user with detailed information separate from the home page about the site itself and the parties it represents.

Figure 12-3: *A pre-home page—the Internet Underground Music Archive*
(http://www.iuma.com/).

Pre-home Page

A pre-home page is shown in Figure 12-3. Given that no site designer can fully anticipate the capacities or interests of his or her potential audience, a number of sites have put up pre-home pages. This page still uses index.htm, but it does not immediately present the main menu. Instead, it gives the user the option to view a full-fledged graphics display or to view a scaled-down text/graphics combination or sometimes a straight text menu. Including a pre-home page is generally the best way to go if your site seeks to cater to a wide range of users, from those using Lynx to those connecting on full T1s. Generally, the pre-home page is little more than a menu allowing the user to select which view of the home page to go to. A pre-home page is also useful if you have a multi-lingual site, as it allows the browser to select a preferred language.

One mistake a number of sites have made in implementing a pre-home page is that only the home page or a few pages have the reduced number of graphics, and as the user moves through the site, she or he encounters pages full of graphics even though she or he selected the option of a limited graphics display. To create a truly flexible site, all the pages should be accessible in the format selected by the user. One easy way of doing this, which requires time and disk space, is to create separate directory hierarchies with identical pages, one with the image tags and one without. A more complex method in the short term, but certainly easier in the long run, is to use a cgi-bin script that tells the browser not to load images on any page in the site if a user selected a "text-only" option at the outset. This process is explained in Chapter 10, "CGI & DLLs: Programming Your Server."

Design & Content Considerations

Once your design and layout skills have drawn users to the first page, your next considerations have to be how to keep them at your site, and how to encourage them to come back after they've left. In this section, we'll provide some suggestions on how to structure your site to keep the users' attention after they have entered the site and how to develop the content and presentation of your site to encourage repeated usage.

One of the most compelling and exciting aspects of hypertext is its ability to create the appearance almost transparently of a unified body of information across machines and domains. For example, by clicking on a link while reading information in California about networking software, the user can pull up a technical document about the World Wide Web located on a machine in Switzerland, without any sense of a break in continuity. However, this sense of continuity can present a problem for some sites. If a software vendor wants the user to browse through its catalog, look at screen captures of the software interface, and read reviews by users of the software, all to get a sense of the company's products and ability, the user's early departure from the site may represent lost potential in terms of exposure or interaction.

One way to avoid this problem from the outset is to be conscious of any external links that you build within the body of the site. For example, if the first line of your home page reads as follows, you run the risk of losing the visitor to the wealth of information that CERN offers about the World Wide Web.

```
<h2>Welcome to ShoopSoft Netware's Home on the <a
href="http://info.cern.ch/hypertext/WWW/
TheProject.html">World Wide Web</a></h2>
```

The problem is not that these links aren't valuable—in some basic sense, any site that does not inform users of the WWW project is leaving out the most important information available on the Web—but that these links should be relegated to a particular area, and anyone creating a Web site should understand that these links are a possible draw away from the site.

The best strategy to allow users to sample the information available about similar topics is to present a "links" page somewhere in the site. It's a good idea to provide a significant amount of hyperlinked text throughout your pages and to configure these links so they move the user around your site in a nonlinear way—allowing the user to choose how and when to receive the information you provide.

It's fairly standard to include a link on the home page of a document, labeled something like "Other resources" or "Links to the WWW," that provides an organized listing of topics that you feel anyone interested in your site would want to explore. It's a good idea to include links to resources that provide services similar or identical to your own, because it allows the user to judge your site against others in the field. By extension, then, if competition is your goal, it's up to you to ensure that users will prefer your site to the others. However, if you're working toward building a general knowledge base, regardless of where the user obtains the information, adding links to similar sites allows the sites to complement each other and collectively cover issues that no single site could fully address. The links page, then, should be accessible as part of the site, but as a marginal part, so that the information you provide can be clearly delineated as your own.

Another way of creating a site that gives the sense of a unified body of information is to use a standard design and layout for your pages. A number of sites standardize their pages through the use of menu bars that allow users to navigate through the various screens, encountering a standard header for every page or a signature and contact line at the bottom of every page. It's always a good idea to include a mailing address, such as webmaster@www.domain.com, on every page, linked to a mail script or a mailto tag if possible. Standardizing your site this way makes certain the user is constantly aware of his or her location and knows when he or she is leaving the site via an external link.

Also, every page on a site should have a "Back to the home page" link with some sort of recognizable icon. This link allows the user to start again at the top and explore new areas of information, without having to use the browser's Back function to page all the way back to the top. It also allows users to navigate to your home page if they bookmark a page deep in your web and then come back at a later date.

Finally, the most important element of the site, above and beyond all design and presentation concerns, is the content. Sites on the World Wide Web can take a number of forms. They can be little more than virtual billboards with pretty pictures and promotional information or online catalogs giving essentially the same information available from a mail-order catalog. However, it is unfortunate—and unprofitable—to use the technology of the Web to such limited ends.

Throughout this book, we provide a number of tips on how to interface your Web site with various features available on the Internet, such as multimedia resources or different types of database programs. When you're developing the ideas for your site, look closely at the resources available to you that you can offer the Internet community. A database of information, such as collections of news articles about certain topics, technical specifications for products or scientific work, and so on, can draw a large number of users to your site, especially if the information is unavailable or difficult to get elsewhere.

This kind of service can establish your site's Web presence—ironically, perhaps—by drawing more potential customers by giving away your services for free. Companies that release information or entertainment that can be used by visitors to their sites generally see those same visitors return as consumers who recommend the site and, by extension, the company, to others. Also, as discussed in the next section, "Choosing & Reaching Your Audience," providing services is its own form of promotion, both online and off. Consider what you have to offer as a company, as a department, or as an individual Web provider, and decide what would be the most valuable information to give away. Using the technologies described throughout this book, you should be able to convert almost any resource at your disposal into data accessible via the World Wide Web. By doing so, you establish yourself both as an entity present on the World Wide Web and as a participant in the benefits that it confers upon both users and providers.

Choosing & Reaching Your Audience

Strange as it may be to say toward the end of a book about creating a World Wide Web presence for yourself, there are no guarantees that the Web will be the "next big thing." The reason it's necessary to keep this point in mind is that, as a new participant in the Web, it's part of your responsibility to make sure this new technology remains an important medium. In this media-driven society, the primary means toward this goal is publicity—both for individual sites and for the Web itself. By talking about the Internet and the Web and by demonstrating the vast potential that it presents to business, education, and individual users, you serve the dual purpose of encouraging the use of a particular site and of the Web itself. While this section focuses primarily on publicity within the Internet itself, it should be remembered that publicity in the print or broadcasting media draws new users to the Internet and broadens the potential audience for your site.

One of the first decisions that has to be made about publicity, online and off, is how much publicity is necessary and who the target audience will comprise. Some sites require very little publicity, such as those serving a particular need for a select group of people. For example, a site that provides software patches and updates for a particular line of products should consider inserting its URL into the documentation distributed with the software, along with information about how to get onto the Web in the first place (that is, where to download a browser or how to use Lynx over dial-up connections).

To publicize the site over all available channels would create more traffic than might be desirable for some sites. If a server is running over a slow connection or expects a large number of FTP accesses, too much traffic will adversely affect the performance and access time of the machine hosting the information. Educational sites, such as university departments running their own servers, would probably want to publicize within the university itself and link to the university's home page, but these departments probably would not want to post to a large number of newsgroups. These are a few examples to encourage thought about an issue that is becoming increasingly important, especially online—namely, that too much publicity can be detrimental to the site and to the Internet community at large, as in the case of "spamming," discussed at the end of this section.

The use of print media to promote a Web site can be extremely helpful in some cases, and in others, its effect is negligible. Some basic steps requiring very little effort can raise general awareness about your site. A number of companies include a line at the bottom of their standard print advertisements saying something like "Be sure to visit us on the Internet at our World Wide Web site: http://www.*domain*.com/." This publicity encourages people who are already familiar with the Web to go to the site and engenders curiosity in those who are not. Simply putting a line like "WWW: http://www.*domain*.com/" in conspicuous places like letterheads or business cards can achieve the same effect.

As a more proactive way of getting attention for a new site, many companies issue press releases announcing the opening of the site. A press release for a Web site should include several items. First, include an explanation of what the World Wide Web is. This explanation can be as simple as "the multimedia front end for the Internet" or as complex as you feel is appropriate for your audience. Second, include an explanation of how to access the site for people on the Internet but unfamiliar with the World Wide Web. Again, this can be as simple as this: "Using software like NCSA Mosaic or Netscape, people connected to the Internet can simply enter our new address (URL) and see all our site has to offer." Finally, some discussion of the implications of this new technology is appropriate, if as nothing more than a way to answer the reader's question, Why should I care?

If you're distributing products online, presenting special information to Internet users, or even just allowing consumers to get product information without having to make a telephone call, discuss these advantages as a way to encourage people to investigate how they can get access to this resource. Keep in mind that, unlike online promotion, any promotion done via print media must assume that the majority of readers are unfamiliar with the technology being described. That's why there's no guarantee that using newspapers or magazines will significantly increase your site's usage. Print media should be viewed as a way of drawing new users online, and to get their attention, you must offer something that's worth their effort. Publicity in print should, above all, emphasize the significance of this new medium to someone who is not yet online but should be.

An easy way to draw people online is to provide a unique service to users, either something new to the Internet or something otherwise not achievable through standard channels like telephone or mail-order. The most obvious benefit of the Web in this regard is multimedia capability. Photographs of your products, brief audio clips of staff or "satisfied customers" discussing whatever your site is focused upon, and other ways of creating a rich description of your goals and organization are all easy to achieve within the context of a Web site. This alone, though, will be purely promotional, and promotional sites are inherently limited. Even if users are so interested in your product or site content that they've come online as a result, their visits will last only long enough for them to look at what they might want and possibly to order the products. A site that is little more than glorified advertising does not encourage repeated usage and does not hold the attention of users who are not interested in a particular product or service.

Another way to create a site that will draw people online is to explore new technologies in the context of a Web site. For example, improvements in audio and video compression and distribution are occurring daily (see Chapter 8, "True Multimedia: Adding Audio & Animation"), and if you can use the newest technology, your site will be of interest by default, as it is exploring the cutting edge of the Internet. This sort of approach can be promoted through print media, and your site will gain a reputation as "one to watch" for users who are excited by the potential of Internet technologies.

This is also true in industries that are not heavily represented on the Web. For example, a film company using high-quality video compression to distribute audio/visual clips would be seen in industry press as a site to watch to find out how this technology can affect or benefit others in the field. If the site also encouraged collaborative efforts—allowing users to edit and upload these clips, creating a sort of community-made film project—the press might use the site as an exemplary case study in articles about the potentials of Web technology. This example is provided simply to reinforce what should be on every Web designer's mind: the draw to a Web site will be in direct proportion to the site's levels of substance, interactivity, and innovation. By emphasizing the new and exciting, you can effectively use print and broadcast media as "free" advertising and, in so doing, increase the population of the Internet itself.

The Mammoth Records Internet Information Center
When North Carolina–based Mammoth Records put up its Mammoth Records Internet Information Center on the WWW, it was still a fairly new idea for record companies. Karen Booth, Mammoth Records's Internet coordinator, focused announcements on nontechnical publications. "If anyone was going to talk about the site being innovative, it was going to be a business journal, if they were running an Internet issue or interactive multimedia issue," she explained, adding that recording industry trade publications also took that approach.

In a press release, Mammoth emphasized unique details of the site ("full-length singles, video, artist photos, CD art, up-to-the-minute tour schedules, and mail-order information") and emphasized some technical details, such as its use of MPEG2 audio compression, "which provides CD-quality music samples." To draw attention to the potential of the Web as a medium, Mammoth stated that "the Internet is fully global," citing accesses from Russia, Japan, New Zealand, and Australia within the first days of operation. And to help writers who were not familiar with the Web itself, Mammoth distributed several pages of a book about the Web.

The focus on nontechnical press had a twofold effect. First, in the industry, Karen noted, "you get a reputation as a trailblazer." Second, it encouraged users who were not yet connected to the Internet to seek a connection so that they could get the information, such as touring schedules for bands.

Publicity on the Internet itself is vital to promoting your site. Print and broadcast media will draw new users to the Internet, the Web, and your site, but since a substantial population already inhabits the Web, drawing these existing users to your site can establish your presence very quickly. Most Web users check for new sites on a regular basis, both at announcement sites and on newsgroups. While there's no centralized registration process for Web sites, there are some newsgroups and pages that are recognized as informal centers for new developments.

Catalogs & Announcements on the WWW

Where do Web users look to learn what's new on the Net? This section provides a rundown of locations most users check.

What's New at NCSA Mosaic
http://www.ncsa.uiuc.edu/SDG/Docs/whats-new.html
What's New at NCSA Mosaic was the first of the "What's New" pages on the Internet and has remained one of the most active. Mosaic was the first of the World Wide Web browsers, and it included from the outset a link to a page where the NCSA staff would list new sites. The page is now updated almost daily, and all of the updates for the current month are kept on a single page. There are two ways to submit to What's New. The first, and probably the simplest for a single page or site, is to go to the URL http://www.ncsa.uiuc.edu/SDG/Docs/whats-new.html and fill out the form. When you submit the form it's automatically added to the list. If you don't have forms capability on your browser or are trying to avoid going from site to site to add to every different What's New page, you can send e-mail. The e-mail should be marked up in HTML with one or two links to your site. The maintainers of NCSA's What's New page ask that submissions be formatted in the following way:

Title (name of resource):

Primary URL (main link to resource):

Organization sponsoring resource:

Location of resource:

City:

State (two-letter code if in United States):

Country:

Contact person:

    Name:

    E-mail:

Category (put an X next to the one that best describes your organization):

Commercial

Educational

Government

Independent

Description:

A single paragraph (30-word limit) that briefly describes your service. You can include HTML links in the description (no repeat of the main link) but please, no bolds, italics, all-caps.

Yahoo

http://www.yahoo.com/

Originally run from Stanford University, Yahoo has rapidly developed into one of the most comprehensive subject-based catalogs on the World Wide Web since its recent inception. Yahoo is a hierarchical menu organized by subject headings that allows users to submit their sites in the area or areas that they feel are appropriate. One can add a site from anywhere in Yahoo by selecting the Add button on the menu bar, but it's a good idea to go to the area you want to have your site included in first. Unless you're already familiar with Yahoo's menu structure, it's not always immediately apparent where to place your new site, and by wandering through the index to find the best location, you save the maintainers of Yahoo the work of placing your entry for you. Be sure to keep in mind that sites can be added in multiple categories, thereby increasing your exposure. The Add form is quite straightforward, and will even assume that you want to add your site to the menu area that you selected Add from and lists that as the default in your form. You receive a confirmation message soon after Yahoo adds your site.

EINet Galaxy
http://www.einet.net/
The maker of MacWeb and WinWeb, EINet Galaxy has a listing for
new sites attached to its home page for the EINet browser software. While MacWeb and WinWeb have declined in popularity as
Netscape has risen in prominence alongside Mosaic, a number of
users still reference this site for its extremely valuable hierarchical
subject menu. As with Yahoo, to submit to EINet Galaxy, wander
through the subject tree until you've found an appropriate place
for your site. Click on Add on the EINet menu bar, and fill out the
form. If you cannot determine a place for your site, simply submit
it from the home page, and the EINet staff will create a new
heading. For help on adding information to EINet Galaxy, look at
the page http://www.einet.net/annotate-help.html.

The GNN Whole Internet Catalog
http://www-e1c.gnn.com/gnn/wic/
A product of the Global Network Navigator, The GNN Whole
Internet Catalog is the World Wide Web outgrowth of the O'Reilly
book *The Whole Internet User's Guide & Catalog*. On the "About this
site" page for the catalog, GNN describes the site as "a collection
of links to 1000 or so of the best resources on the Internet, divided
into easy-to-surf subject areas." The catalog is manually updated,
and all submissions to the catalog are checked out by the GNN
staff before being added. To submit your site, simply send e-mail
with the URL and a description of the site to wic@ora.com.

The WWW Virtual Library
http://www.w3.org/hypertext/DataSources/bySubject/
Overview.html
The WWW Virtual Library is an index of resources on the Web,
organized by subject. Unlike the other catalogs, it is made up of
separate departments that are maintained by volunteer users. It's
intended more as an index of informational sites than an index of
commercial sites. However, it does have a separate section for
commercial services, and commercial servers that address one of
the other informational topics can and should be added to the
listings for that topic. To add your site to the library, you should

contact the maintainer of the particular area into which your site fits. For example, the majority of commercial servers would want a listing in the "Commercial Services" area. To submit to this section, send e-mail with a description of the site to www-request@mail.w3.org. For a complete listing of subject areas and the people maintaining them, look at http://www.w3.org/hypertext/DataSources/bySubject/Maintainers.html.

Robots & Web–Walkers on the WWW

Here is a listing of some robots and Web-walkers on the WWW.

Lycos
http://www.lycos.com
Originally developed by Michael Mauldin at Carnegie-Mellon University, Lycos is a very efficient and extensive indexer. Like other automatically updating indices, it "wanders" the Web and registers the pages that it finds. Lycos locates a home page and follows the links from that page, down to the end of that site, registering the URL, title, and a portion of the text from each page. It's incredibly efficient (and even more popular) and it has the vast majority of sites on the Web within its database. It does, however, need to be told about new domains with Web servers, so that it can add those to its wandering patterns. To add your site to Lycos, go to the URL http://www.lycos.com/register.html, and fill out the form to submit your home page.

The World Wide Web Worm
http://www.cs.colorado.edu/wwww
The World Wide Web Worm is a robot designed by the University of Colorado computer science department and is similar to Lycos in function. It follows links through Web documents and catalogs its findings in a searchable database. Also like Lycos, it requires that the URL of your top-level document be submitted, and from that point on, the process is automatic. To submit your home page, and by extension, all of the pages at your site, go to the URL http://www.cs.colorado.edu/home/mcbryan/WWWWadd.html and fill out the form on that page.

The WebCrawler Index

http://webcrawler.com/

Based at the University of Washington, the WebCrawler Index is another Web-walker designed to maintain a dynamic database of World Wide Web pages. To submit your site for indexing, fill out the WebCrawler URL submission form at http://webcrawler.com/WebCrawler/SubmitURLS.html.

Alta Vista

http://www.altavista.digital.com/

This search engine was created by Digital Equipment Corporation, and boasts 21 million Web pages indexed as of March 1996. With a search index this large, it is possible Alta Vista has already indexed your site, but in case it hasn't you can select the Add/Delete URL option from the main page to add your own site.

Usenet

Here are some Usenet newsgroups you might wish to explore on the Web.

news:comp.infosystems.www.announce

Originally there was a single newsgroup on Usenet for discussions of the World Wide Web. That group has been split into four groups, which have separate purposes. The group currently used for announcements is comp.infosystems.www.announce. It's considered bad form to post announcements of a new site to the other three groups, even though it happens with some frequency. The comp.infosystems.www.announce newsgroup is moderated, meaning that an administrator clears all posts before they go up on the group itself. Announcements should be sent via e-mail to www-announce@medio.com. The announcements should be in plain text, not marked up in HTML. At the beginning of the message, you should include a single line, in the following format:

```
<URL:protocol://site[:PORT]/path/to/file/or/directory/>
```

For example, <URL:http://sunsite.unc.edu/mdw/linux.html> is a valid entry for the beginning of the message. The [:PORT] option should be used only if your HTTP server is running on a port other than the default port (80). In the subject line, use one of the following categories as your first word, in all capital letters, followed by the title of the resource:

ARCHIVE	ART	BOOK
BROWSER	COLLECTION	ECONOMY
EDUCATION	ENTERTAINMENT	ENVIRONMENT
FAQ	GAMES	HEALTH
HUMANITIES	INFO	LAW
MAGAZINE	MISC	MUSIC
NEWS	PERSONAL	POLITICS
REFERENCE	RELIGION	SCIENCE
SERVER	SHOPPING	SPORTS
SOFTWARE		

The newsgroup's charter makes the following recommendations: "The announcement should be short—less than 75 lines—and to the point. The author's signature should be four lines or shorter; the moderator will trim longer signatures. Announcers should not include surveys, polls, application forms, or the like in their posts; such addenda will be excised. Likewise, announcers should not quote price lists or extensive catalog-style descriptions. Instead, a post should provide pointers, in the format described above, to those resources."

news:comp.internet.net-happenings

Originally, the newsgroup net-happenings@is.internic.net was a mailing list started by Gleason Sackman as a way to keep people updated, via e-mail, on the latest developments from all over the Internet. However, user after user complained of the 30 to 50 messages a day that poured in about Gophers, FTP sites, legal updates, and the Web, and so the newsgroup comp.internet.net-happenings was created as an alternative means of retrieval. There are also several FTP mirrors and a WWW site with a searchable index of postings to net-happenings. Net-happenings still remains one of the largest mailing lists on the Internet and is a major source of information for events and new additions to the World Wide Web.

There isn't really a standard format for messages on comp.internet.net-happenings, but you can do a few things to help the moderator organize the messages. First, the subject line should begin with the protocol, in this case "www." The subject line itself should contain a one-line description of the event to be announced, such as "ShoopSoft WWW Site Online." In the body of the message, you can describe your site, services to be offered, interesting features, and include the URL and a contact person. The URL should be in the same format as in messages to the comp.infosystems.www.announce newsgroup, <URL:*protocol*://*site*[:*PORT*]/*path/to/file/or/directory/*>.

news:alt.internet.services

This newsgroup is generally used for announcements about new services being offered to the Internet community at large. New sites are occasionally posted here but far less frequently than on a group like comp.infosystems.www.announce. You should especially consider posting here if your site offers a unique service to the Web community and is not simply a promotional site. The subject line should begin with "ANNOUNCE:" and should include, at the beginning of the message, the URL of your site in standard format: <URL:http://www.*domain*.com/*location*/*filename*.html>.

More on Newsgroups

You'll want to publicize your site on a number of newsgroups in addition to these. Since Usenet is patronized very selectively by most users, the more newsgroups you're visible on, the more attention your site gets.

However, this statement must be qualified: if your site is publicized on inappropriate groups to which it is irrelevant or even tangential, you'll certainly receive attention, but not the sort that you might be seeking. It is absolutely imperative that promotional posts, especially for commercial sites, not be made recklessly. This type of behavior, called "spamming" in Net lingo, is considered one of the worst infractions that users can commit against the Internet population for a number of reasons. One is that, contrary to what many users may think, Usenet is not free to maintain or distribute. Every post takes up disk space and CPU time that has to be paid for by each news host. This is not a problem for information and news, but begins to be a problem for commercial advertisements. Every unnecessary post can be encouragement for news hosts to limit the amount of news that they provide, a limitation which would damage both the users using that particular host and Usenet as a community and a resource.

That said, there's no reason why you shouldn't address appropriate newsgroups when a new site, relevant to the interests of the readers, is created. After posting to the standard announcement sites, think about what newsgroups you read on a regular basis, and decide whether those groups would find this information relevant. Also remember that electronic mailing lists are a valuable means of distribution for new site announcements.

While no advice can be given as to where to begin looking, or exactly which groups would or would not be receptive to an announcement, you can use several methods to determine how you should approach them. Primary to all of these methods, though, is your taking time to read through the group, participating in discussions unrelated to promotion and getting a feel for the community of the group. Ask yourself these questions: First, have other sites been announced on this particular group, and how have those postings been received? Second, is the population of this newsgroup inclined toward Web usage in the first place? If they aren't, should they be, for your site or in general, and might your announcement help encourage them? Finally, how would the members benefit from using your site, outside of just being consumers? Are you providing information that would help them, given that they, as customers and interested investigators, will benefit you by their presence and participation?

This final question should always be considered, not only in your promotional strategies, but in the way that you design your site. As mentioned in "Design & Content Considerations," earlier in this chapter, the quality of the informational content and the general benefits of using your site will be directly proportional to its use by the Internet community. Before promoting your site, and perhaps even before creating it at all, think in terms of mutual benefit: the benefit you'll get by establishing a Web presence and having a new body of potential customers or contacts, and in return, the benefit that you'll give them by providing a new resource for information and ideas. From the outset, we've stressed that the World Wide Web can be much more than a series of billboards or online catalogs. As a new citizen of the Internet (a "Netizen"), it's your responsibility to ensure that it indeed is much more.

Moving On

This book outlines a number of ways to create an excellent Web site, from authoring and style techniques to full multimedia. After creating the site, you should decide how it is to be found and how it will appear upon first impression. Naming your machines and creating an appropriate and attractive home page will lead users to your site and please them upon arrival. The links in your document, laid out with foresight, will guide your users to the pages that you want them to see.

After everything is finished, or at least presentable, new sites should be "advertised" to the Net, using Usenet newsgroups and World Wide Web indices. A number of sites announce their presence on the Internet in the areas listed throughout this chapter, and then place an "Under Construction" icon on their pages. In a way, this is redundant. Every site on the World Wide Web is, and should be, under construction all the time. Instead of putting an "Under Construction" notice on your pages, make it obvious that your site is under construction by providing the newest functions available. The final chapter of this book, "Future Directions," describes the ways that the World Wide Web is changing, and what is becoming possible. Using this information, you can make sure that your site is always under construction, and by extension, on the cutting edge.

13

Future Directions

The World Wide Web is evolving at a faster rate than probably any other medium in history. Between the time that this book is written and when it's on the shelves of bookstores, browsers will be capable of displaying new features of Web pages, merchants will be selling new products for the Web, Web sites will be selling products in new ways, and discussions will be occurring across the globe about how to change the face of the Web.

The discussions in this chapter are intended to give you a peek into the future of the Web, including the following:

- Developments in HTTP, the protocol that clients and servers use to communicate. These developments include an upgraded version and enhancements to HTTP security that are changing commerce on the Web.

- Additions to, and renovations of, HTML.

- A new language, called the Virtual Reality Modeling Language (VRML), describing three-dimensional space on the Web.

- Java extensions.

- New technologies and Web sites that allow new levels of collaboration across the Internet.

The Future of HTML

In discussions about the future of the Web, references to "HTML 3 features" are frequently heard. HTML version 3.0, or "HTML 3," was proposed in an "Internet Draft," a working document that recommends language standards and is open for discussion and debate. The authors of the HTML 3 Internet Draft recommended enhancements to almost every existing HTML tag and the addition of numerous new tags covering everything from representation of complex mathematical functions to new ways of arranging images on a page. Perhaps not surprisingly, it took so long for the Internet Engineering Task Force (IETF) (see "Internet Engineering Task Force (IETF)" in Chapter 1, "What is the Web?") to review a document of that scope that the entire face of the industry had changed before debates about the content of the draft subsided. Inline animations, background and text colors, and other features had been implemented by Netscape, Sun's HotJava browser had introduced a whole new level of functionality with Java applets, and Microsoft had begun to embed Object Linking and Embedding (OLE) support in their Internet Explorer. The IETF, prompted by industry leaders like Netscape and Sun, realized the the language draft model was too inefficient to adapt to such a dynamic environment, and the HTML 3 Internet Draft "expired"; that is, it was taken out of consideration as a standard.

Since the HTML 3 Internet Draft can no longer be revised, there is a new way to propose a change to the HTML language specification. For any new feature or new type of functionality, a team of authors proposes a set of new or enhanced HTML tags and, if the proposal is approved, the IETF integrates the tags into the HTML standard. Once the tags are part of the HTML standard, the companies that produce web browsers (Spyglass, Quarterdeck, Spry, Netscape, Microsoft, and others) will add new functionality to their browsers so the tags will be displayed as recommended by the IETF. Sometimes this functionality exists before the draft is approved—for example, HTML tables have been supported by several browsers for up to a year—but the particular implementation usually differs from the recommended HTML standard, often varying from browser to browser or lacking some of the features that users have requested.

Arena: A Sneak Preview

The new HTML standard will develop and be revised by users and providers, people who look at pages developed with the standard and people who create pages with it. One way to watch the development of the standard and to become a part of the process is to look at pages that use the language.

A browser called Arena, which is being developed by the World Wide Web Organization, is capable of viewing documents that have been marked up according to new additions to the HTML standard. Since Arena is changed when HTML Internet Drafts are approved, its development will always correspond with the latest developments in HTML. Information about Arena is available at the URL http://www.w3.org/hypertext/WWW/ Arena/.

Global Changes to HTML

Even though changes to HTML are now "modular," recommending specific changes rather than global language modifications, some global features from the HTML 3 Internet Draft, such as the CLASS or ID attributes, still exist without being part of any one new proposal. Most of these "leftover" HTML 3 features are really attributes that can (but do not have to) be included inside any HTML "block tag," a tag that defines an entire area of a document, like <H1>, <P>, <OL>, or <DIV>. The attributes do not actually change the appearance or function of that area (or header, or list), but are used as classifiers, describing the nature of the area to the browser or to other features like style sheets. Then, if so instructed, a browser or style sheet or application will make any changes to appearance or function desired by the author or viewer. The authors of the modular proposals to enhance HTML assume that these attributes can be present, and use them when describing how a particular feature might be implemented.

ID and CLASS, two such attributes, are primarily employed to give an area a named identity for reference purposes. You can use ID and CLASS in almost any block tag in the body of the document, and can then refer to using these tags in the header or style sheet. The attributes define a certain area or string in a way that other tags can reference.

Defining something as ID="idname" defines it in a similar way to the <A NAME> tag; in other words, it gives it a unique identifier within the document. However, the ID attribute is not only an anchor but can be used to define any sort of entity within an HTML document: a paragraph, a table, a header, or even the document itself. This definition can be used as a point of reference by several different types of tags, including hyperlinks and style sheets.

The CLASS attribute, on the other hand, is intended for use in multiple locations throughout a document. CLASS is better designed for style sheets and formatting concerns than ID, since it allows a group of objects to be identified as a unit, even if they seem to have nothing in common. Since it is more generic than ID, CLASS could not be used as the destination of a hyperlink—its purpose is to group together elements, whereas the purpose of ID is to distinguish them.

Two more holdovers from the HTML 3 Internet Draft, both used to set certain characteristics, are useful in understanding how revisions of HTML will change the way that a document is broken down: the <LINK> and <DIV> tags. The document's relationship to other documents, that is, what it depends on and how it is positioned in the document hierarchy, needs to be provided, using the <LINK> tag, as is discussed in Chapter 6, "Checking Your Work." The <LINK> tag takes a wide range of arguments. The following <LINK> elements were proposed as additions to the HTML v2.0 <LINK> elements in the HTML v3.0 Internet Draft:

- ❋ **REL=Home** If a <LINK> tag contains this element, it references a home page or the top of a hierarchy.

- ❋ **REL=Copyright** A <LINK> tag containing this element references a copyright statement for the current document.

- ❋ **REL=Up** When the document forms part of a hierarchy, a <LINK> tag containing this element references the immediate parent of the current document.

- ❋ **REL=Help** A <LINK> tag with this element references a document offering help. The help document describes the wider context and offers further links to relevant documents. This element is aimed at reorienting users who have lost their way.

- ❋ **REL=StyleSheet** This element, described in the following section, references a style sheet that defines the way that certain text types are displayed by the browser.

Using these new <LINK> tag elements, you can define your documents both in terms of relationships to other web pages and with stylistic elements, such as the style sheet. Within the document itself, another tag from the HTML 3 Internet Draft is used for internal definitions and delineations. The <DIV> tag breaks up the sections of a document to allow for operations on an entire section.

Three tags explicitly define the layout of a page: the old tags <P> and <BR>, for defining paragraphs and lines, and the new tag <DIV>, which defines larger sections of a document. The paragraph tag, as discussed previously, can take a setting called CLASS, which allows you to give that paragraph a "name." The name can then be referenced by other tags in the document or by an external style sheet.

You can use the <DIV> tag in a similar manner. It can enclose a number of paragraphs and other elements, such as forms and tables, and define the enclosed section with a class. So, for example, a section of an HTML document like the following could be defined as a preface:

```
<DIV CLASS=Preface>
This document seeks to outline ShoopSoft's accomplishments →
in the world of networking software and services. It is not →
intended to be a final copy, but will give you a sense of →
our abilities and potential.</P>
Special thanks to J.R. Dobbs, Bill Jones, Akbar, and Jeff for →
their invaluable contributions to this work.</P>
</DIV>
```

To make the preface designation meaningful, you have to tell the HTML browser what to do with a preface. It can be indented, displayed in boldface, or displayed in a chartreuse color. As noted in the discussion of style sheets, this is defined either in a separate file or in the <STYLE> tag in the header of the document.

You should use the <DIV> and <P> tags to define the sections of your documents as specifically as possible and then give these sections special characteristics in your style sheets. Both <DIV> and <P> share a number of attributes in common, such as CLASS and ID, and both also use the ALIGN attribute.

ALIGN and STYLE are used to determine how an area of the page or an object is displayed by the browser. ALIGN determines where to place an object, usually relative to an adjacent line of text, and has been widely used for images since the first version of HTML was released. The HTML v3.0 Internet Draft contained additional settings for the <IMG> tag, which designate this alignment. The <IMG> tag in HTML v2.0 uses the settings ALIGN=top, ALIGN=middle, and ALIGN=bottom to determine the vertical location of text alongside the image. The additional settings for this tag, ALIGN=left and ALIGN=right, determine the horizontal location of the image on the page, aligning it with either the left or the right margin, respectively. Figure 13-1 shows graphics using the ALIGN=left and ALIGN=right settings. The future of the <IMG> tag is discussed in the "Embedded Multimedia" section, later in this chapter.

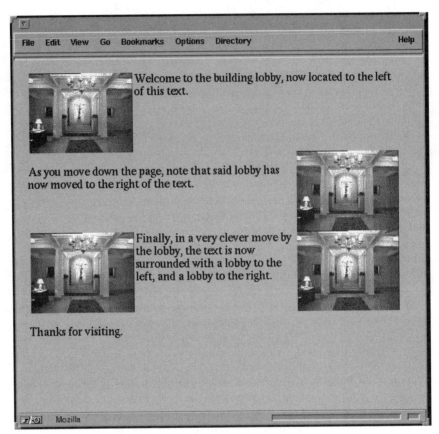

Figure 13-1: *Graphics and text using the ALIGN option.*

The only real change to the ALIGN attribute in the latest revisions of HTML is the generality with which it can be used. ALIGN can be used for tables, paragraphs, Java applets (see "Embedded Multimedia" below), or any other HTML object which is defined with opening and closing tags.

<STYLE> is a tag that allows the author of a page to override the settings specified in the style sheet, or to define a style if none has been defined. The argument for the <STYLE> tag must be in the same syntax as the style sheet itself: if the style sheet for a document is Rich Text Format, then the <STYLE> argument for a paragraph on that page must be a Rich Text Format definition. Examples of the <STYLE> tag can be seen in "Style Sheets," below.

One other attribute can be used to control the appearance of the page, the CLEAR attribute. The paragraph and line break tags, <P> and <BR>, can take the CLEAR setting, which is used in conjunction with a new feature of inline images, the ability to wrap text around the image. You can use the CLEAR setting to wrap text around the left margin or right margin of an image and start the next text line or paragraph below the image rather than alongside it, as described in Chapter 7, "Images on the Web."

These global changes to HTML are only used in the context of other proposals—they will be incorporated into the language by default rather than by election. The IETF is currently considering several modular proposals to expand HTML, some of which are quite interesting and exciting. Proposed style sheets, for instance, are able to determine the style of a document with such granularity that any unique combination of tags (such as a phrase in bold print in a definition list item nested in an unordered list) can be given attributes determining almost any aspect of its appearace. Other proposed features include a generic, but powerful, method of embedding multimedia objects and even small programs ("applets") in a page, a method of sending an entire file in the contents of a form submission, imagemaps that are contained in the web page itself, and a definitive description of tables, with much more flexibility than any current implemention allows.

Style Sheets

Designing an HTML document can be a tricky enterprise. The users viewing the page with their browsers must have input regarding their preferences of background and text color, the browser software itself has certain defaults to keep users from having to define their own preferences, and the HTML designer wants to determine the look and feel of a document for marketability and impact.

HTML as it was originally implemented made no allowance for an author's graphic design considerations—only the end user and the browser had control over elements of a document's appearance like the text color, the font, and the background color. As a reaction to that, Netscape Navigator implemented a rudimentary set of tags to let the author of a page determine the color of a page's background, text, and hyperlinks; several other browsers then adopted this *de facto* standard. However, that particular implementation of document styles did not prove to be very expandable—for example, one paragraph could not be a different color from another—and it lacked the generality necessary for large documents or large bodies of documents, because the style had to be explicitly described each time it was used.

HTML style sheets are an attempt to create a set of stylistic definitions that can be easily reused for entire sets of documents and within a single document multiple times. Using an existing style sheet is very simple, meaning that a corporate style sheet could be created by a company's Webmaster, and the different authors throughout the company could easily use it when creating their documents. A single line in the header of the document using the LINK tag (described above) "turns on" the style sheet for that document, as in the following example:

```
<HTML>
<HEAD>
<LINK REL="StyleSheet" TYPE="text/css" HREF="http://
style.acme.com/marketng.sty">
<TITLE>Acme Marketing Home Page</TITLE>
</HEAD>
```

There are three other ways to activate a style sheet. The style sheet can be retrieved from any URL using an "import" function inside the <STYLE> header tag. The following example would have exactly the same effect as the example above:

```
<HTML>
<HEAD>
<STYLE TYPE="text/css">
@import "http://style.acme.com/marketng.sty"
</STYLE>
<TITLE>Acme Marketing Home Page</TITLE>
</HEAD>
```

If both the LINK and the STYLE tag with an import function were used in the same document, the information imported as a result of the STYLE tag would be appended to the information from the LINK tag.

From an author's perspective, the latter example is more useful than the former because it's simpler to override styles that are defined in the global style sheet. Let's say an author wanted his or her heading 1 text (<H1>) to be red, even though the information in "marketng.sty" only defined the font and size of <H1> text. Only one additional line would be necessary to add that characteristic to <H1>'s style.

```
<HEAD>
<STYLE TYPE="text/css">
@import "http://style.acme.com/marketng.sty"
H1 { color : red }
</STYLE>
```

The "color : red" description is appended to any existing information about H1 in the file marketng.sty.

Note that the first three examples of activating style sheets contain the attribute TYPE="text/css". The TYPE attribute for style sheets, whether the style sheets are called with the STYLE or the LINK tag, defines the language of the style sheet. The examples above feature a style sheet language called CSS, or Cascading Style Sheets, but any style sheet language could have been used in exactly the same way (with the exception of the "color : red" line, which is CSS-specific). Other style sheet languages are Rich Text Format, a long-standing style description language, and DSSSL Lite. CSS seems to be the most promising of the three at this time, but the implementation described above allows any style sheet language to be used.

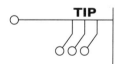
TIP

While it's outside of the scope of this book to go into CSS, RTF, DSSSL Lite, and other types of style sheets, you can check out the growing body of HTML v3.0–based materials that address the development of style sheets. A collection of documents about style sheets is maintained at CERN, at the URL http://www.w3.org/hypertext/WWW/Style/.

The fourth method of defining styles is the use of a STYLE attribute inside a block tag like <H1>. This eliminates the advantages that a document-wide style sheet offers, like the ability to reuse styles consistently throughout a page and the ability to have a site-wide standard. The advantage of this tag is obvious, though, in a scenario where a paragraph, list, or other object must have a unique style. Giving that object a STYLE attribute can override any previous style sheet definitions. Note that the information the STYLE attribute contains must be in the same style sheet language as the style sheet referenced in the header of the document. The example below shows a document which calls a CSS style sheet, but then describes a list with green text, perhaps overriding the style sheet or perhaps just adding a new characteristic to the style of lists.

```
<HTML>
<HEAD>
<LINK REL="StyleSheet" TYPE="text/css" HREF="http://
style.acme.com/marketng.sty">
<TITLE>Acme : Marketing Home Page</TITLE>
</HEAD>
<BODY>
<H1>Acme Marketing Department</H1>
Promoting:
<UL STYLE="color : green">
<LI>Bird-Locating Software
<LI>Bird-Trapping Hardware
<LI>Bird-Cooking Peripherals
</UL>
```

If the author had wanted other lists to be green, though, it would have been a better idea to use the CLASS attribute to define a number of lists as members of the same type, and then refer to that type in the style sheet itself, but the above solution is the most efficient for a one-type description.

The introduction of style sheets will allow for a broad range of possible formatting configurations. Style sheets will be able to define the following characteristics of a file:

- Font family, the base font used for documents, modified by tags like <EM>, <STRONG>, and other text-formatting tags.

- Font color, which can be different for any text font or format.

- Font size, which can also vary according to each type of text format.

- Object alignment.

- Document background color.

- List indention.

- List-numbering style.

These may be added to, or subtracted from, as drafts for HTML style sheets are implemented. However, it's likely that the range of style-formatting possibilities will only increase as the TYPE atttribute for the STYLE and LINK tags allows for more languages with different abilities and limitations to define an HTML document's style. This new level of flexibility will make transitions to new document styles easier, and documents' styles will more quickly reach new levels of sophistication.

Embedded Multimedia

One of the most exciting developments on the World Wide Web in recent months has been the development and implementation of entirely new forms of multimedia. Entire languages like Sun Microsystems' Java and the Virtual Reality Markup Language have given users new ways of conceptualizing the Web, adding interactivity and depth (literally!) to what had originally appeared a very flat, book-like medium. On a slightly smaller scale, the companies that created web browsers for a commercial market have introduced new bells and whistles to give their browser the edge. Microsoft's Internet Explorer began to use its Object Linking and Embedding (OLE) capability to communicate with other applications in the Microsoft Windows environment, while Netscape Navigator introduced animations that use a custom-tailored scripting system to operate.

Unfortunately for the consumer, and for the web provider wanting to please everyone, no clear method of taking full advantage of all of these features seemed to be emerging. No browser used the same tag to implement any feature, and some browsers showed no indication of supporting these types of multimedia—and had no clear reference to show them how if they did decide to include support. Needless to say, the HTML 3 Internet Draft had not anticipated this need, and a team consisting of members from the largest web browser manufacturers and web providers was formed to develop a standard way of getting new technologies out to users via HTML. Once this team determines the HTML standard for embedding multimedia, browsers and HTML authors will have a "right way" to implement these advanced features, and a standard within which to develop entirely new features.

The Internet Draft that has resulted from this team effort recommends only three tags, but these three tags will be able to encompass a broad range of functions, including tags as basic as the <IMG> tag. The three tags work in tandem: the first, <INSERT>, is the core of the embedding process, giving a pointer to, or even the contents of, the multimedia object to be inserted. The second tag, <PARAM>, is used to pass arguments to the object. It's used for Microsoft OLEs and other applications which can behave differently based on the value of their parameters. The final tag, <ALIAS>, is a tag that behaves like the <INSERT> tag, but it does not actually display a multimedia object, just prepares it for later use.

<INSERT> is a block tag, a tag that requires both an opening and closing tag. This means that it, along with other block tags like <UL> or <H1>, can be referenced with the CLASS or ID attributes, or even the ALIGN attribute, allowing control over the inserted object's appearance or position within the document. The simplest implementation of <INSERT> is inserting a basic multimedia object like a picture—the old job of the <IMG> tag. The following example inserts a picture called "family.gif" into the page:

```
<INSERT DATA="family.gif">
</INSERT>
```

The <INSERT> tag can take any of the options traditionally used with images, like HEIGHT, WIDTH, and BORDER, and even ISMAP if the image is to be used as an imagemap.

The <INSERT> tag greatly simplifies one proposed addition to HTML from the HTML 3 Internet Draft, the <FIG> tag, and the two may be used in tandem to create an efficient method of inserting captioned figures into a document. For example, the following markup consisting of a graphic aligned to the left text margin, a caption, and some lines of explanation, would produce the output seen in Figure 13-2:

```
<FIG>
<CAPTION>J.R. "Bob" Dobbs and a friend</CAPTION>
<INSERT ALIGN=left data="bob.gif">
<P>This is a rare photograph of J.R. "Bob" Dobbs and an
otherworldly visitor, discussing the shape of things to
come.</P>
</INSERT>
</FIG>
```

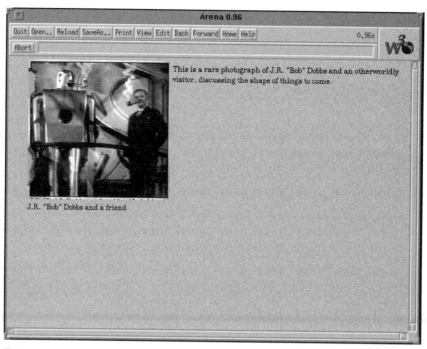

Figure 13-2: *The <FIG> tag with caption and wraparound text.*

The main benefit of the <INSERT> tag over the <IMG> tag is that the <INSERT> tag is flexible enough to accept any type of multimedia object. Using the TYPE option, you can specify the MIME type of an object before it is sent. This means that a browser knows what type of file is embedded in the page, and will load the file if it can. Otherwise, the file will be ignored. The following example shows the code to embed a Video for Windows (.AVI) file in a page, followed by an <IMG> tag, which is to be used for backwards compatibility in case a browser does not support the <INSERT> tag.

```
<INSERT TYPE="application/avi" DATA="/ANIM/FLAPPING.AVI">
<IMG SRC="/GIFS/FLOCK.GIF">
</INSERT>
```

A potentially more complex use of the <INSERT> tag is to embed Java applets. Embedding Java applets does not have to be any more complex than embedding images or other file types. Because Java applets are not just displayed, however, but are actually installed on a local system for future use, an extra attribute, CLASSID, can be used to identify the applet and check whether it is already locally installed before it is reloaded. CLASSID can also be used to identify an object using its *universally unique object identifier* or *uuid*. All CLASSID really does is identify the object being loaded according to a particular naming scheme (Java, uuid, etc.). The following example embeds Sun's Bouncing Heads Java demo. It first uses CLASSID to identify what will be used in case the demo is already installed and so that the system will know that a Java applet is being loaded, and then uses CODE to point to the location of the applet code itself.

```
<INSERT CLASSID="java:BounceItem.class"
CODE="http://java.sun.com/applets/BounceItem.class"
WIDTH=400 HEIGHT=300>
</INSERT>
```

The CLASSID attribute contains two elements, "java:," which indicates that a Java class name follows, and the name itself.

Note that the DATA attribute, used in all of the previous examples, is not used in the one above. If the <INSERT> tag has the CLASSID for an object (that is, information on what type of data it is and how to identify it), and the CODE attribute indicating where to find the CODE itself, then the DATA attribute is not needed. The CODE tells the browser where to get the information and the CLASSID describes how to implement it. This combination is particularly useful for Java applets because the information referred to in the CODE attribute may contain multiple applets, so the CLASSID can be used to indicate which section of code (that is, which applet) actually needs to be executed.

DATA, on the other hand, also has particular advantages. DATA is best used for a simple object like an image or animation that's always implemented the same way by the browser. It can also contain the actual program to be executed using a new URL with the prefix "data:" followed by a base 64 encoding of the object itself. An entire GIF file could be encoded in HTML code like the following example. This is an option designed for super-fast loading of an object:

```
<INSERT TYPE="image/gif"
DATA="data:34j2we3bok4sfj2j0kcq9a4wkc">
</INSERT>
```

The CLASSID, CODE, and DATA attributes can be used in a number of ways, dependent upon the object being embedded, and as such, are far more complex in their implementation than described above. As the proposal moves closer to approval, more thorough documentation of their usage will be available.

As mentioned at the outset, <INSERT> is one of three tags that can be used to embed multimedia, but it always has to be used. Two other tags, <PARAM> and <ALIAS>, are optional tags that complement <INSERT>.

<PARAM> is a simple tag used to pass a value to the object being embedded, just like an option on a command line or a preference set inside an application. Of course, the object or browser has to know what to do with the parameter in the <PARAM> alias to use it; passing a parameter called "duration" with the value "forever" to a Video for Windows animation, for instance, would be meaningless. The <PARAM> tag is used like the <META> tag (see "Creating the Documents" in Chapter 2, "The Basic Pieces"): it is given the name of a variable or property, and then the value of that variable. In the following example, one line has been added to the embedded animation example above to tell the browser to run the loop infinitely.

```
<INSERT TYPE="application/avi" DATA="/ANIM/FLAPPING.AVI">
<PARAM NAME="loop" VALUE="infinite">
<IMG SRC="/GIFS/FLOCK.GIF">
</INSERT>
```

The names and values for the <PARAM> tag are specific to each type of object, and so they will be determined as each object is implemented in browsers.

One other use for the <PARAM> tag is to pass an entire file to an inserted object. The following example shows an embedded Java applet that can accept a parameter called "target." The value of "target" is set to an <ALIAS> tag which has loaded a GIF file used by the applet in its operation.

```
<ALIAS ID="duck" DATA="/GIFS/DUCK.GIF">
</ALIAS>
<INSERT CLASSID="java:SkeetShoot.class"
 CODE:"http://java.acme.com/applets/SkeetShoot.class">
<PARAM NAME="target" VALUEREF="#duck">
</INSERT>
```

Note that VALUEREF is used when the value of the property is actually an object, like an image file, and VALUE is used when the value is a string, like "infinite."

The example above also demonstrates the function of the <ALIAS> tag. The <INSERT> tag displays a multimedia object on the page. The <ALIAS> tag initializes an object but doesn't actually display it. The <INSERT> or <PARAM> tags refer to that object by the information in the ID attributes (ID="duck" in the example above) when the object is actually needed. This is an efficient way of reusing an object in multiple locations on a page.

At first glance, the proposal for embedding multimedia objects may look more complex than the current system—and for the simplest type of objects, image files, it is. However, the proposed system will extend a web page designer's ability to use virtually anything with a MIME type in a page once the browsers are capable of displaying such a wide range of objects. A modular system, like the one introducing Netscape's new plug-ins, is probably the way that new multimedia functionality will be built into a browser. Code that integrates itself into an existing browser will be written by a third-party vendor or by the browser company itself, and the user will download the code and install it for each new type of multimedia that he or she wishes to support. Using this system—flexible tags embedding any type of multimedia and expandable browsers supporting new types of multimedia—it will be simple for the Web community to expand and improve upon the appearance and functionality of web pages *and* for users to quickly take advantage of those improvements.

Uploading Files With Forms

In contrast to the proposal for embedded multimedia, the proposal to include an entire file in the contents of a form submission is a simple one. The proposal is so simple because most of the complexity of this system comes from the client side. The proposal itself only recommends two things: a new setting for the TYPE attributes of the <INPUT> tag inside a form and a new MIME type to handle forms that could be used to send different types of files. What the proposal does not cover is how a browser would implement this file submission mechanism on the client side—the browser manufacturers will have to figure that one out on their own (and, as we'll see, one already has).

A form itself must be changed in the opening tag <FORM...> to allow for a file upload. Forms as they are currently used send back all submitted data in a single text string which is broken up by a CGI script upon receipt by the server (as described in Chapter 10, "CGI & DLLs: Programming Your Server"). This would be an inefficient way of transferring an entire file, so the form has to "encode" the information differently, formatting it in such a way that binary files can be sent more easily. However, a user may also want to send text as part of the form, meaning that multiple types of files must now be supported. To make this possible, a form that will be used to upload a file must be given a special encoding type, or ENCTYPE, called "multipart/form-data." This tells the server that multiple types of files will be arriving in the same submission, and the server needs to be able to break up the submission into those file types.

This may sound more complex than it really is. The following is an example of a form used only to send a file and nothing else:

```
<FORM METHOD=POST ACTION="/CGI-BIN/GETFILE.CGI"
ENCTYPE="multipart/form-data">
<INPUT TYPE=FILE NAME="InputFile">
</FORM>
```

The client will look at the filename of the "InputFile" and try to determine what sort of file it is (for example, a file with the extension .TXT will almost always be a text file). Then the client sends the filename and the MIME type of that file to the server. The CGI script on the server side will receive this block of data in addition to its MIME type as inferred by the client, and will use the variable name "InputFile" to refer to it. Then the CGI script can handle the data any way the author has chosen, perhaps saving it in a directory for uploads, perhaps opening the file and processing its contents.

The above example uses the TYPE=FILE attribute for the <INPUT> tag. This is how the client knows to prompt the user for a filename. As of version 2.0, Netscape Navigator now supports form-based file uploading, and when it sees an <INPUT TYPE=FILE...> tag, it gives the user the option to type in the filename that he or she wants to upload, or to browse through directories for the file (see Figure 13-3). Other browsers may implement the tag in different ways, but the concept will generally be the same: the form is designed to accept a file, the browser allows the user to select a file from his or her local system, and the server receives and processes that file when the form is submitted.

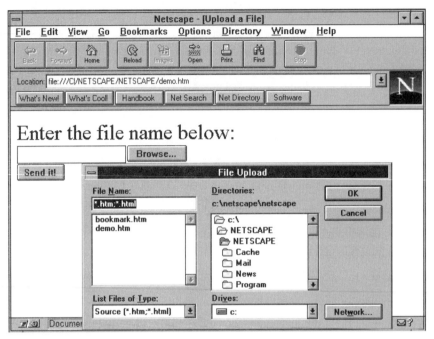

Figure 13-3: *Netscape Navigator displaying a file-upload form.*

Note that the <INPUT TYPE=FILE...> tag could be used inside a form that also had <INPUT TYPE=TEXT...> or <TEXTAREA> tags—the "multipart/form-data" encoding type allows the submitted information to be broken up into normal form data and uploaded files. As long as the CGI script that the form uses knows to process multiple file types, anything can be submitted using this new file upload system.

This particular feature of forms will prove to be very valuable, especially in a corporate intranet inside which application-specific documents like Excel spreadsheets are traded across web servers. This single feature will broaden the potential uses of forms significantly and will probably contribute to the web's speedy takeover of internal information systems inside "trusted environments" where files can be exchanged safely, as well as on the Internet itself where FTP has been historically used to transfer files.

Client-Side Imagemaps

HTML's current implementation of imagemaps is somewhat clumsy. Three distinct files are required: the graphic to be used as the imagemap, the file listing the coordinates on the imagemap that are to be clickable areas pointing to URLs, and the HTML document. The HTML document points to the graphic in an <IMG> tag using the ISMAP attribute to indicate that the graphic is an imagemap. It then links that graphic to a map file with an <A HREF> tag. A proposal by Spyglass, Inc., a leading web browser software company, recommends combining the map file with the coordinates and the HTML document into a single file— and as proof that the concept can work, Spyglass Mosaic (their browser software) supports the feature.

The proposal is really quite simple, containing only two major elements. The first item proposed is the integration of the map file itself into the web page—that is, how the coordinates to be used are inserted into the HTML document. The solution is similar to the map file itself. First, an area of the document is marked as a container for map coordinates using the <MAP> and the </MAP> tags. That area is filled with <AREA> tags, one for each set of coordinates. The <AREA> tag describes the shape, coordinates of that shape's boundaries, and the desired result when that shape is clicked upon. For example, a graphic containing three rectangular areas, each linked to a different site, could be mapped out as follows:

```
<MAP NAME="homepages">
<AREA SHAPE=RECT COORDS="0,0,100,50" ALT="Home Page on the →
Range" HREF="http://home.range.com/">
<AREA SHAPE=RECT COORDS="101,0,200,50" ALT="Home Sweet Home →
Page" HREF="http://home.sweet.com/">
<AREA SHAPE=RECT COORDS="0,51,200,100" ALT="You can't go..." →
HREF="http://home.again.com/">
</MAP>
```

The shape of the area to be linked is given in the SHAPE attribute. Possible settings include CIRCLE, POLY, and RECT. If a circle is being defined, the COORDS attribute is given the coordinates of the center and the radius of the circle: a circle with radius 4 with the center at (20,40) would have the setting COORDS= "20,40,4" in the <AREA> tag. A polygon is given the coordinates of each corner: a triangle would have three sets of coordinates, a hexagon six, and so on. A rectangle only needs to have the coordinates of two opposite corners specified, as in the examples above.

The other attributes used by the <MAP> and <AREA> tags are familiar to the HTML user: the ALT tag is taken from the <IMG> tag, and is used if no graphic can be displayed. The text will be linked to the URL given in the HREF attribute, which is used in all standard hyperlinks (<A HREF>). The NAME attribute is used in named anchors, as in <A NAME="Chapter_2">, which can be pointed to by hyperlinks, as in <A HREF="book.html#Chapter_2">.

To be used, the map information must be linked to a particular graphic. Traditionally, the ISMAP attribute has indicated that a graphic is used as an imagemap, but if the map information is local to the document, you would employ the USEMAP attribute instead. The USEMAP attribute takes one argument: the NAME attribute of the <MAP> tag that contains the relevant map coordinates. So a graphic using the map example above would be embedded in a page as follows:

```
<IMG SRC="HOMES.GIF" USEMAP="#homepages">
```

No surrounding hyperlink is necessary anymore, since all of the required information is contained in the HTML document itself.

If both this proposal and the proposal for embedding multimedia were to be approved and implemented as written, even the graphic could be a part of the HTML document. Remember that the proposal for embedding multimedia allows the image itself to be encoded in base 64 and included in the DATA attribute of the <INSERT> tag. So the following tag could perform the same function as the <IMG> tag above, but without ever having to load an outside file—both the map coordinates and the graphic itself are part of the HTML document.

```
<INSERT TYPE="image/gif"
DATA="data:34j2we3bok4sfj2j0kcq9a4wkc" USEMAP="#homepages">
</INSERT>
```

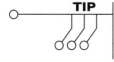

TIP

Client-side imagemaps represent two levels of improvement. The efficiency of an imagemap will improve when one less file is needed. In addition, having an individual ALT attribute for each set of coordinates will finally allow nongraphical browsers to use imagemaps, which is a much-needed feature. It is likely that client-side imagemaps will become more and more prominent in the near future, given their ease of use and the flexibility and efficiency that they add to a document.

Tables

Tables are still technically just a proposal, despite the fact that every major browser now supports them, at least in their most basic form. We'll be providing a description of the full model for creating tables proposed to the IETF, not a description of their current implementation. Each browser has table-related features that only it supports, especially Netscape Navigator, and in many cases, the proposal provides backward-compatibility for these features. However, aside from the most basic features, this description may not apply to all browsers' current implementation of tables—hopefully, though, once the HTML Tables proposal is passed, it will apply uniformly to every browser.

Tables are extremely simple to set up and customize. The opening tag for the table is, not surprisingly, <TABLE>. If you want to include a border on the outside of the table, you can use the FRAME setting inside the <TABLE> tag, and for borders between cells, you can set the RULES attribute. For example, a table with a box border and "rules" (another word for lines) between all of the rows and columns would have the following opening tag:

```
<TABLE FRAME=BOX RULES=ALL>
```

There is a broad range of available settings for the FRAME and RULES attributes, giving the author complete control over the appearance of the table.

The ALIGN setting in the <TABLE> tag can be used the same way as with any other block tag, set to left, right, center, or "justify" (which attempts to justify the text inside the table cell). The CLEAR setting can also be used with the <TABLE> tag and can take the same settings that we described in the discussion of the <P> tag earlier: left, right, and all.

Aside from these more basic settings, you can use other settings immediately after the opening <TABLE> tag that will configure the table layout before the actual content of the rows and cells is specified. The <COLGROUP> tag and optional <COL> tag allow you to configure the width of each column and the alignment of the information in that column to the left, right, or center. It isn't required that you use these tags to configure the widths of columns in a table. In a table in which the <COLGROUP> and <COL> tags are not used, the column width is automatically sized according to the contents of the cells. If you wanted to create a three-column table in which one column had text aligned to the left and was 30 units wide, another column had text in the center and was 15 units wide, and the third column had text aligned to the right and was 45 units wide, you would enter the following opening tags to start the table:

```
<TABLE FRAME=BOX>
      <COLGROUP WIDTH=30 ALIGN=LEFT>
      <COLGROUP WIDTH=15 ALIGN=CENTER>
      <COLGROUP WIDTH=45 ALIGN=RIGHT>
```

Note that the columns are referred to as "COLGROUP" even though there is only one column in the group. To include multiple columns in a group, use the SPAN attribute. For example, if the first <COLGROUP> tag above had ended with SPAN=3, then the first three columns would have all been given the same properties, and the fourth and fifth columns would have been dealt with by the succeeding tags.

The <COL> tag is used inside the <COLGROUP> tag to define exceptions—that is, to indicate if one or more columns in the group are different from the others. The following example would start a table with five columns, all different widths, the first three aligned to the center, the last two to the right:

```
<TABLE FRAME=BOX>
     <COLGROUP ALIGN=CENTER SPAN=3>
     <COL WIDTH="1*">
     <COL WIDTH="2*">
     <COL WIDTH="1.5*">
     <COLGROUP ALIGN=CENTER SPAN=2>
     <COL WIDTH="0.75*">
     <COL WIDTH="0.5*">
```

Note that a different kind of value is used in the WIDTH attributes above. Using a number followed by an asterisk means you are using a relative width rather than an absolute width like the earlier example. The easiest way to think about it is the value times the normal column width, which is "one." So the first column is "one times" as wide as a normal column, meaning it is exactly the same. The second column is two times as wide. The last column is .5 times as wide, or half as wide. This gives the browser more flexibility in fitting the table on the screen since it can always resize the table and keep all of the columns' sizes relative to each other.

After creating a border and setting the widths and alignments of the columns, you'll want to enter the <CAPTION> tag next, which will give the table a title. You can then mark each row in the table with the table row tag, <TR>. The table row can contain one of two types of cell tags, either <TH> or <TD>. The <TH> tag will produce a cell with a table header, in other words, to create a row that contains headers for the other cells in that column. The <TD> tag will indicate that the text is to be table data, in other words, information about the items named in the header row. The following example uses the FRAME and RULES attributes and <CAPTION>, <TR>, <TH>, and <TD> tags to create a simple table, which is shown in Figure 13-4.

```
<TABLE FRAME=BOX RULES=ALL>
     <CAPTION>Produce in stock</CAPTION>
     <TR><TH>Apples<TH>Oranges<TH>Bananas
     <TR><TD>13<TD>15<TD>5
</TABLE>
```

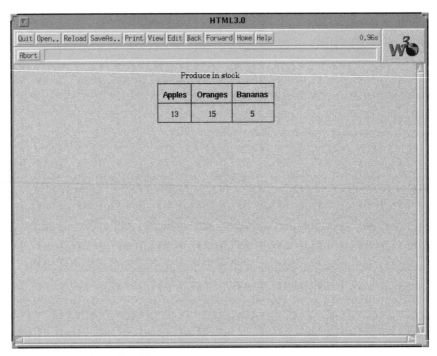

Figure 13-4: *A simple table.*

You can align the cells in a column with the <COLGROUP> tag, or you can set the alignment separately for each cell with the ALIGN setting inside any of the <TD> or <TH> tags. If you want to set the alignment in an entire row, use the ALIGN option inside the <TR> tag. For example, a row of cells all aligned to the center would start off with the following tag:

```
<TR ALIGN=CENTER>
```

One cell can extend over any number of rows or columns. The ROWSPAN and COLSPAN settings designate the number of rows or columns that a cell will occupy. For example, a table row with the following setting has two columns, one that is two column widths across and a second that is the normal size.

```
<TR><TD COLSPAN=2>400,000<TD>10
```

A table row with the following setting would have a table cell that is two rows tall, and another that is normal size.

```
<TR><TD ROWSPAN=2>Hi!<TD>there
```

Since tables are automatically sized according to the contents of the cells, it's not necessary to increase a cell's width for a large amount of information. The ROWSPAN and COLSPAN settings simply allow you to control a table's appearance.

You can include anything inside a cell, not just text. Images, lists, forms, and any other objects that can be specified with HTML markup can be included by putting the appropriate markup tags after the <TH> or <TD> tag. For example, the following markup creates the table in Figure 13-5. The table includes two images, a list, and headers that are hyperlinked to other web pages.

```
<TABLE FRAME=BOX RULES=ALL>
<TR><TH><A HREF="bob.html">Bob's Picture</A><TH><TH>
<A HREF="http://www.shoop.com/services/">ShoopSoft Services
</A>
<TR><TD><IMG ALT="Bob" SRC="bob.gif"><TD>
<IMG ALT="Shoop" SRC="logo.gif">
<TD>ShoopSoft supports:
    <UL>
    <LI>Macintosh
    <LI>PC
    <LI>UNIX Workstations
    </UL>
</TABLE>
```

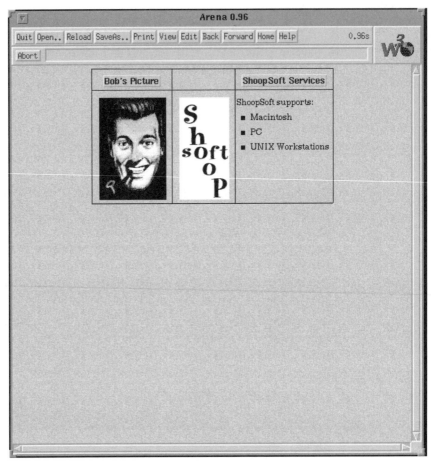

Figure 13-5: *A table with hyperlinks, images, and a list.*

Note that the second use of the <TH> tag, between the headers "Bob's Picture" and "ShoopSoft Services," has no text or HTML markup after it. This markup produces the filled-in cell that appears in the top row of the table in Figure 13-5. You can use this feature with either the <TH> or the <TD> tag. Also, you can see in the example markup that all of the information for a cell does not have to appear on a single line, as in the case of the embedded list, which contains several lines of entries.

For larger tables, the table may be divided up into a header and a body. A browser may choose to display the header and the body differently or not, but it is a useful way to delineate the information, especially in larger tables. The following example would produce exactly the same output seen in Figure 13-5 above, but the header and body are now clearly marked:

```
<TABLE FRAME=BOX RULES=ALL>
<THEAD>
<TR><TH><A HREF="bob.html">Bob's Picture</A><TH><TH>
<A HREF="http://www.shoop.com/services/">ShoopSoft Services
</A>
</THEAD>
<TBODY>
<TR><TD><IMG ALT="Bob" SRC="bob.gif"><TD>
<IMG ALT="Shoop" SRC="logo.gif">
<TD>ShoopSoft supports:
      <UL>
      <LI>Macintosh
      <LI>PC
      <LI>UNIX Workstations
      </UL>
</TBODY>
</TABLE>
```

The <THEAD> and <TBODY> tags mark the header and body; the <TFOOT> tag can also be used to demarcate a footer.

Using these tags and options, you can produce lots of different types of tables. Inside the cells, you can include anything that a browser is capable of displaying. A number of tutorials on table design are on the Web. One of the best is the NCSA Mosaic Tables Tutorial, which includes some fancy examples of table design, at the URL given in the following tip.

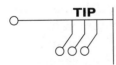

TIP

Most every web browser on the market currently supports tables. Two popular web browsers, NCSA Mosaic and Netscape, both support tables but implement them slightly differently. To see how tables are implemented in Netscape, look at the help page at the URL http://home.netscape.com/assist/net_sites/tables.html. To see how tables implemented in Mosaic, see the Tables Tutorial, at http://www.ncsa.uiuc.edu/SDG/Software/Mosaic/Tables/ tutorial.html.

Math

Another proposal before the IETF is a direct holdover from the HTML 3 Internet Draft, a proposal to display mathematical characters and equations in great detail. The proposal includes an extensive set of math characters as *entities*, that is, icons that are referred to with a series of special characters. When you see a less-than sign (<) on a web page, for instance, it is an entity and is called by the string < in the HTML itself. (The reason for this is fairly obvious: if you just type a < character on your page, the browser could mistake it for a new tag being opened.) This proposal recommends a set of mathematical entities, and a new structure to be used to arrange these entities into equations and functions. In this section, we'll briefly describe some of the math features in the proposal.

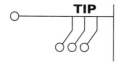

TIP

While it's beyond the scope of this chapter to describe every mathematical tag that HTML v3.0 offers, a complete listing and explanation is available in the proposal, at the URL http://www.w3.org/ pub/WWW/TR/.

The <MATH> tag allows you to enter a number of abbreviations for mathematical symbols and syntactical markers for formulas and, in combination with the math entities, creates a complete system for displaying functions. You begin a section of mathematical markup with the <MATH> tag. You then use combinations of the other tags to lay out your information in correct mathematical syntax. The HTML v3.0 Internet Draft listed the following tags for mathematical markup:

◈ **<BOX>** Used for hidden brackets, stretchy delimiters, and placing one expression above another (as in numerators and denominators), the <BOX> tag can take a number of internal settings, which allow formatting of complex fractions, placing functions above or below one another, and other layout specifications. The shortcut characters for the opening and closing <BOX> tags are { and }, respectively. An example demonstrating the use of the shortcut characters is provided at the end of this list.

⁂ **<SUB>** and **<SUP>**   The subscript and superscript tags are also used for limits. The shortcut character for the superscript tag is ^, and the shortcut character for the subscript is _.

⁂ **<ABOVE>** and **<BELOW>**   The <ABOVE> tag is used to draw an arrow, line, or symbol above an expression, and the <BELOW> tag draws the same elements below the expression.

⁂ **<VEC>, <BAR>, <DOT>, <DDOT>, <HAT>, <TILDE>**   These tags are convenient for marking common accents as an alternative to using the <ABOVE> tag.

⁂ **<SQRT>** and **<ROOT>**   These tags are used for square roots and other roots of an expression.

⁂ **<ARRAY>**   You can use the <ARRAY> tag for matrices and other kinds of arrays.

⁂ **<TEXT>**   Used to include a short piece of text within a math element, the <TEXT> tag is often combined with the <SUB> or <SUP> tags.

The use of the shortcut characters for <SUP>, <SUB>, and <BOX> makes simple equations reducible to a single line of HTML code. The following lines are separate functions and equations, which are shown in Figure 13-6.

```
<MATH>{1<OVER>1 + x}</MATH><P><HR>
<MATH>2^3^</MATH><P><HR>
<MATH>{x^2^<OVER>1 + {3<OVER>y - z}}</MATH><P><HR>
```

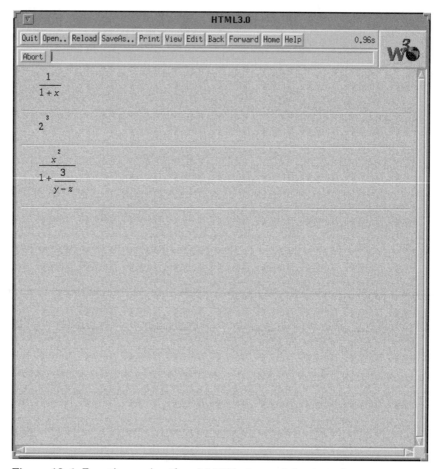

Figure 13-6: *Equations using the <MATH> tag and shortcut characters.*

Note that the character for superscript (like subscript, which is not shown in the example) has to be used twice, once as an opening tag and once as a closing tag. The first function is "one over one plus x," which must be enclosed in the <BOX> tags (or their shortcut equivalents) because it is rendered as a fraction. The second function is "two to the third power." The third equation is "x squared over one plus three over y minus z." In this function, the fraction "three over y minus z" must be put inside the <BOX> tags even though it's in the denominator of another fraction.

The level of complexity of the <MATH> tag increases with the complexity of the functions being expressed. Every level of expression is possible, from simple algebra and arithmetic, as shown in the example, to complex matrices and chemical notations. As the proposal nears approval, it will change and expand, so the document containing the proposal should be consulted for any new developments.

HTTP–The Next Generation

HTTP-NG (HyperText Transfer Protocol-Next Generation) is the proposed replacement for the Web's current underlying transport, HTTP. Before we can explain the function and features of HTTP-NG, we need to look at the current standard from an Internet protocol designer's point of view.

Inner Workings of HTTP

HTTP, described in Chapter 2, "The Basic Pieces," is one of the most important factors in the success of the Web. Its popularity and ubiquity are a result of the protocol's one big advantage: simplicity. As we demonstrated in Chapter 2, HTTP follows an easy-to-understand request/response paradigm. The client, your web browser, connects to the server and issues a plain-text request for a file; the server sends the file, preceded by several lines of textual header information, and closes the connection. This entire process, both request and response, is referred to as a transaction.

When the client wants another file from the same server (an inline image referred to in the HTML document it just retrieved, for example), it opens a new connection and goes through the whole process again. The simplicity of HTTP has delivered tremendous dividends. As a text-only protocol, it is easy to implement and debug, and this has resulted in dozens, if not hundreds, of web browser and server implementations.

HTTP Problems

Unfortunately, HTTP's simplicity comes at the cost of performance and efficiency. This was a reasonable trade-off when the protocol was originally designed to be used by a few hundred physicists sharing ideas and data, but now that the Web represents the bulk of traffic on the Internet, this inefficency has become a problem. And the problem has been worsened by the way browsers make use of the protocol.

Although the verbosity of HTTP's textual protocol contributes to it, the main source of HTTP's inefficiency is its need to open a new connection for each requested file. For one thing, there is a fixed cost for opening a new connection across the network. It doesn't matter how long the connection is kept open; the cost is a result of the time that it takes for the transmission back and forth of the messages that initially set up the connection. There is also a time delay for every network packet that passes between the client and server—since each packet must be acknowledged, the delay is the amount of time it takes light to make the round trip.

These costs add up. With all the traffic and delays, you find that when you load a Web page, both the client and server spend most of their time waiting around unnecessarily. Modern browser writers have partially addressed this problem by having the client issue multiple HTTP requests at the same time. To the user, this seems to improve performance, as it allows the browser to get more quickly the basic information needed to render the page, such as the sizes of the inline images. In fact, though, this behavior only really improves perceived performance when relatively few people on the network engage in it, but browsers that don't utilize this technique don't get their fair share of the bandwidth. Now that everyone does it, HTTP's inefficiencies are multiplied, the Internet backbones are becoming congested, and everyone suffers: the classic "tragedy of the commons."

The Next Generation

Luckily, there is a solution on the horizon: HTTP-NG. This new protocol proposal (http://www.w3.org/pub/WWW/Protocols/HTTP-NG/Overview.html) by Simon Spero of Enterprise Integration Technologies and University of North Carolina's SunSITE addresses all of HTTP's problems and throws in some great new features at the same time. It's being seriously investigated by the clever people at the World Wide Web Organization (http://www.w3.org) and may soon become HTTP's anointed successor.

Unlike HTTP, HTTP-NG is not a human-readable protocol. It's a complex binary language specially designed to solve many of the Web's biggest problems. The first of these problems should be obvious by now: a separate connection for each request. So, an HTTP-NG connection, once opened by the client, may be kept open for as long as desired, while many transactions are proceeding across it.

One of the protocol's major advantages is that it is asynchronous, which means that the client may issue a bunch of requests at the same time, without waiting for the server's response each time. Since several requests will fit in a single network packet, this dramatically reduces the number of round trips made over the course of a session.

Interestingly, asynchronicity works both ways: once the connection has been opened, the server doesn't have to wait for a client's request in order to send data. Spero predicts that will facilitate "smart" servers, which guess what files a client is going to ask for next. For example, the request for a Web page is usually followed by requests for all of the inline images referred to on that page. If the server guesses right, then all the round trips for the client's requests are eliminated—giving you better than speed-of-light performance: a good trick indeed.

"Wait!" you say, "What if the server guesses wrong? The client will have to wait until the server is done sending data before it can inform the server of the error of its ways." That would indeed be a problem. Fortunately, HTTP-NG is implemented over a *session control layer*. This networking technique allows several virtual connections to be multiplexed over a single real connection—so clients and servers may send messages to each other at the same time, therefore allowing clients to cancel any individual transaction at any time. This multiplexing also gives browser writers a way to retrieve a page's inline images in parallel, so that they aren't tempted to open several separate connections at the same time; this too will improve the Internet's overall performance.

In addition to all of these fundamental advantages over the original HTTP, HTTP-NG offers several other perks:

- *Advanced Caching Proxies:* HTTP_NG enables easy use of caching proxy servers, which can trade information on client usage. More service providers will implement proxies to reduce use of their network connections, which will also help relieve the Internet's growing congestion.

- *Mandatory Display:* HTTP-NG allows the author of a document to attach information, such as payment and licensing conditions, that the browser must display and the user must accept before the primary document can be retrieved.

- *Logging:* An HTTP-NG server can inform the client what transaction information is being logged, giving the user the opportunity to terminate the connection. In addition, caching servers can communicate "hits" back to the originating server, which is especially important to commercial servers.

- *Security:* Although HTTP-NG doesn't specify any particular security scheme, there is built-in support for plugging in any encryption method the client and server can agree upon for the transmission of sensitive information.

- *Payment:* HTTP-NG provides plug-in support for online payment schemes such as First Virtual and DigiCash (discussed in "Security & Commerce," below), without dictating which scheme to use.

All of this new functionality comes at a cost, of course: simplicity. The description and implementation of HTTP-NG is much longer and harder to understand than for the original HTTP. The axiom that you can't have everything proves doubly true for network protocols. Still, HTTP-NG is an excellent protocol which will improve the Web's performance and capabilities.

Implementation is the sincerest form of flattery, though, and there are a few projects in progress to implement the HTTP-NG specification. One is sponsored by Hewlett-Packard Labs, Bristol (http://www-uk.hpl.hp.com) and is led by Andy Norman. The W3O is sponsoring HTTP-NG research as well, along with further research into combining HTTP-NG with a distributed object system (http://www.w3.org/pub/WWW/Protocols/HTTP-NG/Activity.html). There is also an academic project implementing NG clients and servers at Carnegie-Mellon University (http://nusselt.me.cmu.edu/http-ng).

Security & Commerce

Thus far, the focus of this book has been to show you how to provide information that can be freely accessed by anyone on the Internet. However, a number of businesses use the Web for commercial transactions as well, selling goods, such as software and information, that can be sent over the Internet and goods that are ordered over the Internet and physically shipped to the consumer. There are, however, security issues involved with transactions over the Web. Using forms, as described in Chapter 9, "Simple Forms," and Chapter 10, "CGI & DLLs: Programming Your Server," a user can select his or her order, enter a credit card number and a shipping address, and send that information to a vendor. In Chapter 4, "System Security," we discussed the popular security protocols SSL and S-HTTP. Beyond basic security, there are some new ideas for exchanging valuable information over the Internet. Each of these models offers a way to conduct commercial transactions over the Internet.

CyberCash

CyberCash (http://www.cybercash.com/) is a method that complements having a secure HTTP server running at a merchant's site and a secure browser submitting information to that site. CyberCash uses encryption to protect private messages and then sends those messages on top of another protocol, like Secure HTTP or SSL. A user establishes a "CyberCash persona," which sends information about the user to CyberCash after downloading the client application via anonymous FTP. The CyberCash client application is a standalone interface on a user's machine that is launched whenever a purchase needs to be made using CyberCash. When a purchase is requested, the user is sent an online invoice form with the total charge for that purchase. The user then enters her or his credit card number and credit card information and submits it to the CyberCash server. All of this information is encrypted using public and private key encryption technology. When the CyberCash server receives this request, the credit card is authorized by a bank or credit processing center, and the merchant's account is credited.

CyberCash can also be used between individuals, not just between a merchant and a consumer. CyberCash maintains accounts for every user who registers his or her client software. Any two CyberCash users can send money between CyberCash accounts. The electronic cash can be exchanged for real cash through a demand deposit in a bank, and the funds in CyberCash accounts are certified by participating banks (currently only Wells Fargo Bank).

Figure 13-7: *The CyberCash home page.*

DigiCash

DigiCash (http://www.digicash.com/) uses another model for electronic financial transactions: "ecash," or electronic cash. The idea behind ecash is that users have an account at an ecash bank, from which they can withdraw ecash, in the form of electronic coins. Each coin carries a bank signature to authenticate it. The ecash is certified by a bank, and the bank can exchange real money for whatever amount of ecash is spent. Like CyberCash,

DigiCash uses its own client and server software, which can be used in conjunction with any Web browser.

Figure 13-8: *The DigiCash home page.*

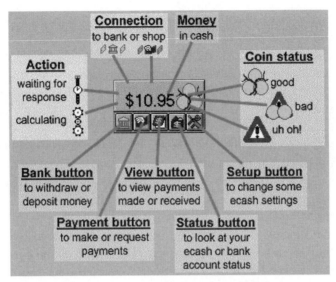

Figure 13-9: *The DigiCash client, with explanations.*

The client software can be used to withdraw a certain amount of cash from the bank account, in other words, taking ecash from a server and storing on the local disk of the user. Then, the client software can send the ecash from the local disk to a vendor to pay for a product or service. The user makes a connection to a vendor's "shop" using a regular Web client. When the user selects a link that requires payment, a CGI script launches the DigiCash shop software, which then makes a request to the user's DigiCash client for payment.

The DigiCash shop software is simply the text-based version of the DigiCash software, which can be used as either a server or a client, in other words, for a vendor or for a customer. The graphical interface, shown in Figure 13-9, is a client-only program. Currently, UNIX servers are the only servers that can use DigiCash shop software, but software is being developed for Macintosh and Windows HTTP servers. For HTTP servers that cannot run the DigiCash software, DigiCash runs a remote shop server that will automatically handle transactions. The remote shop server uses a special directory setup on the Web server. DigiCash's remote server accesses this directory over the Internet to get information about a store, such as the identity of the shop and owner, the goods for sale, and the prices of those goods.

The bank account and local ecash are both protected using public and private key encryption. This means that no one but the user can withdraw money from their bank account or from his or her local ecash. Also, every payment in ecash is unique, using authentication (as described in "Secure HTTP," earlier) to identify the payment. If a user attempts to copy his or her local ecash supply into a second file, and spend that ecash twice, the bank will recognize that the ecash coins have been used before, and will not clear the payment.

All payments made with ecash are anonymous, just like payments with real cash. The ecash is "blinded," that is, made anonymous by the bank, when it is issued, meaning that there's no way for the bank to connect a particular coin that has been issued to that same coin when it's spent. The value of the coin is verified by the bank without any reference back to the user. In essence, the bank says, "Yes, this is real money," without asking, "Who are you and where did you get this money?"

A user includes an e-mail address when setting up a DigiCash account, allowing the bank to communicate with the user. The contact address is for administrative purposes only, not for purposes of identification. For example, if a bank needed to tell a user to look at a set of transactions, or to tell a user that his or her key needed to be changed, this e-mail address would be used.

DigiCash is working on other ways of using ecash, aside from transactions over the Internet. For example, a card with a computer chip on it, or "smartcard," can read an amount of ecash from a user's disk, and then that card can be used to make payments like a credit card. While the cards with computer chips were developed by DigiCash several years ago, DigiCash's cooperation with major credit card companies is leading to a wider acceptance of the ecash system. This type of innovation could fully integrate electronic financial transactions and real-world purchases, in effect, making every personal computer an automatic teller machine combined with a shopping mall.

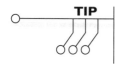

TIP

For discussions about buying and selling on the Web, check out the archives of the www-buyinfo mailing list at the URL http://www.research.att.com/www-buyinfo/archive/, or subscribe to the list by sending the message "subscribe www-buyinfo" to the e-mail address www-buyinfo-request@allegra.att.com.

First Virtual

The First Virtual (http://www.fv.com/) solution to secure financial transactions on the Web uses no encryption whatsoever. Users establish an account with First Virtual by sending it electronic mail with information about themselves. After this information is submitted, the user calls a toll-free number and enters his or her credit card number using a touch-tone phone. After these two steps, the user is sent an account number and complete details about using the new account. Whenever a purchase is made using First Virtual, the user transmits only the account number, and First Virtual automatically charges his or her credit card for that amount.

The process is not much more complicated for vendors. First, the vendor submits the initial application just like a regular user. Then, the vendor sends information about its checking account to First Virtual, and from that point on, any purchases made using First Virtual will be deposited directly to that e-mail account.

To prevent people from intercepting and using a First Virtual account number to make unauthorized purchases, every First Virtual purchase is confirmed by e-mail. A user makes a purchase, submitting only his or her account number. First Virtual uses that account number to retrieve the user's e-mail address and automatically send a letter requesting confirmation. Charges are made only after a reply is received from that user's e-mail address.

There's one major restriction on using First Virtual to authorize purchases, however: the only thing that can be paid for with a First Virtual account is information, in the broadest sense of the word. Nothing that First Virtual merchants sell is ever physically shipped to the consumer—it's sent over the Internet. This means that First Virtual can be used to buy anything from electronic artwork to software to literary works, so long as that information can be transmitted to an electronic mail account. Also, First Virtual can be used to make donations and pay fees. This specialization reduces the possibility of fraud, because any information purchased will be sent to the account holder's electronic mail address, and not to a third-party impostor, even if the account number was used without authorization.

First Virtual hosts all of its merchants in its "InfoHaus," at the URL http://www.infohaus.com/. First Virtual purchasing capability can also be built into Web pages on a merchant's server, however. Essentially, Web pages have to be configured to mail a MIME-typed message that is recognized by First Virtual's InfoHaus software, which initiates the automated electronic mail confirmation process. Full technical information about First Virtual, including documentation on the implementation of First Virtual purchasing on your own pages, is available at the URL http://www.fv.com/tech/.

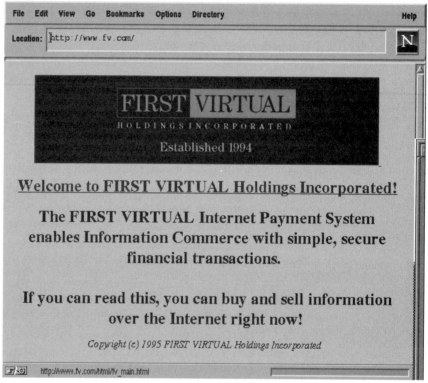

Figure 13-10: *The First Virtual home page.*

CommerceNet

CommerceNet (http://www.commerce.net/) was founded in 1993 with a federal grant designed to promote the commercial use of defense-related technology. It is, primarily, a consortium of corporations, organizations, and individuals committed to developing commerce on the Internet.

CommerceNet has organized a number of task areas and working groups to develop different resources and technologies involved in Internet commerce. These areas include topics from Internet connectivity and engineering groups to marketing and payment services, and participants are drawn from CommerceNet member organizations. The consortium of organizations has also provided funding for the development of new technologies for commercial usage. One of the technologies developed with CommerceNet funding is Secure HTTP, discussed earlier in this chapter.

CommerceNet's WWW site has a broad collection of information about commerce gathered from across the Web, as well as a number of original documents. Some of this information, however, is restricted to subscribers. Subscribers can participate in CommerceNet under a number of different subscription plans that allow access to different types of information and subscription benefits. For full information about subscribing to CommerceNet, send e-mail to subscriber-info@commerce.net or look at the CommerceNet subscriber information page at the URL http://www.commerce.net/information/sb/overview.html.

Virtual Reality Modeling Language

There has been quite a bit of speculation and, dare we say, hype about the emergence of "virtual reality" as a widely used communication medium. The image of complete immersion in a three-dimensional, computer-generated virtual world is indeed a strong one, and many media outlets and entrepreneurs have romanticized about and capitalized on this vision. The increasing popularity of the Internet has only furthered the romanticization of this ideal, as can be seen lately by (often outlandish) portrayals of VR technology in popular media.

The obvious problem with implementing virtual reality communication systems is the amount of computing power and bandwidth they would require. Thankfully, computers with enough processing power to display complex graphical environments are dropping in price and becoming more commonplace. However, the networks that connect these machines are becoming increasingly strained by the growing demand for bandwidth as multimedia applications become more popular. Even though these networks are limited by the amount of information they can transfer, the demand for distributed 3D environments and "sensualized" interfaces of virtual reality is stronger than ever. Not satisfied with waiting for high-bandwidth fiber-optic networks, some software developers have proposed techniques for distributing 3D graphical worlds over the existing Internet infrastructure.

In the spring of 1994, Tim Berners-Lee (see Chapter 1, "What Is the Web?") and Dave Raggett organized special sessions at the First International Conference on the World Wide Web (see http://www.w3.org/) to encourage discussion about virtual reality interfaces to the Web. At the conference, Mark Pesce and Tony Parisi first proposed a networked 3D Web interface based on previous virtual reality and networking research. Since many of the conference participants were already working on 3D visualization tools, they agreed upon a need for a common protocol with which different visualization applications could communicate over the Internet. The participants realized that the maturation of the virtual reality industry would bring with it the need for some method of utilizing existing technologies and protocols for shared virtual environments.

An electronic mailing list was set up soon after the conference to facilitate discussion among the numerous researchers who expressed an interest in the proposed interface. After much debate, it was decided that the Virtual Reality Modeling Language (VRML) would be based on Silicon Graphics's Open Inventor ASCII file format. Open Inventor and its predecessor, IRIS Inventor, are 3D modeling toolkits that have been used for a number of commercial 3D graphics applications.

The decision of the VRML developers to base version 1.0 on Open Inventor has prompted Silicon Graphics to strongly support the VRML standard. It released the first VRML browser, WebSpace (see Figure 13-11), in the summer of 1995. In its original announcement, Silicon Graphics stressed the broad support VRML received from numerous members of the business and research communities, including CERN, Brown University, NEC Technologies, and Netscape Communications.

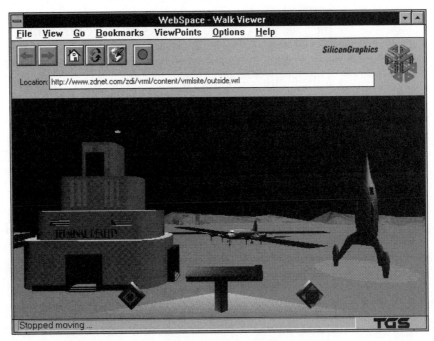

Figure 13-11: *The Silicon Graphics WebSpace VRML viewer.*

The current VRML implementation is designed to function as a platform-independent language for three-dimensional graphic scene design. It describes 3D objects much like the PostScript language describes images and text. Objects' descriptions, not their entire graphic representations, are communicated between machines. This technique greatly reduces the amount of bandwidth necessary for distributing virtual worlds. It also enables objects to be infinitely scaleable, meaning that as you navigate within a 3D environment and move closer to objects, greater levels of detail emerge. Once an object's parameters (description and coordinates) have been defined, it can be viewed from every imaginable range and orientation.

There are many 3D object file formats, but what sets VRML apart is its ability to incorporate hyperlinks for use with the World Wide Web. Any object in a VRML world can be defined as a *WWWanchor*, which will link the object to some URL on the Web. It's the dream of the VRML creators that much of the information available on the Internet in the form of two-dimensional text and pictures will come to be represented by three-dimensional hyperlinked objects. And since VRML browsers are designed to work in conjunction with current Web browsers as helper applications, information providers don't have to worry about conflicts arising between HTML and VRML files distribution. In the words of Mark Pesce, "VRML is a language for describing multi-user interactive simulations—virtual worlds networked via the global Internet and hyperlinked within the World Wide Web." Not a bad start for a language that's less than a year old, eh?

To handle 3D objects, VRML defines a set of objects called nodes. Objects can theoretically contain any file format type, but nodes are designed specifically for 3D graphics. Each node is defined with certain characteristics:

- *Type:* This could be a cube, sphere, cone, light source, texture map, transformation, and so forth.

- *Fields:* These are characteristics that differentiate the node from other nodes of the same type, such as the radius of a sphere, the intensity of a light source, or the image used for a texture map.

- *Name:* Although not necessary, naming nodes can assist in the manipulation of the scene. Named nodes are commonly used within worlds that are hyperlinked to other worlds.

- *Node hierarchy:* This allows parent nodes to contain children nodes, the combination of which are referred to as group nodes.

Luckily, you don't have to worry about these technical specifics if you're just looking to serve some worlds. Since VRML is designed to be used in conjunction with existing Web protocols, you just need to add the MIME type world/x-vrml to your server's configuration files. The file extension that you should associate with the MIME type is .WRL.

If you want to browse the Web in 3D, or if you're aching to design your own three-dimensional worlds, there's never been an easier time. Numerous companies have released 3D modelers, translators, and viewers, many of which are freeware or shareware and available for Windows NT. To find a complete list of VRML software, example applications, press releases, job postings, and research projects, check out the San Diego Supercomputer Center's VRML Repository at http://sdsc.edu/vrml/.

So you're probably saying, "That's all fine and good, but it's gotta be called version 1.0 for a reason, right?" How good of you to ask. There's been a rush by numerous software developers to come up with an enhanced verion of VRML that will win the coveted 2.0 position. The enhanced VRML-based language that is receiving the broadest support is Moving Worlds, proposed by— you guessed it—Silicon Graphics. This is the most likely candidate to be elected VRML 2.0, since it has the blessing of many of the VRML 1.0 architects, as well as that of more than 50 leading software and hardware manufacturers. Moving Worlds includes support for many features that will greatly enhance the VRML 1.0 language, including the ability to add dynamic movement to worlds by allowing Java applets (see "Catching the Java Buzz," below) to interact with them. To get the lowdown on Moving Worlds, including the current specification and a list of companies that are supporting it, see http://www.sgi.com/Headlines/1996/ Feb/moving-worlds.html. Not suprisingly, Netscape has already released a plug-in that allows users of Netscape 2.0 to view Moving Worlds scenes within their Web browser (see Figure 13-12).

VRML Resources

This has been only a brief introduction to VRML and should by no means be considered complete. For more complete details, see the VRML version 1.0 Specification at http://www.eit.com/vrml/vrmlspec.html.

To learn more about the theories behind the development of VRML, see the EIT VRML overview at http://www.vrml.org.

The main VRML forum is at http://vrml.wired.com.

The VRML mailing list Hypermail archive is at http://vrml.wired.com/arch/.

The VRML Forum at *Wired*, including a Hypermail archive of the VRML mailing list and links to the VRML Technical Forum, is at http://vrml.wired.com/.

For a great listing of VRML sites, see WebFX What's Cool at http://www.paperinc.com/wrls.html.

For more information on Silicon Graphics's Webspace viewer, as well as specifications and history of VRML, see http://webspace.sgi.com/.

To learn more about Netscape's Live3D, visit http://home.netscape.com/comprod/products/navigator/live3d/intro_vrml.html.

Want to see one of the earliest, coolest applications of VRML? Check out WAXweb at http://bug.village.virginia.edu/. It's a hypermedia version of David Blair's feature film, "WAX or the Discovery of Television Among the Bees," which incorporates multimedia clips, MOOs, and VRML worlds.

Figure 13-12: *The Netscape Browser with the Live3D VRML plug-in.*

Catching the Java Buzz

Multimedia has been the refrain of the desktop-oriented '90s; it's Java that has created the buzz (and it's not just the caffeine!) that heralds a new era of computing. In this new era, we're told, the network is the main appliance, while PCs are merely cups, receiving a server's piping hot bounty.

"Enough with these percolating analogies and strained metaphors," you say, "what exactly is Java?" We'll tell you—Java is a new object-oriented programming language, similar to C++, created at Sun Microsystems. This language and its associated technologies not only are capable of solving several of the Web's current problems, but also create a new platform that will speed the Internet's already dizzying pace of technological improvement.

Everyone knows that online, content is king. The problem with the Web's content is that it's largely static. Web pages, despite their hyperlinks, are essentially like pages in a book; they offer little in the way of interactivity. Although HTML forms and server-side CGI scripts provide a way of creating new content on the fly, they are limited by the Web's underlying technology, which makes it extremely difficult to write complex applications.

Another problem with the pre-Java Web is the way updates and upgrades are handled. Content is constantly evolving; there are new and better compression schemes, file formats, browser features, and HTML extensions all the time. But when a programmer has invented a new technology, no users can take advantage of it until their Web browsers have been upgraded, or until they've downloaded and installed a new helper application.

Java changes all that. Java-enabled Web browsers can be updated dynamically because they have the ability to download and run little programs called *applets*. Here's the way it works: when your browser retrieves a page with a Java applet embedded in it (using the new HTML tag, <APPLET>), it asks the server for a copy of the code and runs it. The code your browser downloads is in a format called *Java byte code*, which is like machine language for an imaginary computer. Since it runs within the browser's Java interpreter, it can run on any type of computer.

These little programs can do almost anything. Programmers can use the Java class libraries (collections of useful, ready-to-use software components) to easily display and manage multimedia, network services, and graphical user interfaces. Applets can create cool new effects like online animation for your Web pages, display heretofore unknown multimedia formats, or turn your Web browser into any type of application: a spreadsheet, a collaborative whiteboard, a shared scheduler. With Java, you no longer have to wait for Netscape (or any other browser company) to release a new version of their software in order to take advantage of all the Web's best; online publishers will instantly provide a new applet that gives your existing browser a new ability on the fly.

There is one thing that Java applets can't do: violate your system security. The Java language and the Java interpreter inside your browser have built-in security. Untrusted applets cannot access any data on your system or anywhere on the network, except on the host from which you downloaded it. That means that Java applets can't read, write, or delete files on your local system, nor can they act as Trojan horses; you needn't worry that the interactive physics simulation you're using is secretly sending hate mail to president@whitehouse.gov.

Creating the Brew

It's obvious that Java is an important development for Web programmers and surfers. Programmers get an elegant object-oriented language that allows them to create entirely interactive applications, while users get to enjoy these new applications. The question is: what does Java give the middle-men: the page designers, HTML writers, and Web publishers?

The answer is *lots*. Java applets are objects: modular, reusable pieces of software. The <APPLET> tag makes it easy to embed any Java applet into a Web page—you just provide the URL that points to the applet you want to include, and the browser's Java interpreter takes care of the rest. As Java applets proliferate (and it's already happening), Web publishers will have thousands of new page elements to choose from when designing a Web site.

"All this sounds great," you say, but you're still wondering why this may be heralding a new era of computing. Well, that bit of hype was started by George Gilder in *Fortune* magazine, in an article called "The Coming Software Shift," reprinted online at http://homepage.seas.upenn.edu/~gaj1/ggindex.html. In this article, Gilder envisions a time (perhaps not too far away) in which shrink-wrapped applications are replaced with Java-based applets that are loaded over the network as you use them.

This scenario would have the following advantages over the current way software is developed:

❧ *Platform independence:* Java byte-codes will run on any computer that has a Java interpreter. So programmers can write a program once and it will run under Windows, MacOS, UNIX, and anything else you can think of. Microsoft is including direct Java support in their ActiveX Internet architecture, so that Java applets will function in the broader ActiveX scope.

❧ *Incremental upgradability:* Currently, you buy a piece of shrink-wrapped software. In six months to a year, the company releases a new version. Not only do you have to buy the upgrade, but the new release may mark an enormous change from the previous version. There are usually plenty of new bugs, which is a result of inadequate testing and tight development schedules. Java-based software could be improved a little bit at a time. Customers would get updates quickly and automatically over the Internet, while developers would get immediate feedback on their latest changes.

❧ *Distributed development:* Java applets are written as self-contained objects that can be linked together on the fly to create a full-fledged application. For example, you might grab an editing object, a drawing object, and a spell-checking object in order to construct a word processing application. These various objects could all be written by different people or companies. This feature allows the user to choose the bits that best suit his or her needs, rather than being tied to a single company's way of doing things.

❧ *Diverse market:* The software industry is dominated at present by large software houses with the resources to maintain worldwide retail distribution channels, while small companies make do in niche markets. If the Internet were used as the primary channel for distributing software, all players would have equal access to the market.

❧ *Pay-per-use:* Currently, to buy a piece of software, you go to the store, plunk down a (usually large) chunk of change, and take it home. You own a license to use that software as long as you like, but you can't make copies for your friends. This model has always served to frustrate both users and software companies. The user has a cool piece of software and wants to let a friend try it out, while the company is hell-bent on stopping them—either through copy protection or legal intimidation.

In a Java-based software market, payment would probably be based instead on actual use. Each time you used the software, you would automatically be charged a small amount (using a micro-payment system, like Digital's Millicent). If you wanted your friend to try it, you could just give him the URL, and he could try it out for the same small charge. If you found another object that did the same job better, then you could easily switch, without feeling tied in to your current application by a monetary investment.

This may or may not be the future model of software development, but either way, it highlights the obvious advantages of Java: it's secure, networked, object-oriented, and portable—just the thing to bring greater flexibility and interactivity to the Web!

To view and use Java applets, you need a Java-capable browser. Currently, the only browser fitting this bill is Netscape 2.0 (http://www.netscape.com), which supports Java on all platforms except Macintosh. All other major browser vendors, like Microsoft and IBM, have announced their intention to support Java, as well. In addition, Sun will soon be releasing a new version of their HotJava browser (which is written completely in Java); the current version only handles an earlier, incompatible version of the Java byte codes.

Once you've got a Java-enabled browser, you'll want to find examples of interesting applets. There is an index of applets kept at Gamelan (http://www.gamelan.com), but soon the best place to find an interesting Java applet will be at your favorite Web site.

If you want to start writing Java applets, check out http://www.javasoft.com. This site has all the documentation and software you'll need to get started, found in the Java Development Kit, which is available for Windows 95, Sparc Solaris, Linux, and other UNIX platforms. Advanced development tools, such as visual GUI, will soon be released by Sun and other companies. You can find a listing of companies that have signed onto the Java bandwagon at http://www.javasoft.com/licensees.html.

Conclusion

The future of the World Wide Web is promising. The protocol that clients and servers use to communicate is undergoing major changes, changes that will improve the speed, efficiency, and security of the Web. HTML, the language in which Web pages are designed, will expand dramatically and change from being a simple layout language to a language capable of complex interactions and flexible design. Other developments, from teleconferencing to commercial transactions, will change the face of the Web, allowing for a broad range of uses that no other technology has made possible. In the near future, you will see the evolution of the Web into a highly interactive, personalized medium. Microsoft's ActiveX, NeXT's WebObjects, and Netscape's JavaScript will help us all reach this next level of Web functionality.

Using the information in this book, you can create a site that is among the best on the Web. By using advanced features like multimedia, databases, and complex forms, you can make your Web pages rival those of the largest companies with an Internet presence. By incorporating developing technologies, and by looking ahead to the newest advances on the Internet, you can also make sure that your site never becomes obsolete. So put your best out there for the world to see, and you will enjoy the rewards of building a strong presence on the world's fastest growing medium—the World Wide Web.

SECTION V

Appendices

About the Online Companion

Information is power! *The Windows NT Web Server Book Online Companion* supplements the book, exploring the best server-side information on the Net.

You can access the special Web site at http://www.vmedia.com/ntweb.html. Some of the valuable features of this special site include information on other Ventana titles and links to other valuable Internet sites.

The Windows NT Web Server Book Online Companion also links you to the Ventana Bookshop where you will find useful press and jacket information on a variety of Ventana Communications Group's offerings. Plus, you have access to a wide selection of exciting new releases and coming attractions. In addition, Ventana's Online Bookshop allows you to order online the books you want without leaving home and at a special rate!

The Online Companion represents Ventana Communications Group's ongoing commitment to offering the most dynamic and exciting products possible. And soon Ventana Online will be adding more services, including more multimedia supplements, searchable indexes, and sections of the book reproduced and hyperlinked to the Internet resources they reference.

Free voice technical support is offered but is limited to installation-related issues and is available for 30 days from the date you register your copy of the book. After the initial 30 days and for non-installation-related questions, please send all technical support questions via Internet e-mail to **help@vmedia.com**. Our technical support staff will research your question and respond promptly via e-mail.

About the Companion CD-ROM

Installing the CD-ROM

The CD-ROM included with your copy of *The Windows NT Web Server Book* contains a wealth of valuable software, including Alibaba Lite, CGI PerForm, Cool Edit, and GoldWave. Also included is a collection of sample code taken from the text.

To run the CD-ROM, load the CD and with Windows running, select File | Run from the Program Manager. Then type **D:\VIEWER** (where D: is your CD-ROM drive) in the command-line box and press Enter. You'll see a menu screen offering several choices. See "Navigating the CD-ROM" below for your option choices.

Technical Support is available for installation-related problems only. The Technical Support office is open from 8:00 A.M. to 6:00 P.M. Monday through Friday and can be reached via the following methods:

- Phone: (919) 544-9404 extension 81
- E-mail: help@vmedia.com
- FAX: (919) 544-9472
- World Wide Web: http://www.vmedia.com/support
- America Online: keyword *Ventana*

Navigating the CD-ROM

Your choices for navigating the CD-ROM appear on the opening screen. You can Exit from the CD, get Help on navigating, view the CD Contents, learn more about Ventana, or view the Hot Picks.

If you click the CD Contents button, you will see a scroll box with the contents of the CD-ROM. As you click on each piece of software, you'll see its description in the text field at the bottom.

There is a Copy button in the middle of the CD Content screen. You can click on the button to install individual programs on your hard drive. First click on the software you would like to copy to your hard drive, then click once on the Copy button. Or you can use the Copy All button to install all of the programs at one time. Click Menu to return to the Main Menu.

Alibaba Software

The Companion CD-ROM contains two versions of the Alibaba web server software: lite and full.

Alibaba (Lite Version)

This special "development edition" of Alibaba for Windows NT (for the Intel processor), licensed from the manufacturer, is included on the Companion CD-ROM. What makes this version special is that it is not a demo that will time out after a certain period; it is limited to four simultaneous IP connections. This development edition server can be very useful for creating a web and testing it. Please contact Ventana Technical Support for installation problems with Alibaba Lite.

Alibaba (Full Version)

The full version of the Alibaba web server is locked. You can obtain the key by contacting Computer Software Manufaktur, the makers of Alibaba. You can contact CSM through e-mail or by fax. Their address is sales@scm.co.at and their fax is ++43-1-317 30 40. The upgrade price is $99.

If you decide to upgrade to the full version of Alibaba, please contact CSM for technical support questions. Please refer to the readme text on the CD-ROM.

CSM Alibaba WWW Server
End User License Agreement

This Agreement applies to both the Lite and Full versions of the Alibaba software.

BY OPENING THE PACKAGE, YOU ARE CONSENTING TO BE BOUND BY AND ARE BECOMING A PARTY TO THIS AGREEMENT. IF YOU DO NOT AGREE TO ALL OF THE TERMS OF THIS AGREEMENT, CLICK THE "DO NOT AC-CEPT" BUTTON OR RETURN THIS PRODUCT TO THE PLACE OF PURCHASE FOR A FULL REFUND.

Grant

CSM hereby grants to you a non-exclusive license to use its ac-companying software product ("Software") and accompanying documentation ("Documentation") on the following terms: You may:

- use the Software on any single computer;
- use the Software on a second computer so long as the first and second computers are not used simultaneously; or
- copy the Software for archival purposes, provided any copy must contain all of the original Software's proprietary notices.

You may not:

- permit other individuals to use the Software except under the terms listed above; modify, translate, reverse engineer, decompile, disassemble (except to the extent applicable laws specifically prohibit such restriction), or create derivative works based on the Software or Documentation.

- copy the Software or Documentation (except for back-up purposes);

- rent, lease, transfer, or otherwise transfer rights to the Software or Documentation; or

- remove any proprietary notices or labels on the Software or Documentation.

Software

If you receive your first copy of the Software electronically, and a second copy on media, the second copy may be used for archival purposes only. This license does not grant you any right to any enhancement or update.

Title

Title, ownership rights, and intellectual property rights in and to the Software and Documentation shall remain in CSM and/or its suppliers. The Software is protected by the copyright laws of the United States and international copyright treaties. Title, ownership rights, and intellectual property rights in and to the content accessed through the Software is the property of the applicable content owner and may be protected by applicable copyright or other law. This License gives you no rights to such content.

Limited Warranty

CSM warrants that for a period of ninety (90) days from the date of acquisition, the Software, if operated as directed, will substantially achieve the functionality described in the Documentation. CSM does not warrant, however, that your use of the Software will be uninterrupted or that the operation of the Software will be error-free or secure and hereby disclaims any and all liability on account thereof. In addition, the security mechanism implemented by the Software has inherent limitations, and you must determine that the Software sufficiently meets your requirements. CSM also warrants that the media containing the Software, if provided by CSM, is free from defects in material and workmanship and will so remain for ninety (90) days from the date you acquired the Software. CSM's sole liability for any breach of this warranty shall be, in CSM's sole discretion: (i) to replace your defective media; or (ii) to advise you how to achieve substantially the same functionality with the Software as described in the Documentation through a procedure different from that set forth in the Documentation; or (iii) if the above remedies are impracticable, to refund the license fee you paid for the Software. Repaired, corrected, or replaced Software and Documentation shall be covered by this limited warranty for the period remaining under the warranty that covered the original Software, or if longer, for thirty (30) days after the date (a) of shipment to you of the repaired or replaced Software, or (b) CSM advised you how to operate the Software so as to achieve the functionality described in the Documentation. Only if you inform CSM of your problem with the Software during the applicable warranty period and provide evidence of the date you acquired the Software will CSM be obligated to honor this warranty. CSM will use reasonable commercial efforts to repair, replace, advise, or refund pursuant to the foregoing warranty within 30 days of being so notified.

THIS IS A LIMITED WARRANTY AND IT IS THE ONLY WARRANTY MADE BY CSM. CSM MAKES NO OTHER EX-PRESS WARRANTY AND NO WARRANTY OR CONDITION OF NONINFRINGEMENT OF THIRD PARTIES' RIGHTS. THE DURATION OF IMPLIED WARRANTIES, INCLUDING WITH-OUT LIMITATION, WARRANTIES OF MERCHANTABILITY AND OF FITNESS FOR A PARTICULAR PURPOSE, IS LIMITED TO THE ABOVE LIMITED WARRANTY PERIOD. SOME STATES DO NOT ALLOW LIMITATIONS ON HOW LONG AN IMPLIED WARRANTY LASTS, SO LIMITATIONS MAY NOT APPLY TO YOU: NO CSM DEALER, AGENT, OR EMPLOYEE IS AUTHO-RIZED TO MAKE ANY MODIFICATIONS, EXTENSIONS, OR ADDITIONS TO THIS WARRANTY. If any modifications are made to the Software by you during the warranty period; if the media is subjected to accident, abuse, or improper use; or if you violate the terms of this Agreement, then this warranty shall immediately be terminated. This warranty shall not apply if the software is used on or in conjection with hardware or Software other than the unmodified version of hardware and Software with which the Software was designed to be used as described in the Documentation.

THE WARRANTY GIVES YOU SPECIFIC LEGAL RIGHTS, AND YOU MAY HAVE OTHER LEGAL RIGHTS THAT VARY FROM STATE TO STATE OR BY JURISDICTION.

Limitation of Liability

UNDER NO CIRCUMSTANCES AND UNDER NO LEGAL THEORY, TORT, CONTRACT, OR OTHERWISE, SHALL CSM OR ITS SUPPLIERS OR RESELLERS BE LIABLE TO YOU OR ANY OTHER PERSON FOR ANY INDIRECT, SPECIAL, INCIDENTAL, OR CONSEQUENTIAL DAMAGES OF ANY CHARACTER, INCLUDING, WITHOUT LIMITATION, DAMAGES FOR LOSS OF GOODWILL, WORK STOPPAGE, COMPUTER FAILURE OR MALFUNCTION, OR ANY AND ALL OTHER COMMERCIAL DAMAGES OR LOSSES, OR FOR ANY DAMAGES IN EXCESS OF CSM'S LIST PRICE FOR A LICENSE TO THE SOFTWARE AND DOCUMENTATION, EVEN IF CSM SHALL HAVE BEEN INFORMED OF THE POSSIBILITY OF SUCH DAMAGES, OR FOR ANY CLAIM BY ANY OTHER PARTY. THIS LIMITATION OF LIABILITY SHALL NOT APPLY TO LIABILITY FOR DEATH OR PERSONAL INJURY TO THE EXTENT APPLICABLE LAW PROHIBITS SUCH LIMITATION. FURTHERMORE, SOME STATES DO NOT ALLOW THE EXCLUSION OR LIMITATION OF INCIDENTAL OR CONSEQUENTIAL DAMAGES, SO THIS LIMITATION AND EXCLUSION MAY NOT APPLY TO YOU.

Termination

This license will terminate automatically if you fail to comply with the limitations described above. On termination, you must destroy all copies of the Software and Documentation.

Miscellaneous

This Agreement represents the complete and exclusive agreement concerning this license between the parties and supersedes all prior agreements and representations between them. It may be amended only by a writing executed by both parties. THE ACCEPTANCE OF ANY PURCHASE ORDER PLACED BY YOU IS EXPRESSLY MADE CONDITIONAL ON YOUR ASSENT TO THE TERMS SET FORTH HEREIN, AND NOT THOSE CONTAINED IN YOUR PURCHASE ORDER. If any provision of this Agreement is held to be unenforceable for any reason, such provision shall be reformed only to the extent necessary to make it enforceable. This Agreement shall be governed by and construed under Austrian law as such law applies to agreements between Austrian residents entered into and to be performed entirely within Austria, except as governed by Federal law. The application of the United Nations Convention of Contracts for the International Sale of Goods is expressly excluded.

U.S. Government Restricted Rights

Use, duplication, or disclosure by the Government is subject to restrictions set forth in subparagraphs (a) through (d) of the Commercial Computer-Restricted Rights clause at FAR 52.227-19 when applicable, or in subparagraph (c) (1) (ii) of the Rights in Technical Data and Computer Software clause at DFARS 252.227-7013, and in similar clauses in the NASA FAR Supplement. Contractor/manufacturer is Computer Software Manufaktur, Bindergasse 5/24 A-1090 Vienna/Austria/Europe.

Computer Software Manufaktur GmbH.
Bindergasse 5/24
A-1090 Vienna/Austria
phone: +1-43-3194246
fax: +1-43-3173040

Index

D

J

436 The Windows NT Web Server Book

Internet Resources

Internet Business 500

$29.95, 488 pages, illustrated, part #: 287-9

This authoritative list of the most useful, most valuable online resources for business is also the most current list, linked to a regularly updated *Online Companion* on the Internet. The companion CD-ROM features the latest version of *Netscape Navigator*, plus a hyperlinked version of the entire text of the book.

Walking the World Wide Web, Second Edition

$39.95, 800 pages, illustrated, part #: 298-4

More than 30% new, this book now features 500 listings and an extensive index of servers, expanded and arranged by subject. This groundbreaking bestseller includes a CD-ROM enhanced with Ventana's WebWalker technology; updated online components that make it the richest resource available for Web travelers; and the latest version of Netscape Navigator along with a full hyperlinked version of the text.

Quicken 5 on the Internet

$24.95, 472 pages, illustrated, part #: 448-0

Get your finances under control with *Quicken 5 on the Internet*. Quicken 5 helps make banker's hours a thing of the past—by incorporating Internet access and linking you directly to institutions that see a future in 24-hour services. *Quicken 5 on the Internet* provides complete guidelines to Quicken to aid your offline mastery and help you take advantage of online opportunities.

Windows 95 Revealed!

Windows 95 Power Toolkit

$49.95, 500 pages, illustrated, part #: 319-0

If Windows 95 includes everything but the kitchen sink, get ready to get your hands wet! Maximize the customizing capabilities of Windows 95 with ready-to-use tools, applications and tutorials, including a guide to VBA. The CD-ROM features the complete toolkit, plus additional graphics, sounds and applications. An *Online Companion* includes updated versions of software, hyper-linked listings and links to helpful resources on the Internet.

The Windows 95 Book

$39.95, 1232 pages, illustrated, part #: 154-6

The anxiously awaited revamp of Windows is finally here—which means new working styles for PC users.
This new handbook offers an insider's look at the all-new interface—arming users with tips and techniques for file management, desktop design, optimizing and much more. A must-have for moving to 95! The companion CD-ROM features tutorials, demos, previews and online help plus utilities, screen savers, wallpaper and sounds.

Internet Guide for Windows 95

$24.95, 552 pages, illustrated, part #: 260-7

The *Internet Guide for Windows 95* shows how to use Windows 95's built-in communications tools to access and navigate the Net. Whether you're using The Microsoft Network or an independent Internet provider and Microsoft *Plus!*, this easy-to-read guide helps you started quickly and easily. Learn how to e-mail, download files, and navigate the World Wide Web and take a tour of top sites. An *Online Companion* on Ventana Online features hypertext links to top sites listed in the book.

Books marked with this logo include a free Internet *Online Companion*™, featuring archives of free utilities plus a software archive and links to other Internet resources.

Web Pages Enhanced

Shockwave!

$49.95, 350 pages, illustrated, part #:441-3

Breathe new life into your Web pages with Macromedia
Shockwave. Ventana's Shockwave! teaches how to
enliven and animate your Web sites with online movies.
Beginning with step-by-step exercises and examples, and
ending with in-depth excursions into the use of Shockwave
Lingo extensions, Shockwave! is a must-buy for both
novices and experienced Director developers. Plus, tap
into current Macromedia resources on the Internet with
Ventana's *Online Companion*.

Java Programming for the Internet

$49.95, 500 pages, illustrated, part #: 355-7

Create dynamic, interactive Internet applications with Java
Programming for the Internet. Expand the scope of your
online development with this comprehensive, step-by-step
guide to creating Java applets. Includes four real-world,
start-to-finish tutorials. The CD-ROM has all the programs,
samples and applets from the book, plus shareware.
Continual updates on Ventana's *Online Companion* will
keep this information on the cutting edge.

Exploring Moving Worlds

$24.99, 300 pages, illustrated, part #: 467-7

Moving Worlds—a newly accepted standard that uses
Java and JavaScript for animating objects in three
dimensions—is billed as the next-generation
implementation of VRML. Exploring Moving Worlds
includes an overview of the Moving Worlds standard,
detailed specifications on design and architecture, and
software examples to help advanced Web developers
create live content, animation and full motion on the Web.

Macromedia Director 5 Power Toolkit

$49.95, 800 pages, illustrated, part #: 289-5

Macromedia Director 5 Power Toolkit views the industry's hottest multimedia authoring environment from the inside out. Features tools, tips and professional tricks for producing power-packed projects for CD-ROM and Internet distribution. Dozens of exercises detail the principles behind successful multimedia presentations and the steps to achieve professional results. The companion CD-ROM includes utilities, sample presentations, animations, scripts and files.

Internet Power Toolkit

$49.95, 700 pages, illustrated, part #: 329-8

Plunge deeper into cyberspace with *Internet Power Toolkit*, the advanced guide to Internet tools, techniques and possibilities. Channel its array of Internet utilities and advice into increased productivity and profitability on the Internet. The CD-ROM features an extensive set of TCP/IP tools including Web USENET, e-mail, IRC, MUD and MOO, and more.

The 10 Secrets for Web Success

$19.95, 350 pages, illustrated, part #: 370-0

Create a winning Web site—by discovering what the visionaries behind some of the hottest sites on the Web know instinctively. Meet the people behind Yahoo, IUMA, Word and more, and learn the 10 key principles that set their sites apart from the masses. Discover a whole new way of thinking that will inspire and enhance your own efforts as a Web publisher.

 Books marked with this logo include a free Internet *Online Companion*™, featuring archives of free utilities plus a software archive and links to other Internet resources.

To order any Ventana title, complete this order form and mail or fax it to us, with payment, for quick shipment.

TITLE	PART #	QTY	PRICE	TOTAL

SHIPPING

For all standard orders, please ADD $4.50/first book, $1.35/each additional.
For software kit orders, ADD $6.50/first kit, $2.00/each additional.
For "two-day air," ADD $8.25/first book, $2.25/each additional.
For "two-day air" on the kits, ADD $10.50/first kit, $4.00/each additional.
For orders to Canada, ADD $6.50/book.
For orders sent C.O.D., ADD $4.50 to your shipping rate.
North Carolina residents must ADD 6% sales tax.
International orders require additional shipping charges.

SUBTOTAL = $ _____
SHIPPING = $ _____
TOTAL = $ _____

Name_____
E-mail _____ Daytime telephone_____
Company _____
Address (No PO Box) _____
City_____ State_____ Zip_____
Payment enclosed ___VISA ___MC ___ Acc't # _____ Exp. date_____
Signature _____ Exact name on card _____

Mail to: Ventana • PO Box 13964 • Research Triangle Park, NC 27709-3964 ☎ 800/743-5369 • Fax 919/544-9472

Check your local bookstore or software retailer for these and other bestselling titles, or call toll free:

800/743-5369